Handbook on
Learning
Disabilities

Handbook on Learning Disabilities

A PROGNOSIS FOR THE CHILD, THE ADOLESCENT, THE ADULT

New Jersey Association for Children with Learning Disabilities

ROBERT E. WEBER, EDITOR

Prentice-Hall, Inc.　　　　　Englewood Cliffs, N.J.

Prentice-Hall International, Inc., *London*
Prentice-Hall of Australia, Pty. Ltd., *Sydney*
Prentice-Hall of Canada, Ltd., *Toronto*
Prentice-Hall of India Private Ltd., *New Delhi*
Prentice-Hall of Japan, Inc., *Tokyo*

Third Printing . . . . . . June, 1975

The New Jersey Association for Children with Learning Disabilities gratefully acknowledges the contribution of the Editor and Authors to this book. Their work as it appears in this manuscript is not a statement of support, endorsement or recommendation by the Association. Instead it is hoped these contributions will serve to promote constructive debate.

Library of Congress Cataloging in Publication Data
Main entry under title:

Handbook on learning disabilities.

    1. Mentally handicapped children--Education--Handbooks, manuals, etc. 2. Mentally handicapped children --Handbooks, manuals, etc. 3. Learning ability--Handbooks, manuals, etc. I. Weber, Robert E., 1922-   ed. II. New Jersey Association for Children with Learning Disabilities. [DNLM: 1. Child development. 2. Learning disorders. WS107 W364h 1974]
LC4661.H29   371.9'2   73-22441
ISBN 0-13-380287-6

FOREWORD

BY
SENATOR MIKE GRAVEL
(ALASKA)

"We try harder" could be the motto of every child with a learning disability. I know from watching my son, Marty. In a regular classroom our children start out trying to compete, to keep up, and yet suffer the frustration, heartache, and humiliation of falling farther behind.

The drive our children have should be an example to us, for only if we try harder will we be able to help their dream come true—to help them run home and say, "Mommy, Daddy, I got an A!"

As a father, I am convinced that if we all tried as hard as our kids, we could overcome *our* disability—our inability to help our children.

We must try harder as concerned parents, teachers, and friends to be educators to the outside world.

We must try harder to bring the statistics to the forefront of national concern. The federal government recognizes that from six to ten percent of all school-age children suffer from some type of learning disability. Some experts say the figure is as high as twenty percent. That is twelve million children—more than the total population of New York City!

We must try harder to let others know that children with learning disabilities are not "lazy," "retards," or "stupid," as they are often named. Learning disabled children generally have average or above average intelligence and they begin life with little or no emotional problems or obvious physical handicaps. It is the constant failure and ridicule that often results in anger, hostility, poor self-concept, and serious emotional problems.

Marty started the first grade an average, inquisitive boy. Every time he jumped up to ask questions he was told to sit down. He was yelled at for being disruptive, and then something happened. . .the negative change began.

We must try harder to bring pressure to bear on our representatives at all levels—aldermen, school board members, state legislators, congressmen, senators, and President—to get legislation passed and monies appropriated to provide for diagnosis and special classes for our children.

We must try harder to call to the attention of our public officials that the right of every child to an education is unqualified—

that the right to an education does not belong only to the normal child—that the right to an education for every child was guaranteed in the Equal Protection clause of the Constitution.

This summer we were fortunate enough to be able to send Marty to the George Washington University Speech and Hearing Clinic. Twenty lessons and the examination fee cost $235.00. It was expensive, but it was well worth it for Marty. We were fortunate, but what about parents who cannot afford it.

We must try harder to encourage teachers to specialize in learning disabilities. There are very serious shortages of teachers with the special skills needed even to recognize the problem. I remember Marty's teachers telling us how he daydreamed in class, sometimes not even opening his book. His mother called it inventing. She knew that when he did not understand what was going on around him he thought about his hero, General Patton.

We must try harder to convince our government of the economist's cliche, "You have to spend money to make money." Studies have shown that in some instances it takes only two years of special help before a child can be returned to a normal classroom, can succeed, and can become a productive member of society. The cost of two years of special education is very little when one considers that many children with learning disabilities who do not receive help end their frustrations by dropping out of school and becoming delinquents—a cost to the government which may have no end.

We must try harder to organize to keep a concerted effort, for only then will we succeed. The organization of the New Jersey Association for Children with Learning Disabilities was a stepping stone; the publication of this book is another step along the way; but we are not there yet.

I say, we must try harder, yet I know our energies are not limitless. When I begin to run down and feel that I've hit a brick wall and it is time to quit, I look at Marty and see how hard he tries to read his book on General Patton that he spent his allowance on and I know, we must try harder.

For

John Brian Weber

*who taught me much of what I've
learned about learning disabilities*

ROBERT E. WEBER

PREFACE

It is estimated by the Department of Health, Education and Welfare that there are up to ten million children in the United States afflicted with learning disabilities (other experts place the number at twelve million). The problem is not confined to the poor or the wealthy—it is found in every strata of economic and social life in the nation, and may affect only one or all children of a family.

The magnitude of the problem for the child is fully as great as that of heart disease or cancer is for the adult. A survey of one middle-sized community school district indicated that 40 percent of the children were underachievers, and of the 40 percent, 15 percent had moderate to severe learning disabilities. Other surveys indicate similar or worse situations.[1]

The National Advisory Committee on Handicapped Children defines specific learning disabilities as disorders resulting in imperfect ability to listen, think, speak, read, write, spell or do arithmetic. These disorders include perceptual handicaps, brain injury, minimal brain dysfunction, dyslexia, developmental aphasia, etc. They do not include learning problems which are due primarily to visual, hearing or motor handicaps, or to mental retardation, emotional disturbance, or environmental deprivation.

The opening chapter of this book, "The Nature of Learning Disabilities," illustrates an incredible array of dysfunctions—hyperactivity, hypo-reactiveness, audio and visual perceptual impairment, gross and fine motor impairment, poor attention span, impulsivity and many other disorders of memory and thinking. The

---

[1] Betty Bader, *Learning Disabilities: A Study in Programs.* Polk County, County Board of Education Des Moines, Iowa. January, 1970, p. 16.

sheer complexity of the problem has hindered researchers seeking simple answers to the causes and remediation of learning disabilities.

The contributors to this handbook have researched programs and strategies that, if used effectively, are important tools that sometimes can lead to a good prognosis for the child. However, learning disabilities do not disappear when the child reaches adolescence or the legal age of eighteen. On the contrary, the condition of learning disabilities reaches a most critical stage of adolescence and young adulthood; a stage at which life-long decisions of personal development, social management and education must be made.

There has been little written about the adolescent and young adult with learning disabilities. Part of the problem has been that research priorities in special education have been devoted to early identification and intervention. As a consequence, studies of programs for adolescents with learning disabilities and adult social planning have been generally neglected.

The development of new knowledge about the child with learning disabilities and the increased concern by parents and professionals for program growth have created an immediate need for additional knowledge about the secondary-age child with learning disabilities. The chapters in this book that address the concerns of the adolescent and young adult are truly pioneering efforts to create change.

One example of the need for this handbook came to mind after this writer had the opportunity to observe a counseling session at the offices of the New Jersey Association for Children with Learning Disabilities. A family came to the office requesting advice that would be useful for the planning of the education of their youngest child, who suffered from specific learning disabilities.

The child, an attractive boy of ten, did not speak until he was six years of age and had many gross motor coordination and perceptual problems. The parents, who could not afford to send their child to a private educational program, were seeking to find the answers relating to the future of the child, what they should look for in his development, how they should handle the problems that arise in the family regarding the child, and how to ensure that he would be socially accepted as he progressed along in life. The answers, of course, were not easily found and, in some cases, were not easily hypothesized. The organization was successful in assisting in the placement of the child by utilizing rules and regulations existing in the State legislation of which the parents were not aware. The problem was not so much finding an appropriate educational placement for the child; it was answering the social and counseling questions presented by the parents.

The authors of this book now present a document which looks at the child from infancy through adulthood, and which provides the parents and professional with a source of information most useful in serving the child with specific learning disabilities.

Children with learning disabilities are powerless young people. They rely completely upon the pediatrician's ability to identify the problem early, upon the parents' ability to adjust to and manage the problem, upon the teacher to make correct educational decisions, upon the State legislators' power to provide free public education for the exceptional child, and upon society's recognition of specific learning disabilities as a critical problem that must be handled and dealt with appropriately.

Robert H. Winnerman, President of the New Jersey Association for Children with Learning Disabilities, says: "The salvation of the child with learning disabilities requires the in-depth planning of parents and professionals from the time the child is born until it is time for the child to sustain himself as a contributing member of society."

This requires parents and professionals to think together, work together and advocate that a long-range prognosis be developed for each and every child. The authors of this handbook on learning disabilities are answering the need presented by professionals and by parents everywhere. Their insightful thinking and practical suggestions for educational programs, medical plans, and social awareness, offer a realization that the future of the child with learning disabilities can be improved substantially.

Professionals in the field of medicine, social work, psychology and allied health and education professions should not be without a copy of this book. It will assist in answering the critical questions which often dictate the success or failure in relationships between client and professional.

Much of the change and forward developments in the area of specific learning disabilities is the direct result of the advocate work of parent and professional organizations such as the New Jersey Association for Children with Learning Disabilities, a non-profit, non-sectarian organization dedicated to education, medical and social research for the learning disabled.

Parents, all across the country, who have learning disabled children, through organization and action, can effect improvements in services, secure justice and influence legislation for their children.

As an example, the New Jersey Association for Children with Learning Disabilities has created major legislative programs, innovative technological language arts centers, early childhood education centers, child evaluation centers, post-graduate training courses for pediatricians, and computer-based resource and referral programs. All these were accomplished by parents and caring professionals.

This book is another step in that direction. It should be read and discussed by all the parents of brain-injured children, all of the professionals who serve those children, and all of those young people who are preparing to enter the helping professions.

L. Jay Lev
Executive Director
New Jersey Association for
Children With Learning
Disabilities
Convent Station, New Jersey

CONTENTS

Chapter 3—EFFECTS OF EARLY MALNUTRITION AND STRUCTURE AND FUNCTION: THE CASE FOR SECONDARY PREVENTION

Chapter 4—EARLY CHILDHOOD DEVELOPMENT

Chapter 5—EMOTIONAL AND SOCIAL PROBLEMS OF CHILDREN WITH DEVELOPMENTAL DISABILITIES

Chapter 6—EMOTIONAL AND SOCIAL PROBLEMS OF THE FAMILY WITH A CHILD WHO HAS DEVELOPMENTAL DISABILITIES 121

Chapter 7—PHYSICAL EDUCATION FOR THE HANDI-CAPPED: A NEGLECTED APPROACH 131

1

THE NATURE OF LEARNING DISABILITIES

Catherine E. Spears, M.D.
Neurological Pediatrician
Child Evaluation Center
Morristown Memorial Hospital
Morristown, New Jersey
            and
Robert E. Weber, Ph.D.
Special Consultant
New Jersey Association for
Children with Learning Disabilities

DEFINITION

The practitioners who work with the neurologically impaired child—pediatricians, teachers, learning disabilities specialists, visual and audio perception trainers, psychologists, remedial reading teachers—have coined almost 40 different labels to describe the neurologically impaired child. Some of these terms are moderately helpful, but most fail to accurately describe the damage to the nervous system and the range of consequences. Listed below is a brief sampling of some of the terms used in the literature:

Minimal brain damage
Cerebral dysrhythmia
Minimal cerebral dysfunction

Developmental disability
Perceptually handicapped
Specific learning disability
Delayed neural maturation
Developmental dyslexia
Hyperkinetic behavioral syndrome
Behavioral disorders
Language disorders
Choreiform syndrome
Strauss syndrome
Educationally handicapped
Hyperkinetic impulse disorder

We should keep in mind, when using these terms, that the neurologically impaired child often has average or above average intelligence. For the purposes of this book it is convenient to think of neurological impairment as flaws in the neural circuitry, ranging from minor (subclinical) to catastrophic (severe disablement), that proceed from a variety of causes (see The Etiology of Neurological Impairment, P. 21), which give rise to a range of specific performance consequences (see The Symptomatology of Neurological Impairment, P. 26).

In all likelihood a satisfactory two- or three-word definition of neurological impairment may never arise, unless such definitions are clearly understood as shorthand for a complex subject. We can, however, single out the two key ingredients: 1) an aberration in the neural network (brain, sensors, and related neural apparatus) that delays, complicates, and impedes the development of the human organism on various levels of functioning, and 2) an impairment in learning which gives rise to a deficiency in quality of production, which, in turn, lessens the value and strength of an individual's self-concept and/or self-image.

The description of neurologically impaired children given in the NINDB Monograph #3, entitled "Minimal Brain Dysfunction in Children,"[1] is a complete and comprehensive compilation of terminology and identification. The term "Minimal Brain Dysfunction" is used to designate a large group of children whose

---

[1] U.S. Department of Health, Education and Welfare (Washington, D.C.: U.S. Government Printing Office, 1966).

neurological impairment is "minimal," subtly affecting learning and behavior without necessarily lowering of general intellectual capacity. The term "Minimal Brain Dysfunction Syndrome" refers to children with near average, average or above average general intelligence, with certain learning or behavioral disabilities ranging from mild to severe which are associated with deviations of the function of the central nervous system. These deviations may manifest themselves by various combinations of impairment in perception, conceptualization, language, memory and control of attention, impulse or motor functions.

In addition, we offer the following definition: a neurologically impaired child is one who demonstrates maturational, developmental and biological clocks whose timing does not conform to accepted normal standards and whose behavior, social drives and educational achievement is affected.

ETIOLOGY OF NEUROLOGICAL IMPAIRMENT

In addition to the causal factors in neurological impairment, we are also concerned with the severity and degree of handicap and the prognosis for habilitation. The time at which a difficulty arises determines the above. Hence, four time phases will be explored.

Phase one is the prenatal period, known as the growth period of the unborn child from the time of conception to the time of delivery. The course of the developing fetus depends greatly upon the health of the mother at the time of conception, the formation of the placenta and throughout the pregnancy. An important factor is the reproductive age of the mother and the parity of the fetus. The teenager and the premenopausal female or the advanced aging female present more hazards to the fetus than females of any other age. Whether the child is the first, second, third or fourth child (parity) is likewise an important factor. Poor nutrition, drug ingestion and possibly excessive chronic smoking seem to play as large a role in prenatal causes of difficulties as maternal diseases and infections (about which more is known). For instance, there is a great awareness of the difficulties encountered in pregnancy when the mother is a known diabetic, a hypothyroid or hyperthyroid, has other glandular dysfunctioning, neoplasms, cardiac or pulmonary difficulties, anatomical abnormalities of uterus and cervix and/or toxemia. With the increase in drug abuse and teenage pregnancies, more chromosomal abnormalities are occurring. The problems of poor nutrition in the adolescent mother, who has not fully matured herself, influence the size and maturity of the newborn. Virus diseases such as rubella (German measles) play an important role in the formation of the fetus, also.

Placental abnormalities such as toxemia, tumors, hydramnios (excessive amount of fluid in utero), placenta previa and abrupto (the "after birth" separating from the uterus or womb before the birth of the baby, causing excessive bleeding) cause the baby to have insufficient nourishment and oxygen.

Phase two is the perinatal or paranatal period (labor and delivery time). Long hard labors, toxemia and/or convulsions due to the toxemia, hemorrhage and infection cause fetal distress. Administration of drugs and hypotonic fluids to the mother along with operative complications at the time of delivery also present problems. Hence, the importance of good prenatal care with early identification of difficulties cannot be stressed enough.

Phase three is the neonatal period (the first four weeks of the life of the baby). Viral infections of the neonate (new baby) can cause serious difficulties, especially the "Herpes Simplex Hominis" type. Subdural hematoma (blood clot or collection of blood between the linings of the brain and the brain itself), convulsions, cyanotic (blue) spells and metabolic imbalance can also contribute to later neurological impairment.

Phase four is the postnatal period, which extends from four weeks of life to two years. Severe dehydration, meningitis or other infections of the central nervous system, head trauma, convulsions, nutritional deficiencies and inborn errors of metabolism, such as phenylketonuria (P.K.U. disease), interfere with the normal maturation and development of the nervous system.

With the development of newer laboratory techniques and bio-chemical procedures, along with new concepts of the role viruses play in the human body, particularly in utero and in the neonate, we are able to make earlier identification of difficulties.

The technique of amniocentesis enables us to obtain cellular constituents of the amniotic fluid for diagnosis of chromosomal abnormalities and inborn errors of metabolism before the fetus is four months old.

In summary, then, we can list the causative factors in neurological impairment as follows:

1. Genetic aberrations
2. Disease
3. Birth complications/trauma
4. Environmental trauma (e.g., head injury)
5. Poor nutrition

We should also note that, taking these causative factors to gether, the incidence of neurological impairment for the school-age population has been estimated to range from 8 percent to over 15 percent. In terms of the sex breakdown, four to ten times as many males are afflicted as females.

DIAGNOSIS OF NEUROLOGICAL IMPAIRMENT

In order to be able to diagnose an impairment, and more particularly, what specific areas are impaired, the examiner must know how to diagnose the "normal" child and be familiar with developmental schedules. A child grows in four areas simultaneously at approximately the same rate of speed. Let us say that a round wheel that is divided into four quadrants represents normal growth. One quadrant would represent physical growth, one would be intellectual growth, another would be emotional growth and the fourth would be social growth. If a child is not developing in all four of the above-mentioned quadrants at the same rate of speed, he no longer is a perfect round wheel. The shape of the circle becomes distorted. A mis-shaped circle or square can be seen as representing neurological impairment. In this construct one corner could be allotted to all the children with obvious motor difficulties or deficits (e.g., cerebral palsy). Another corner could be the convulsive disorders or epilepsies; a third corner could be for the panretarded child whose greatest deficiency is in intellect (mental subnormalities). The fourth corner would be for the gross disorders of behavior, blindness, deafness and severe aphasias. All these disabilities would represent *major* cerebral dysfunction syndromes. Minimal cerebral dysfunction is considered to be the main cause of the hyperkinetic behavioral syndrome characteristic of many neurologically impaired children. The child will usually show a history of a group of the following symptoms in varying degrees and in varying combinations known as soft signs: 1) hyperactivity, which is abnormal motor activity, including speaking in disorganized torrents; 2) incoordination, poor coordination with clumsiness in gait, in hopping, heel walking, toe walking, riding a bicycle, eye-hand movements, right-left disorientation, poor or unestablished lateral dominance, digital awkwardness, tremors or athetoid movements; 3) impulsiveness or poor impulse control; 4) distractibility or inability to concentrate on appropriate stimuli and function in logical sequence; 5) short attention span or concentration; 6) impaired perception and concept formation—visual, auditory, tactile and kinesthetic senses, and memory deficits; 7) language disorders which give rise to a learning disability; 8) labile emotions—tolerance of failure and frustration is low; 9) perserveration—where the child repeats needlessly (verbally or behaviorally) until helped to stop, and 10) irregularities on the electroencephalogram (EEG) without actual seizures or with possibly subclinical seizures associated with fluctuations in behavior or intellectual function.

In neurological examinations, gross motor coordination is checked to determine whether there is an abnormal delay in the maturation of motor function (unless this can be explained on the basis of factors outside the central nervous system). We must also examine the child's large muscle coordination. Next, fine motor coordination would be tested—individual finger movements, finger to thumb opposition, buttoning, tying shoes, eye-hand coordination, throwing, catching and kicking a ball, writing with a pencil. We would also note whether he has difficulty with spatial perception. In the meantime, the examiner is asking questions, evaluating the responses as to accuracy, speed of response and use of words to express a thought. The hyperactive motor activity and short attention span should be evaluated relative to the level of parental tolerance and the child's effect in relation to parents, siblings and other children. Rapid and skilled movements of the tongue should be noted, as well as the movements of the eyes. Test for color vision is also important. Particular attention should also be paid to involuntary movements, tremors, habit spasms or tics.

In addition to the medical examination delineated above, there is another set of metrics which supplements the medical analysis and evaluation. These are test batteries variously administered by psychologists, teachers, and learning disability specialists on child study teams, in schools, child evaluation clinics, and hospital settings.

Dr. Donald D. Hammill, writing in *Academic Therapy,* a journal devoted to learning disabilities, provides a description of a typical test battery.[2]

1. Intelligence—WISC, Stanford-Binet
   Intelligence Scale (revised), Slosson
   Intelligence Test for Children and Adults
2. Language—ITPA
3. Achievement—California Achievement Test, Metropolitan Achievement Tests, Stanford Achievement Tests, Jastak-Bijou
   Achievement Test, Durrell-Sullivan Reading Capacity and Achievement Tests, Gates Reading Readiness Scales
4. Speech—The Templin-Darley Tests of Articulation
5. Perceptual Motor—Bender Visual-Motor Gestalt Test, Marianne Frostig Developmental Test of Visual Perception, Wepman Auditory Discrimination Test, Graham-Kendall Memory for Designs Test, and the Benton Visual Retention Test

In some evaluation centers other tests are used as indicated, such as the Peabody Picture Vocabulary, forms A and B, the Leiter Test of Performance, the Hiskey Test, the Harris Test of Laterality, the House-Tree-Person Exercise, the Goodenough Draw-A-Man Test and the Rorshach. It is essential, of course, that the proper tests be used for the age group being tested.

When all the above information is compiled, it is important to obtain the observations of the classroom teacher and the feelings

---

[2] Donald D. Hammill, "Evaluating Children for Instructional Purposes," *Academic Therapy,* Vol. VI, No. 4, Summer, 1971, p. 343.

of the child about himself. When all this information is analyzed, it enables us to determine degrees of impairment and specific deficit areas. This then becomes the basis for making prescriptions for education and training (e.g., perceptual training) and for delineating major life management problems.

THE SYMPTOMATOLOGY OF NEUROLOGICAL IMPAIRMENT

We are all born with nervous systems—which is to say, a set group of cells, a set group of structures, but we have to develop both the functions of these structures and the continuity and integration of these structures. Let us think of the brain as a computer which depends on sensing mechanisms for its information, and drive mechanisms to carry out its responses. With regard to sensing mechanisms, we are talking about types of perception—audio, visual, tactile, etc. Let us examine some perceptual forms, using visual perception as our first example. Let us say an eye perceives an image for the first time. The image goes through the eye mechanism and is recorded on what is known as Area 17 of the occipital cortex or the visual receptive cortex. The second time the eye sees the image the same way it goes back to Area 17, where it was recorded initially, and is then transferred to Area 18 of the same occipital cortex (known as the visual associative cortex), with the notation, "I've seen this before." (See Figure 1)

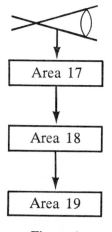

Figure 1

The third time the eye sees the same image in the same way, in the same sequence, the information is then forwarded to Area 19 of the occipital cortex, only higher up, where we have sound beginning its entry (hearing) and exit (speech) and other sensory involvement. The response of this neural registration is, "I recognize this."

By the fourth time the eye sees the same image in the same sequence, an emotional response is generated. The child might say, "I know what this is," and, in a didactic situation, he gives a correct answer. This is what breeds security and the feeling of confidence that comes from success.

Suppose, however, that something untoward happens in the passage of the image through the eye so that a different pathway is established, with the result that the child produces a "wrong" answer. It is a bewildering experience to the child not to have his perception confirmed by a teacher or family adult or sibling. Moreover, enough "wrong" answers eventually produce a neurotic and failure-oriented child.

The child with a visual perceptual disorder may experience many more failures than successes. When he enters school, after having been through a series of failures in the visual perceptual modality, it will be difficult for him to succeed at reading and writing. Only if one can learn to see and recognize what one sees, can one hope for success in reading and writing.

Let us look at auditory perception. Sound enters the ear and proceeds through the auditory canal till it encounters and activates the eardrum. The drum vibrates so that the three little bones behind it get the message and carry the signals to the inner ear, through the semi-circular canals and the cochlea, and then to the eighth nerve and, ultimately, to the auditory reception center (temporal lobe) of the brain. Sometimes these normal pathways are blocked (e.g., malfunction, disease, wax) or the message is not understood when it reaches its cerebral destination. This results in poor phonic learners and, perhaps, good visual learners who, not having learned to listen, concentrate mightily on receiving visual clues. Obviously, if a child does not hear (correctly) the sounds on which speech is based, he is not able to reproduce useful (i.e., correct) sounds.

There are numerous other brain functions—too numerous for delineation here. The point is that the functions of each lobe or area of the brain, plus the neural pathways and sensors, have to be developed and integrated with one another if the organism is to function adequately. Damage (insult, aberration) to the total neural system, including the neuroanatomy, or to any of the neural subsystems (e.g., a given perceptual modality) result in dysfunctional and dis-integrated individuals. Damage to the basal ganglia, the occipital cortex, or the motor cortex, for example, produces the child with cerebral palsy; similarly, damage to the thalamus can produce petit mal and damage to the motor cortex can produce grand mal; also, aberration of the limbic system and chemical imbalance will produce emotional difficulties and deleterious mood swings.

While the full range of mechanisms involved in neurological impairment is not well understood, we do have a good grasp of the range of symptoms that may be attributable to central nervous system (brain, spinal cord, and related nervous apparatus) damage and/or malfunction. Without getting into an exhaustive list of symptoms, let us now examine a few symptoms in several key areas of development and performance.

In terms of the visual modality, the neurologically impaired child often has poor visual recall, poor visual discrimination (e.g., figure-ground relationships), poor form perception; he may also have strabismus, nystagmus, ambloyopia, or poor acuity, and he will very often exhibit the full range of disabilities in the visual area of language development (e.g., dyslexia, poor spelling, etc.). The child may pass acuity tests with glasses but his visual information may still be garbled.

In terms of his audio functioning, the child might have poor audio recall, poor auditory discrimination, and expressive language dysfunction; moreover, his audio functioning (also his visual functioning) may be exacerbated if he has a convulsive disorder wherein the flow of information is interrupted—even for very brief periods.

The child's perceptions of and sense of relatedness in space is another area of concern. In this area of development and performance, the child might have poor body image, poor spatial concepts, a poor sense of laterality, directionality, balance, and, in general, a spatial disorientation.

Motor functioning (fine, gross, hand-eye coordination) is another problem area. The average neurologically impaired child is generally a clumsy child. He often has difficulties in running, climbing, hopping, skipping, holding a pencil, picking up small objects, etc. Part of his problem is sometimes the problem of "mixed dominance" (confusion about and delayed choice of left-handedness or right-handedness) and confused laterality. Obviously, the prognosis for such a child, with regard to participating in sports requiring high degrees of coordination, such as baseball, are very bleak.

It is worth inserting here a brief remark on the temporal relationships of the neurologically impaired child. Generally, the child has a much slower learning style/pace. Thus, time-related tests, for example, penalize him. He also suffers from a general temporal disorientation that precludes the adequate development of temporal assessment equipment. It is almost impossible to get across concepts of yesterday, a week from Tuesday, and fifteen minutes from now to many of these children. Similarly, mothers of neurologically impaired children will postpone the announcement of a trip until one-half hour before departure to forestall hours of "Is it time yet?" "Are we almost ready to go?" Perceptions of time and space, the basis of Einstein's Theory of Relativity, are two immutable basic facts of human existence; when both are disoriented, we see an individual who is profoundly disabled in his universe.

When one adds to the above deficits such neurological elements as tremors, convulsive disorders, the abnormal EEG, and the negatively synergistic factors of poor inter- and intra-sensory integration and the presence of multiple handicaps, one can only be amazed at the adaptability and survivability of the neurologically impaired child.

At the level of behavioral functioning, the neurologically impaired child is sometimes an explosive child whose behavior is both hyperkinetic and unpredictable. In some cases, though, his behavior is hyperactivity. For the most part, however, we see bizarre and frenetic behavior—poor control over one's impulses,

ramdom tactile and motor activity, and a large amount of perseverative (senseless and misdirected) repetitious repertoire, we see
delayed speech and locomotion, and, as a consequence, sometimes
delayed public school entry.

It should be no wonder, then, in view of the foregoing, that
the emotional and academic development of the neurologically
impaired child is in great jeopardy. Consider what the neurologically impaired child brings to the educational scene. He brings:
short attention span, running-amok behavior, the full range of language acquisition impediments, and delayed readiness for a variety
of academic tasks. His teacher might well perceive him as an anti-
learner. She will note that he has poor sequential learning and
/or recall abilities, poor association of ideas, poor concept formation
and inability to handle abstractions, poor ability to concentrate
and follow directions, poor ability to integrate in group activities,
and is very unready for training in basic arithmetic and communications skills, and so forth.

The emotional consequences, at this point, should be clear.
The average neurologically impaired child has a poor self-image,
manifests more anxiety and over-reactiveness, is overly sensitive,
shows lower frustration thresholds, and is noticeably maladaptive
when it comes to coping with stress (e.g., a new student in the
class) and change (e.g., a gift of new clothing).

It should also be noted here that the basic *social* drives of the
disabled learner—curiosity, the need for status and companionship
—are also often blunted and frustrated. When curiosity is not satisfied, it is discouraged; when the achievement of status, which
comes through performance and mastery, is thwarted (as in massive
blockages to learning), feelings of self-worth are diminished; and
when the drive for companionship and "belongingness" goes un-
fulfilled by being "put down" or not accepted by one's peers, the
child's world becomes more lonely and his social resources more
barren. The variables of his existence become negatively reinforcing.

Over the past few years, psychiatrists have been emphasizing
the effect of a malfunctioning Limbic System on behavioral and
emotional responses. This system is located in the thalmus, where
the integrative processes are also developing, and can account for

the mood swings observed in the neurologically impaired child. This also can explain why sometimes the neurologically impaired child is often first diagnosed as emotionally disturbed or behaviorally maladjusted.

Let us conclude our section on symptomatology by noting that the neurologically impaired child who survives the public educational offerings is the child/learner victorious. He has had to surmount obstacles that the teachers in his schools have seldom either experienced or understood. He is, in some ways, the supreme learner who has refused to abide by the conditions of damage and who has, at least in part, contradicted his prognosis. Let us marvel at his strength and his adaptability.

TREATMENT APPROACHES TO NEUROLOGICAL IMPAIRMENT

Because neurological impairment is a basic physiological problem, anything that has a bearing on the child's physiology is of paramount importance. Attempts at the medical control or regulation of the behavior of neurologically impaired children center in the administration of several types of drugs. Typical are the following: anti-depressants, such as thioridazine (Mellaril); quieting agents, such as methylphenidate (Ritalin); amphetamines, such as Dexedrine;[3] tranquilizers, such as chlordiazepoxide (Librium) and chlorpromazine (Thorazine); and anti-convulsants, such as diphenylhydantoin (Dilantin). This list is illustrative and is not meant to show the full range of pharmacologic prescriptions.

Linked to the concept of medical regulation is the nutritional approach. In addition to a well-balanced diet, and without getting into the regimens specified by the advocates of mega-vitamin therapy, it would be fair to cite the fact that several of the B vitamins are used extensively as part of the therapeutic regimen. These are as follows: niacinamide (B2), thiamin (B1), and pyridoxine (B6). These are administered in varying dosages depending on the child's needs and toleration threshold.

---

[3] It should be remembered that stimulating drugs such as amphetamines work in reverse fashion in young children.

As was mentioned earlier, "perceptual handicap" is one of many synonyms for neurological impairment. Thus, it is centrally important to discuss therapy as it involves various perceptual modalities. Let us begin with the area of visual perception. The optometrists, as distinct from the opthamologists, have done the bulk of the work in developing orthoptic training programs (i.e., the development of normal binocular vision). While these programs are popular among parents, medical people continually cite the absence of scientifically rigorous data (e.g., the establishment of control groups). Part of the orthoptic training programs involves various types of visual-motor training (e.g., hand-eye coordination). In addition, many school programs, through the use of Frostig, Winterhaven, and parquetry materials, also provide visual perceptual training.

The area of audio perceptual training, though lacking some of the techniques employed in the area of visual perceptual training, nevertheless has some treatment approaches. Among these are the audio-visual-tactile programs involving the talking typewriter, the talking page, and the voice mirror. In addition, the "Tomatis Effect" equipment utilized by Dr. Alfred Tomatis in Paris and by Dr. Agathe Sidlauskas at the University of Ottawa is worthy of mention. Other treatment approaches in the audio area include amplification equipment, conventional recording equipment, and speech therapy.

There are also other perceptual training areas, such as tactile perceptual training, which involve a great deal of tactile stimulation and the use of materials such as the sandpaper alphabet figures.

Probably the most famous of the motor training programs is the one developed by Doman and Deliccato at the Institute for the Development of Human Potential in Philadelphia, wherein neurologically impaired persons retrace their steps (crawling, creeping) through the various stages of ontogenetic development. In a school setting, motor training may take the form of physical exercises, the use of balance boards, playing games (e.g., bean bag), and various hand-eye coordination exercises.

In terms of the child's academic development (including behavior and socialization) a number of special measures must be taken. Some states (e.g., New Jersey) have laws which make special education mandatory—that is, individual school districts must provide special classes for children with learning disabilities, either in the district of the child's residence or by sending him to an adjacent district where special classes are available. These classes, necessarily, have a low student/teacher ratio (e.g., 6:1 or 8:1) and are generally taught by a teacher with special training in learning disabilities. This special teacher is often aided by a remedial reading teacher, a speech therapist, etc.

Obviously, given the prevalence of audio and visual perceptual deficits, adequate development of communications skills—speaking, listening, reading, writing, and spelling—is the largest single problem of the school-age neurologically impaired child. This child will often enter the school system with a poorly developed speech and a visual perceptual set which makes him confuse "13" and "B", and which makes him see "b" as "d" and "p" as "q", etc. Thus, the teacher has to use a variety of language development approaches (e.g., look-say, phonics, language experience), sometimes in combination, and provide additional visual training through the use of Fostig and Winterhaven materials.

Where the parietal lobe of the child's brain has been impaired, the teacher has to experiment with a variety of materials in the area of computational skills (e.g., the Stern arithmetic materials), although in cases of severe insult to the parietal lobe, the child may never master computational skills.

The teacher of the neurologically impaired child has to get into many areas that the teacher of normal children ordinarily would not. For example, the teacher of the neurologically impaired child might have to devote considerable attention to memory training. Even the environmental design has to be reckoned with. The walls have to be painted in quiet colors and be uncluttered, and sometimes windows must be partially covered to aid in extending the attention span of the hyperdistractable and hyperactive child. Every aspect of the teaching-learning process must be grappled with in conscious, meaningful ways.

Let us share, for example, some observations of Mrs. Judy Bartholomew, a teacher of neurologically impaired children in Brookside, N.J..

1. The inability to make figure-ground distinctions makes it difficult for the child to focus on one word in reading.

2. Distortions in form constancy, which take place from minute to minute or day to day, mean that things appear different, which makes reading and spelling especially difficult.

3. Poor concepts of spatial relations and body position in space lead to a lack of confidence in being able to cope with the environment, to poor body image (and thus to poor self image), to poor athletic performance, and an inability to meet peers on an equal footing.

4. In the area of visual-motor performance, poor hand-eye coordination results in difficulty in writing, drawing, and focusing on small areas for fine work. When one adds to this ataxic (balance) involvement, a simple task such as *standing* before an easel and painting becomes extremely complicated; the child must make his hand move to where the eye wants it and concentrate on maintaining his balance at the same time.

5. The auditorily handicapped child whose perceptions of sound (i.e., acuity is not a problem), as in the visual figure-ground difficulty, might not be able to focus auditorily to screen out unwanted audio stimuli or he might have difficulty in clearly distinguishing vowel and consonant sounds (between "o", "e", and "u", for example). In addition, he might have poor audio memory.

Now, what about the emotional problems of the neurologically impaired child, which are exacerbated upon school entry (where certain performance standards are expected)? It should be remembered that the learning disabled child is destined for more than his share of failure experiences. As a result he becomes failure-oriented, failure-prone, has a poor self-image, and develops a fair amount of anxiety in learning (especially testing) situations. It is probably a truism that any child with a handicap develops a secondary emotional problem as a result of not fitting the mass production mold of public education. The neurologically impaired child, even though his disability may be "invisible," is no exception. There are four main approaches to this problem in current use. These are as follows:

1. One-to-one psychiatric care.
2. Group work with a school psychologist.
3. The modification of behavior through operant conditioning (i.e., contingency management or techniques of positive reinforcement).
4. Parental counseling, which attempts to treat the "patient" by intervening in the lives of "significant others."

While all of the above approaches are valid, probably the most effective way to combat the development of emotional problems in disabled learners—a technique which *is not* in current use—is to provide sensitivity training to all non-disabled school-age children and teachers and parents of normal children. The emotional make-up of the child is influenced by the trauma itself, his performance difficulties, and *by how he is perceived and treated by those around him.*

It is very important, then, to determine how a child learns before making his educational prescription. The following would have to be known: 1) does he have inner language and experience background; 2) what is his sensory input; 3) is there neurological integration; 4) does he have retention and memory so that he can relate past experience and look forward to a new one; 5) how does he express himself academically, behaviorally and emotionally; 6) what is his emotional involvement and effort?

WHAT NEUROLOGICAL IMPAIRMENT MEANS TO THE CHILD AND HIS PARENTS

The problems of neurological impairment—for the child and his parents—begins, generally, in the pre-school years. The parents, detecting developmental differences between the neurologically impaired child and his siblings or observing untoward behavior, report their concerns to the family physician. When a general practitioner is consulted rather than a neurological pediatrician, the parent is sometimes told that there is nothing wrong with the child or that he will "grow out of it." This is generally followed by an admonition to the parent not to be over-anxious.

When the diagnosis of neurological impairment is eventually made by a pediatric neurologist, a member of a child study team (part of the public school system), pediatrician or other specialist, parents feel a number of deep emotions —pity or rejection of the child, shame, disbelief, and other emotions—but almost always a feeling of aloneness, often to the point of despair. Many times the initial reaction of parents is mainly fear of what 'the world' will think. What will the grandparents, the neighbors, the teachers, the playmates say (or worse, think and feel)? Not only what will be their reaction to the child involved, but what will be their reaction to us —the parents?

After the initial shock of diagnosis and, of course, the length of this period differs greatly with the individuals involved, parents often feel a sense of something close to relief. There is the old saying, "Ignorance is bliss." That may be, but many parents have had a sneaking suspicion, if not an absolute gnawing realization, that something was "wrong" or at least "different" in the child involved. Others have had the abrupt experience of being summoned to the school to be told, "Your child has a serious problem." After the initial blow—the diagnosis—which in many cases is less serious than our unspoken fears, is made, it at least gives us a place to start. It is the unknown that is difficult to cope with.[4]

Once the diagnosis has been made and accepted,[5] the real *work* of child development begins for the parents—work in which parents must steer a careful course between overprotectiveness and too strict a delimiting of the child's activities and being so casually permissive as to expose the child to danger.

Perhaps the first order of business is to educate the child's siblings (and playmates and neighbors and teachers) about neurological impairment—the range of the child's performance difficulties, his limitations, and his feelings about himself. Primary

---

[4] There is a general move, in various parts of the country, for parents of children with learning disabilities to get together and develop handbooks that will help other parents, delineate educational rights, and so forth. The above quotation, written by parents of neurologically impaired children, was taken from draft sections of a handbook which is currently being developed.

[5] Since neurological impairment is often invisible, some teachers and parents have difficulty in accepting the diagnosis, believing that the child is just spoiled.

in this effort is the attempt to prevent the development of feelings of shame among the siblings and to foster understanding and attitudes of helpfulness.

If patience is a virtue in the normal population, it is an absolute requisite in the family which has a neurologically impaired child as one of its members. The relatively simple tasks of early childhood—tying shoelaces,⁶ putting on clothing, buttoning clothing—are all disaster areas for many neurologically impaired children. Extreme patience is required of everyone with whom the child interacts.

Coping with the child's untoward behavior—hyperactivity, distractability, poor audio processing, perseveration (especially verbal perseveration), tantrums resulting from poor performance, poor control of impulsivity, exaggerated ego needs or greatly diminished ego—all are extremely trying for the parents and the family constellation.

Another area of extreme frustration for parents and others in the life of the neurologically impaired child is what we might call "discontinuities in performance and achievement." A neurologically impaired child may know something one day and not the next (e.g., 2 x 4, how to read a story, recognizing the word "meadowland" and not being able to decode"was").

Also, in the area of behavior, the child might be able to master a relatively difficult task (e.g., roll down a hill) and fail to do a relatively simple task (e.g., hop on one foot). These discontinuities are also manifested in the phenomenon of plateauing, as opposed to continuous progress. They can also become rather bizarre, as in the case of children who have learned to read and then "forget" how to read.

The crises milestones for the parents of the neurologically impaired child might be set forth as follows:

1. Securing an accurate diagnosis of the child's problems.
2. Getting the child ready for public education.
3. Finding a *proper* educational placement and supplementary therapeutic program.

---

⁶ With regard to tying shoelaces, most kids learn how to do this from other kids. The neurologically impaired child, however, might only be able to learn through untying.

4. Finding (almost non-existent) programs for the neurologically impaired adolescent.
5. Finding vocational education and life management programs for neurologically impaired youths.
6. Finding post-parental-death[7] programs for the neurologically impaired youth or adult.

One group of folks in Iowa—parents of children with learning disabilities—summarized their feelings as follows:

1. Please do not make the parents feel guilty, they already do.
2. Please do not make the parents feel inadequate, they already do.
3. Please do not sympathize, and then offer no help.
4. Please do not blame the home—it exists adequate or inadequate, and your criticism only places more stress on family relationships.
5. Please do not say, "This information is highly confidential and too technical for you to understand." *He is their child and they are entitled to know all about him.*[8]

If the parents think they have problems—and, obviously, they do—the learning disabled child has them in spades: he cannot learn in the same styles or at the same rate that others do; he behaves in a different style, and, as a result, he finds many achievement areas shut off from him. He will never excel or even adequately compete in such sports as baseball, football, basketball, and hockey—sports which require high degrees of gross and fine motor coordination. He might, however, compete successfully in swimming—but how many among us have swimming pools or access to pools on a year-round basis?

He has difficulty flying kites and riding bikes—in short, in most areas where other children do not have a problem. He approaches a given task or activity expecting to fail, and, in terms of the "expectancy conditioning" of himself and those around

---

[7] A haunting question for the parents of neurologically impaired children (and mentally retarded and emotionally disabled children) is: "What will happen to my child when I die?"

[8] Learning Disabilities: A Handbook for Parents and Teachers (Des Moines, Iowa: Polk County Board of Education, 1970), p. 2.

him, he probably loads the deck against himself. The perform-
ances of siblings and playmates all outshine him, and he is left
to his own (sometimes barren) resources. He is literally dying for
his environment to provide him with any kind of success experience, so that he can attain the feeling of self-worth that comes
from achievement. We are reminded here of the story by Anatole
France called "The Juggler of Notre Dame," about a simple-
minded person who came to Notre Dame to worship the Virgin.
He could do almost nothing except juggling and yet the statue
of the Virgin in the cathedral wept when he juggled as his adora-
tion.

The neurologically impaired child rarely ever learns the
techniques of juggling, but there are aspects of his existence that
validate his humanity. Endeavors to identify these and enter into
"a conspiracy" to aid him in finding meaning and self-worth should
be a continuing process.

BIBLIOGRAPHY

A Quarterly, Academic Therapy Publications, San Rafael, California.

Anderson, C. M., Playmate, H. B. Management of the Brain Damaged Child, Am. J. Orthopsychiatry, XXXII (April 1962), 492-501.

Ashlock, Patrick and Alberta Stepher, *Educational Therapy in The Elementary School* (Springfield, Ill.: Chas. C. Thomas, 1966).

Baker, H. J. Introduction to Exceptional Children (New York: Macmillan Co., 1959).

Behrman, R. E. et al., "In Utero Disease and the Newborn Infant," *Advances in Pediatrics,* Vol. 17 (Philadelphia: Year Book Medical Publishers, 1970).

Birch, H. G. (ed.) Brain Damage in Children—the Biological and Social Aspects (Baltimore, Maryland: Williams and Wilkins Co., 1964).

Boder, Elena, "Neuropediatric Approach to the Diagnosis and Management of School, Behavioral and Learning Disorders," Learning Disorders, Vol. 2 (Seattle, Wash.: Special Child Publications, 1966).

Central Processing Dysfunction In Children: *A Review of Research,* MINDS Monograph No. 9 (Washington, D.C.: Superintendent of Documents, Government Printing Office) 1967.

Chaney, Clara, and Newell C., Kephart. *Motoric Aids to Perceptual Training* (Columbus, Ohio: Charles E. Merrill Publishing Company, 1968).

Clements, Sam D., *Minimal Brain Dysfunction in Children*: *Terminology and Identification* (Chicago: National Society for Crippled Children and Adults, 1966).

Clements, Sam D. *Minimal Brain Dysfunction in Children. Phase I* (Washington: U. S. Goverment Printing Office, 1966).

Clements, Sam D. Lehtinin, I. E., and Lukens, J. E., *Children*

With Minimal Brain Injury—A Symposium (Chicago: National Society for Crippled Children and Adults, 1964).

Clemmens, R., "Minimal Brain Damage in Children—An Interdisciplinary Problem," *Children,* 8:179-183, 1961.

Crosby, R.M.N., M.D., Robert A. Liston, *The Waysiders* (New York, N.Y.: Delacorte Press, 1968).

Cruickshank, W. M., Bontzen, F. A., Ratzebury, F. H., and Tannhauser, M. T. *A Teaching Method for Brain Injured and Hyperactive Children* (Syracuse: Syracuse University Press, 1961).

Cruickshank, William M. and others. *Misfits in the Public Schools* (Syracuse: Syracuse University Press, 1969).

Edgington, Ruth and Liliam Blackman (Little Rock, Arkansas: Child Study Center, University of Arkansas Medical Center, 1962).

Ellingson, C. C., *The Shadow Children* (Chicago: National Society for Crippled Children and Adults, 1967).

Frierson, E. C. and Barbe, W. B. (eds.) Educating Children With Learning Disabilities (New York: Appleton-Century-Crofts, 1967).

Gordon, Sol, Facts About Sex (Plainview, New York: Charles Brown Inc., 1969).

Gross, Mortimer D., and William Wilson, "Behavior Disorders of Children with Cerebral Dysrhythmias," *Archives of General Psychiatry,* 2:610-619, December, 1964.

Haring, N. G., and Whelan, R. J. (eds.) *The Learning Environment: Relationship to Behavior Modification and Implications for Special Education* (Lawrence, Kans.: University of Kansas Press, 1966).

Hellmuth, Jerome, *Learning Disorders,* Vols. I and II, Seattle, Wash.: Special Child Publications, 1966.

Journal of Learning Disabilities, A Monthly, Chicago: Professional Press Inc.

Kephart, Newell C. *Learning Disability: An Educational Adventure* (Danville, Illinois: The Interstate Printers and Publishers, Inc., 1968).

Kephart, Newell C., The Slow Learner In The Classroom (Columbus, Ohio: Charles E. Merrill, 1960).

Kirk, S. A. *Educating Exceptional Children* (Boston: Houghton Mifflin Co., 1962).

Knobloch, H., and Pasamanick, B.: Syndrome of Minimal Cerebral Damage in Infancy, J.A.M.A., 170: 1384, 1959.

Kronick, Dorothy, *They Too Can Succeed: A Practical Guide For Parents Of Learning Disabled Children* (San Rafael, California: Academic Therapy Publications, 1969).

Kronick, Dorothy, et al., *Learning Disabilities—Implications for a Responsible Society* (Chicago: Developmental Learning Materials, 1970).

Krupp, G. R., and Schwartzberg, B. "The Brain-injured Child —a Challenge to Social Workers," *Social Casework,* February 1960.

Lewis, Richard, et al., *The Other Child* (New York: Grune and Stratton, 1960).

Mager, Robert F. Preparing Instructional Objectives (Palo Alto: Fearon Publishers, 1962).

Millichap, J. G., "Drugs in Management of Hyperkinetic and Perceptually Handicapped Children," J.A.M.A. 206, 1527, 1968.

Money, J. (ed.), *Reading Disability—Progress and Research Needs in Dyslexia* (Baltimore: The John Hopkins Press, 1962).

Nahmias, A. J. et al., "Infection of the Newborn with Herpes Virus Hominis," Advances in Pedatrics, Vol. 17 (Philadelphia: Year Book Medical Publishers, 1970).

Paine, Richard S. "Organic Neurological Factors Related to Learning Disorders," *Learning Disorders,* Vol. I (Seattle, Wash.: Special Child Publications, 1969).

Prechtel, H. F. R., and Stenimer, C., "The Chloroform Syndrome in Children," *Dev. Med. Child Neuro.,* 4:119, 1962.

Radler, D. H. and Newell C. Kephart, *Success Through Play* (New York: Harper and Row, 1960).

Reger, Roger, "Programs and Participants," *Selected Papers On Learning Disabilities, Progress in Parent Information, Professional Growth, and Public Policy* (San Rafael: Academic Therapy Publications, 1969), pp. 145-151.

Rimland, B., Infantile Autism—*The Syndrome and its Impli-*

cations for a Neural Theory of Behavior (New York: Appleton-Century-Croft, 1964).

Siegal, Ernest, "Special Education In The Regular Classroom" (New York: The Johnson Day Company, 1969).

2

GENETIC COUNSELING: THE CASE FOR PRIMARY PREVENTION

Theodore Kushnick, M.D.
Professor of Pediatrics
Director, Division of Human Genetics
New Jersey Medical School
Newark, New Jersey

INTRODUCTION

Every state of normalcy or of disease is a reflection of the interplay between the genetic composition of an individual and his environment. There is marked variation with regard to the percentage of each component's influence in a particular condition, but the manifested spectrum extends from states which are primarily of environmental influence to those which are primarily of genetic causation. An individual presents himself or herself to a physician because of an affliction or presumed affliction. The physician, on the basis of numerous factors elicited by history, family history, physical examination, and laboratory studies must decide whether the patient's status is within the wide range of normalcy or if he has an abnormality. If there is abnormality, the doctor must determine the cause of that abnormality, i. e., make a diagnosis. When the physician has established an accurate diagnosis for the patient's condition, he proceeds to inform the patient with regard to available treatment, if any; expectations with regard to the future course of disease; the impact on the individual's life; how to avoid future complications from the illness, if such are preventable; and he tries to insure that the patient has understood the information.

Despite outcries from colleagues who might wish to retain an exalted status for genetic counseling, the basics include: determination of normality or abnormality; accurate diagnosis of an abnormal condition; prescribing therapy, if available; counseling with regard to the future outlook for the afflicted individual; assessing the risks for future similar complications in the family's life; and offering assistance to all involved to ensure full understanding of the situation. None of these procedures is beyond the capabilities of a competent physician who is provided with proper laboratory facilities for the necessary appropriate tests.

DIAGNOSIS

In order to assure an accurate diagnosis, a great deal of time may be required during the initial work-up. This entails a detailed history of the patient's chief complaint and his entire previous life; a family history, which is directed toward those peculiarities which are associated with numerous genetic disorders; a family pedigree with details as to specific illnesses that the family has been involved with for as many generations as possible; a meticulously detailed physical examination, including determination of the fingerprint (dermatoglyphics) patterns of the afflicted individual; and the initiation of those laboratory studies which appear indicated, i.e., chromosome analysis, biochemical tests, X-ray investigation. Very frequently the abnormal condition does not have an associated laboratory abnormality and further investigation is impossible. Instead, those multiple features which have been noted by history and physical examination provide a clinical picture which can be classified by virtue of previously reported patients with similar particular clinical features. These multiple findings are thus equated to one of the numerous clinical syndromes in medicine.

Once the diagnosis has been made, it then becomes possible to predict (to some extent) the future patterns of the patient and his family. These predictions are not based on magic and mysticism, but are dependent upon varying numbers of reports of similar patients and families recorded in the medical literature. Thus, in order to accomplish effectively any evaluation, a physician must keep abreast of the medical journals.

Despite all our present knowledge, however, there will be an inability to provide a diagnosis in approximately 20 percent of the patients. It is impossible to provide complete counseling in such instances, i.e., inheritance patterns, recurrence risks, etc., but the family can be assisted with regard to psycho-social and educational management.

For the majority of situations, where the diagnosis has been established, the genetic and/or environmental aspects can be explained to the family. It is necessary, therefore, to define various inheritance patterns and give proper perspective regarding their frequencies.

GENETIC INHERITANCE PATTERNS

General

Each individual inherits 23 chromosomes (see Glossary), including one sex chromosome, from each of his or her parents, with the resultant normal total of 46 chromosomes. An excess or a deficiency of chromosomal material is harmful. While chromosomes can be visualized, there are thousands of invisible genes located on each chromosome and comparatively few genes have been localized. The manifestation of their coded messages for features such as eye color, etc., are visible. These effects, as well as others such as biochemical enzymatic functions, blood groups, etc., are the results of the activities of single pairs of genes—one of each pair inherited from each parent. Traits and characteristics such as height, weight, intelligence and body build are an expression of multiple—not single—gene pair activities, and therefore are classified as polygenic or multifactorial-type inheritance. The latter expression is more accurate, in the sense that it indicates the environmental interplay with these multiple genes.

Even prior to conception, there has been an interaction in

the gametes—sperm and ovum—between genes, their carrier chromosomes, and the environment. This constant interplay determines whether the subsequently fertilized egg will be involved with a hidden, previously non-expressed deleterious gene that a parent might carry, or with a new genetic mutation; whether the chromosomes will be normal in number or in their individual configuration; and finally, after fertilization, whether the sex chromosome composition will be such that there will be a higher risk for the appearance of certain genetic diseases in which the expression depends upon the sex of the child.

Polygenic Inheritance

As indicated previously, there are polygenic multifactorial inheritance patterns for many normal traits and many diseases. These features are derived by small contributions from multiple genes, no one of which can be implicated for the normal or abnormal state. In essence, this means that there is a large spectrum of normal variability, and there may not always be a clear-cut distinction between normal and abnormal. Normal standards are defined by the distribution of measurements of particular traits in a *particular* population. This distribution produces a bell-shaped curve for each trait that is being measured, with the midportion (50th percentile) wide peak of the bell curve comprised of the largest group of individuals with the trait being measured. The curve falls off at either end, with plus or minus deviations from the mean (50th percentile), and the entire bell contains approximately 95 percent of the population with the characteristic being studied. Thus, the norm for that trait in that group is defined. There is extreme *normal* variation at each end of the curve, e.g., a twelve-year-old girl might weigh 125 lbs. or 62 lbs. and still be considered at normal weight.

The individuals who are above or below the accepted ranges in this type of curve represent abnormal situations for that particular trait. If it is intelligence that is being measured, the outer limits represent either mental retardation at the lower end of the scale or genius at the higher end of the scale. Ultimately, one of the problems in dealing with normal variability is to define whether a particular characteristic *is* normal or abnormal in comparison to the acceptable extreme variations of the bell curve. If the characteristic is definitely abnormal, then the problem is to define the extent of the contributions of genetic or environmental causations, with the realization that both are involved in varying degrees. As an example, short parents will produce short, slow-growing, slow-maturing, but normal children. If the child is truly dwarfed, one must diagnose whether this is genetic and, if so, on a *de novo* sporadic or an inherited basis, or whether it is environmental in origin.

In attempting to define the incidences of genetic diseases, the lay person tends to overestimate the frequencies of major mutant (abnormal) gene diseases and chromosomal abnormalities. The fact is that the vast majority of genetic disorders are classifiable as those with polygenic or multifactorial inheritance patterns. If an individual has an increased number of contributing factors for a polygenic disease, he has an increased risk for expressing the abnormality. These genetic diseases afflict from 10 to 20 percent of the population and include such disorders as club foot, pyloric stenosis, hypertension, diabetes mellitus, schizophrenic and manic depressive psychoses, rheumatoid arthritis, asthma, hydrocephalus, and myelo-meningocoele, and many of the learning disorders, etc.. The recurrence risks in that family for subsequent afflicted individuals are, for the most part, quite low and in the range of 2.0 percent to 5.0 percent. In addition, nearly all of the conditions are amendable to satisfactory treatment, and the families should not be deterred from having further children.

Approximately 1 to 2 percent, i.e., a much lower incidence of the newborn population, will have a major abnormal gene disease with such aberrations being responsible for approximately 1,500-2,000 diseases. Thus, most of these numerous diseases are very rare as individual illnesses in the population, but collectively, they do represent one to two individuals in one hundred newborns. Many of the major gene abnormalities do lead to early deaths prior to school age, but there are numerous conditions that are compatible with long-term survival. These conditions are nearly equally divided between what is termed an autosomal dominant and an autosomal recessive type of inheritance pattern, with a small percentage being sex-linked (X chromosome) recessive disease. Autosomal means that the genetic disorder is believed to be located on a chromosome other than the sex (X) chromosome; such non-sex chromosomes are called autosomes. Parenthetically, there are no Y sex chromosome *gene* disorders, although entire extra Y chromosome abnormality does occur.

Autosomal Dominant Inheritance

An example of an autosomal dominant condition can be illustrated by one particular form of dwarfism known as achondroplastic dwarfism. Only one of the pair of genes need be abnormal and the disease is expressed because it is dominant over the normal partner gene. However, most children with this affliction represent sporadic new gene mutations and their parents are generally normal. In such a circumstance the chance for subsequent recurrence for the partners is extremely low and virtually zero. On the other hand, the affected child has the gene, and when she has children, there is a 50 percent chance of transmitting her affliction to her offspring. This 50 percent risk occurs with *each* pregnancy so that the birth of one achondroplastic offspring does not preclude the possibility of a second achondroplastic dwarf being born subsequently to that individual. Obviously there is also the 50 percent chance of a normal offspring in each pregnancy. Thus, with the exception of sporadic mutations, an autosomal dominant pattern is one which extends vertically through the generations.

Caution must be exercised because many of these conditions are not fully expressed in every afflicted individual. In essence, the parent may show mild physical abnormalities which are compatible for the presence of the abnormal gene, but this may not be detected until his offspring shows the full-blown picture for that particular affliction.

Autosomal Recessive Inheritance

An autosomal recessive condition is one which both parents' phenotypes (what an individual looks like) are completely normal, but they are both carrying, in an unexpressed fashion, one of a pair of genes which is normal. The normal partner of the gene pair maintains normalcy in all respects, with the abnormal partner in the genotype (what the individual is genetically) being carried without manifestation. It should be noted that each of us carries between three to ten hidden genes which are deleterious or lethal and may be expressed with any pregnancy if the spouse has a similar non-expressed abnormal gene. In essence, the two carrier parents will have a one in four chance in each pregnancy of having the two abnormal gene partners come together in the fertilized egg and produce an afflicted child. There is a two in four chance in each pregnancy for the offspring to be carriers of one abnormal gene but phenotypically normal individuals like the parents. There is a one in four chance in each pregnancy that the child will have a completely normal genotype without carrying the abnormal gene.

As examples of this autosomal recessive type of inheritance, there are illnesses such as cystic fibrosis, PKU (Phenylketonuria) and most forms of Gargoylism. These diseases also offer biochemical markers in the afflicted child. However, there are many other disease states which are transmitted in autosomal recessive patterns which have no biochemical markers, but which can be defined by clinical examination and comparison with previously described patients with the same disorder. The transmission of an autosomal recessive condition reflects a horizontal type of inheritance, i.e., there may be siblings with the disease, but the parents are not afflicted with any disability.

Sex-Linked Recessive Inheritance

The small percentage of disorders with sex (X) chromosome-linked transmission are, for the most part, X-linked recessives. These disorders include conditions such as most forms of hemophilia and progressive muscular dystrophy. In these conditions the carrier female demonstrates no abnormality, but she can transmit the disease with a 50 percent risk of an afflicted son for each pregnancy with a male fetus, and has a 50 percent risk of producing a symptomless carrier daughter, similar to herself, in each pregnancy with a female fetus.

Perspectives

Despite the infrequent individual occurrence of each of the above numerous conditions and the tremendous amount of publicity given to particular diseases, the most common major gene aberrations in the United States population are the autosomal recessive pattern for *expression* of sickle cell disease in Blacks, and the autosomal recessive transmission of Tay-Sachs disease in Ashkenazic Jews.

Chromosomal Abnormalities

Even *less* frequent than the illnesses cited above are those associated with the numerous types of chromosomal abnormalities. These afflictions *in toto* represent 0.5 percent to 1.0 percent of the newborn population. Many of the individuals with chromosomal abnormalities expire early in life, especially those with the non-sex chromosomal conditions, with the notable exception being the majority of those children afflicted with Down's syndrome (Mongolism). Most individuals with sex chromosomal abnormalities can survive for a normal life span. Despite this, the vast majority of chromosomal aberrations are discarded prenatally as spontaneous abortions or are stillbirths.

The individuals with sex chromosomal abnormalities who do survive comprise a subsequent 10 percent of infertile couples, approximately 30 percent of those seen for abnormal sexual development, and nearly 50 percent of the females with primary lack of menstruation.

In summary, most genetic illness belongs to the polygenic inheritance pattern group. Less genetic illness is due to the major abnormal gene category, and even smaller numbers are due to chromosomal aberrations.

GENETIC COUNSELING

Once an accurate diagnosis of the patient's condition has been established, genetic counseling may then ensue. The counseling should be done with the same empathy and sensitivity that the physician utilized during the course of history-taking and physical examination. These families have been distraught with concern over the condition of the afflicted individual for a long period of time.

Prognosis for the Patient

The probable future course of the patient's life must be outlined for the family. The facets dealt with include approximate length of life to be expected, and the quality of life—whether it will be a progressively downhill course with severe mental retardation, or a stable situation with moderate degrees of mental retardation, or a progressively improving course with or without therapy. Definition is required as to whether or not there is therapy available for the condition and, if so, of what nature, i.e., medical, surgical, educational, vocational, etc.

Prognosis for the Family

Subsequent to discussion with regard to prognosis for the patient, the other family members must be counseled with regard to the prognosis for the family *per se*. If the condition is mainly environmental in etiology, there would be no risk of recurrence in that family. Such an entity might include measles encephalitis with its devastating effects on the patient's brain. If the condition is primarily genetic in origin, the type of genetic inheritance pattern should be defined for the family, with indications as to whether they are at high risk, i.e., over 10 percent, or low risk, less than 10 percent, for recurrence in future offspring or in the offspring of their other children. As stated previously, most genetic illnesses are of the multifactorial inheritance pattern. These are mainly single defects or illnesses and are low and generally of the range of 2 percent to 5 percent, so that the families can be encouraged to have further children. If there is more than one afflicted individual in the particular family, the risks do increase to a level of approximately 10 percent. However, it must be re-emphasized that most polygenetic illnesses can be treated with satisfactory outcome.

If the disease is of autosomal dominant category, and it is not a sporadic new mutation, the risks are 50 percent with each pregnancy, as explained previously. Fortunately, many of the autosomal dominant genetic diseases do arise as new mutations with little risk for recurrence.

Autosomal recessive conditions carry a one in four chance for recurrence in each pregnancy and are therefore of high risk. The sex-linked recessive conditions are similarly high risk for recurrence with a 50 percent chance of afflicted male offspring. While female offspring have a 50 percent chance of being carriers, one can be optimistic that many of the X-linked recessive conditions will be amenable to treatment in future years, when the girls are of child-bearing age.

Gene Detection

The next phase of genetic counseling is concerned with whether or not the carrier state for various conditions is detectable. Comparatively few of the numerous genetic diseases are detectable by physical or biochemical markers, chromosome studies of X-ray examinations. There are numerous clinical syndromes in which the patient has multiple physical features which identify his particular disease, but for which there are no markers to establish the carrier state in his parents.

Prevention and Treatment

When there are means of detection, subsequent counseling deals with prevention, if possible, and the mechanism for such. For example, prophylactic therapy by the use of a low phenylalanine diet in a PKU woman (even pre-conception) can prevent damage to her fetus. High levels of phenylalanine severely affect the developing fetus' brain, even if that fetus' genes are of the carrier PKU type, i.e., normal phenotype. Of greater import for the general population should be the use of good prenatal care; a decrease in the high-risk teenage pregnancies; treatment of veneral disease; previous immunization against German measles; and improved nutrition so as to ensure an optimum intrauterine environment for any fetus. These latter measures are mainly prophylactic environmental manipulations for the prevention of damage to genetically normal fetuses.

A second mechanism for prevention of detectable conditions would be the use of amniocentesis (obtaining fluid from the uterus) during the seventeenth to eighteenth week of pregnancy. This fluid can then be tested for biochemical markers of the type indicated by the particular affliction in the family; chromosomal abnormality, again, as indicated by the particular affliction in the family; and sex constitution of the fetus with regard to the sex-linked recessive conditions. In addition, the procedure should be offered to pregnant women who are in the age range of 35 to 40 years. This latter group accounts for 13.5 percent of all pregnancies, but they produce 50 percent of all of the children with Down's syndrome (Mongolism). The implication of amniocentesis is that if an abnormal fetus is detected, it will be subject to therapeutic abortion. Despite the clamor both for and against this method, one must remember that the families involved with amniocentesis are having the procedure performed for exactly the opposite reason: they are parents who desire more children, but wish to ascertain that they will have normal children, having been through the emotional and financial disaster of dealing with a previously born abnormal child.

A third technique for prevention is the use of intrauterine diagnosis and treatment of a very few conditions, such as the severe form of Rh disease.

Lastly, if the affliction is not amenable to intrauterine diagnosis, but is detectable in the newborn and early infancy period, such diagnosis could lead to the early institution of appropriate therapy to prevent the complications of the disease, e.g., low phenylalanine diet for PKU.

In similar fashion, the more numerous non-preventable polygenic abnormalities can be detected at their varied ages of onset (from the newborn period to old age) and there are adequate treatments available. Cleft lip can be repaired in early infancy; club foot can be managed orthopedically at the same stage of life; the aging individual with diabetes mellitus can receive diet and insulin therapy, frequently with the oral forms of insulin. In addition the polygenic diseases do have low recurrence risks, even if it has been "100 percent" for the first child afflicted with illness. Certainly many of the conditions in which there is no associated mental retardation, e.g., club foot, should not preclude having further children.

In rare instances a family may be apprised of a high risk of recurrence for a particular non-detectable condition which is associated with stillbirth or early neonatal death. Such parents may very well decide to have further pregnancies with the realization that they will have either normal, living children or produce another afflicted child, stillborn or with early demise. In essence, such a pregnancy would be viewed as a delayed spontaneous abortion, and the family would not be subjected to a disastrous childrearing situation.

Follow-up

It is quite obvious that no family will be able to comprehend all of the information concerning the patient's illness in one or two visits to the physician. Follow-up is essential and this can be carried out very effectively by genetic counselor associates. They are trained individuals who maintain contact with the family, and through subsequent repeated sessions can ascertain that the family has understood the concepts regarding the patient's affliction. In addition, families may be quite at ease with the genetic counselor associate after repeated sessions and can then indicate their varied but expected emotional reactions to the situation.

Repetition is required in order to educate the parents to the meaning of high risks as opposed to low risks for recurrence; the social implications of the affliction; the social agencies that are available to assist the family; and, in time, to impart newer information regarding a particular illness, as it unfolds by virtue of research investigations.

In many instances, follow-up necessitates subsequent physical examinations by the physician; biochemical determinations to ensure that the metabolic disease is being controlled by the medical therapy; and repeated ascertainment as to whether or not the mother is again pregnant in the light of whether a previously undetectable disease has become detectable and treatable.

Screening for Genetic Disease in the General Population

There has been increasing pressure on the part of a poorly informed population to provide screening tests for *all* genetic diseases. With the realization that there are over 1,500 to 2,000 such illnesses, such requests are obviously impossible to fulfill in every respect. Some of the diseases are extremely rare, and the afflicted individuals described in the medical literature are numerically quite few. Another factor is that the vast majority of genetic disease carrier states are *not* detectable by any biochemical or other markers. A prime example of this dilemma is the adrenogenital syndrome, which is a metabolic error in the formation of adrenal gland hormones. There is no screening test to detect the carrier parents but the child that is afflicted can be managed very adequately with treatment, has above average intellect, and can have a normal life span.

The wisest course in utilizing genetic screening techniques would appear to be to detect those conditions with the greatest frequency in the population, i.e., sickle cell carrier state in the Blacks, Tay-Sachs carriers in the Ashkenazic Jews, and cystic fibrosis of the pancreas in Caucasians. For the latter disease, unfortunately there is no screening test available as yet, although one is in the process of development.

As an adjunct to these few biochemical screening techniques, and probably of greater value to the general population, would be the use of a family pedigree questionnaire which could be filled in by the applicant and quickly sorted out by computers. Thus, any conditions that might be of possible importance to that *particular* individual and family could then be dealt with by more specific approaches, be it physical examination, biochemical tests, chromosome analysis, or X-ray examination.

It should be pointed out that there is a flaw in the fantasies on the part of most of the general population in their desire to have a "perfect" child. Many of the hidden, non-expressed genes that are carried for genetic diseases have been demonstrated in the past to have been selected by virtue of a survival value in an environment which is detrimental to the normal pairs of genes. Thus a carrier state for some of our present genetic diseases may prove to have a much greater survival value in a changing future environment that is detrimental to "normal" genes. It will lose the advantage of selection and survival in a future environment which is not stereotyped, but ever changing.

Genetic Counseling Applied to Learning Disabilities

As all of the previous background material has indicated, the keystone to therapy with regard to learning disabilities is, once again, accurate diagnosis. However, educators and physicians find themselves in the confusing morass of the numerous etiologies that lead to learning disabilities. These causations can be broadly classified into:

1. Intellectual factors

   a. Mental retardation, which can be due to hundreds of etiologies.

   b. Superior intelligence with an inability to adjust to a classroom environment which is directed toward less capable individuals.

2. Developmental disorders

   a. Language, in all its aspects.

   b. Motor functioning, including the clumsiness and hyperactivity manifested by the child with minimal brain dysfuncton (the brain-injured child).

3. Physical defects

   a. Visual.

   b. Auditory.

   c. Cerebral damage.

   d. Chronic illness.

4. Emotional problems, including those attributable to poor early intellectual stimulation in a low socioeconomic background.

All of these conditions reflect the genetic endowment which has been interacting with adverse environmental influences and which the child brings to the classroom.

Diagnosis

In order to make an accurate diagnosis in the face of these numerous possibilities, the physician and the educator must be mutually involved in obtaining the child's history, family history, physical examination, and laboratory determinations that may be applicable. Such laboratory examinations must include intelligence and achievement testing.

Incidences

It is extremely difficult to define the incidences of these various disorders in the school-aged population. However, as a perspective, slightly more than 3 percent of the population will be classified as mentally retarded at one time in their lives. This reflects the fact that the definition of mental retardation is based on psychosocial concepts, and essentially consists of a deficit in intellectual capacity which prevents an individual from making an adequate independent social adjustment in the environment in which he is expected to live. Thus, the child who is unable to demonstrate abstractive or thought-synthesizing abilities will be noted to make an *in*adequate adjustment in the average classroom environment. In later years, he may make a very good independent adjustment in a vocational, concrete-performance type of environment. More than three-quarters of the individuals classified as "mental retardates" are those in the mildly educable group who can be trained to make such an adjustment.

Included in the developmental disorders is specific reading disability, or developmental dyslexia, which is a defect in the ability to interpret the written word. This is a frequent cause of school difficulty involving about 16 percent of the males and 4 percent of the females, and such children are not retarded in general intelligence. That there is some genetic basis for this disability is revealed by the sex incidence differences. In addition, maturation occurs in some of the children with a "catch-up" period at nine years of age, and there is frequently a positive family history for the disorder. Although most workers are persuaded that a polygenic type of inheritance for this particular group of children with reading disability is correct, some recent investigation has suggested the possibility that it is an autosomal dominant condition with partial sex limitation, in that the gene is manifested less frequently in females.

Included in the group of dyslexic children are those whose reading disability is primarily the result of environmental causation. They are children from lower economic and social backgrounds with reduced home reading interests and intellectual stimulation.

In addition to the above mixed group with dyslexia, one frequently encounters the child who has minimal central nervous system damage with "soft" abnormal neurologic signs and normal I.Q.—the minimal brain dysfunction child.

Therapy

After diagnosis is established, educational therapy can be appropriately applied to overcome the learning disability. However, the family must be apprised of the future course for such a child, especially those with minimal brain dysfunction. Such children—and only those particular children—do benefit from the use of anti-depressant drugs to control the hyperkinetic aspects which make the learning experience unavailable and inadequate for them. The major objective of such drug use is to ensure the child's ability to benefit from the educational process. In addition, there are biochemical effects which appear beneficial to their brains, especially to the median forebrain bundle which is an important element in aiding the consolidation of learning. The parents can be reassured that if the child's I.Q. is over 90, he will be able to do quite well in later life, with completely independent, adequate adjustment and excellent employment possibilities in various professions. They should also be apprised of the fact that the troublesome impulsivity and low frustration tolerance will tend to disappear as the child grows older and enters his teens. Thus, what seems like an interminable harrassment to the family can be given some degree of optimism by constant reassurance with regard to the expected progressive improvement as the child grows older. The parents can be informed also that recurrence risks for subsequent afflicted children are extremely low.

Screening

Many of the learning disabilities are detectable conditions and are amenable to screening techniques even when applied at pre-school age. Psychological testing, as represented by appropriate for age intelligence tests, Frostig Developmental Test, etc., can define whether the child has learning disabilities by virtue of mental retardation, poor visual perception, or has organic brain damage. Detection of deafness or reduced visual acuity can lead to early appropriate therapy. Intellectual stimulation for those with poorly stimulating homes by means of pre-school training can be beneficial as partial prevention and treatment. Lastly, there is recent evidence that application of the Frostig screening and therapeutic regimen can be utilized even in a standard classroom setting with beneficial results.

In summary, the educator and the physician can easily collaborate in an effort to provide accurate diagnosis of the underlying cause of a child's learning disability, and then provide appropriate therapy which is tailored to deal with that underlying etiology as well as the learning disorder.

GLOSSARY OF CYTOGENETIC TERMS

Chromosome—carrier of genetic information within the cell nucleus, visible in a dividing cell as rod-shaped structures; composed of DNA on a framework of special proteins.

Gene—basic invisible unit within the human chromosome; a portion of DNA molecule coded for the synthesis of a particular partial protein chain.

Polygenic—many genes at different loci (sites), producing a cumulative effect.

Multifactorial—polygenetic and environmental causation.

Myelo-meningocele—cystic protrusion of the spinal cord.

Autosomal dominant—a gene not carried on a sex chromosome, expressed despite the presence of a normal partner in the gene pair.

Biochemical makers—biochemical indication that condition is genetically transmitted.

Sporadic mutation—non-inherited change in genetic material appearing for the first time.

Adrenogenital syndrome—treatable condition causing overproduction of abnormal and normal adrenal hormones.

Expressed genes—the observable manifestations of genes.

Achondraplastic—dwarfism due to a genetic defect in skeletal bone formation.

3

EFFECTS OF EARLY MALNUTRITION AND STRUCTURE AND FUNCTION: THE CASE FOR SECONDARY PREVENTION

Joseph H. DiLeo, M.D.
Director, Developmental Clinic
New York Foundling Hospital

INTRODUCTION

During recent years increasing attention has been directed to the effects of environmental factors on mental competence. Among the influences studied are poverty, sensory deprivation, and especially malnutrition. The three are not always interrelated.

We shall concern ourselves here with malnutrition before and after birth and its effects on the child's ability to learn. Fetal malnutrition is an effect of qualitative and/or quantitative dietary deficiency during pregnancy. After birth the deprivation is direct.

It may be well to recall the overall daily caloric requirements (RDA) at various ages as recommended by the National Research Council.

infants up to 1 year:	1200 calories per kilogram body weight
children from 1 to 3:	1300
4 to 6:	1700
7 to 9:	2100
10 to 12:	2500
boys 13 to 15:	3100
girls 13 to 15:	2600

boys   16 to 19:   3600
girls   16 to 19:   2400

Especially important for the maintenance of health and for growth are proteins, minerals, and vitamins.

Proteins provide the amino acids for the synthesis of body tissues. Meat, fish, beans, cheese, and grain products are chief sources of proteins. Calcium is provided almost entirely from milk and its products; iron from potatoes, meat, dark green leaves, liver, and fish. Where there are pockets of endemic cretinism, iodine must be included as an additive, usually to salt.

While the poor are main targets for malnutrition because of inadequate caloric intake, dietary deficiency is also prevalent among the privileged because of unbalanced diets deficient in essential nutrients so that malnutrition occurs paradoxically among those who are obese from excessive intake and insufficient motion.

NUTRITIONAL STATUS OF THE ADOLESCENT GIRL

Studies of the nutritional status of adolescent American girls have shown that large numbers are deficient in the intake of protein, vitamins, and minerals. Judgment of dietary adequacy is based on a comparison with the National Research Council Recommended Dietary Allowances (RDA). Poor food patterns are responsible for the widespread malnutrition among teenagers in general but inadequate intake is a serious problem among the poor. Girls are more likely to be poorly fed than boys and girls are more disturbed by complexion problems and weight gain. Many shun milk, regarding it to be the source of acne and fatness. The result is a pronounced deficiency in calcium. Many strive, regardless of their frame, to attain the sinewy figure of the models pictured in fashion magazines. Strange dietary fads may result in the desired weight loss but not without danger to health and well-being. Some girls have stopped menstruating for over a year; others have never regained their lost freshness and lovely curves. Nature abhors a straight line.

In contrast, there are those who insist, and often rightly so, that they do not overeat and are yet obese because of unbalanced diet or lack of activity.

These are the mothers of today and of tomorrow.

Malnutrition during a girl's early years may have far-reaching effects. Rickets is no longer common in this country but where it does occur, it tends to retard and distort the development of bones. Rickets in childhood may cause faulty development of the pelvis, with inadequate space for the easy passage of a fetal head and the complicated delivery may result in damage to the brain, all traceable to malnutrition in childhood.

More direct effects on the child's neurological integrity are the result of failure to provide adequate nutrients during the actual pregnancy.

MALNUTRITION IN THE PREGNANT ADOLESCENT

The incidence of complications is significantly high in adolescent pregnancy. Toxemia is an outstanding complication, often resulting in stillbirth or miscarriage and the rate of prematurity is notably elevated. Also in recent years there has been an increase in venereal disease among teenagers. The hazards of adolescent pregnancy are not due to a single cause; attempts to conceal the pregnancy and lack of prenatal care are overall factors. Malnutrition plays a specific role since among adolescents in general, there is widespread malnutrition just at a time when there is increased need for nutrients. Pregnancy always brings an additional need for protein, vitamins, and minerals, which are especially deficient in the dietary patterns of many adolescent girls. Nutritional studies of programs in Syracuse showed that half of 125 girls had protein deficiences and practically all had vitamin deficiencies. Anemia was a common finding. Obesity as the expression of an emotional problem occurs at all socio-economic levels and it has been noted that the overweight person was also an overweight baby. I mention obesity to indicate that malnutrition can be qualitative as well as quantitative.

As a result of intensive educational programs and the increased provision of prenatal care, the rate of complications, prematurity, and neonatal mortality has fallen. These programs provide medical, educational, social, and psychological services.

NUTRITION AND GROWTH

The adverse effect of malnutrition of stature was clearly demonstrated in Japan when comparisons were made between pre- and post-war adolescents. The latter, who were better nourished, were significantly taller, a difference that could not be ascribed to altered genetic factors. Similar observations have been made on inhabitants of Central America. Animal experiments show that restriction of the mother's diet during pregnancy reduces the growth rate of her young; newborn mice, for example, are not only smaller than average but fail to attain adult average dimensions. Growth retardation in animals can result from quantitative restriction of nutrients or from selective reduction of protein intake. Human studies indicate that abnormally small newborns who are not prematurely born tend to remain smaller than average despite adequate nutrition given post-natally. There is evidence that the overall growth retardation extends also to elements of the nervous system; brain cells, for example, have been noted to be reduced in size and number. This observation raises the likelihood of impairment of brain function and its effects on cognitive development and behavior.

NUTRITION AND BRAIN FUNCTION IN ANIMALS

Numerous animal experiments have clearly demonstrated that quantitative or selective dietary restriction during pregnancy results in stunted physical and mental growth in the offspring. These effects are especially evident when the protein intake was low during pregnancy and lactation and the brain has been shown to be the organ most affected by the amino acid deficiency. These deleterious effects on the progeny of malnourished rats and dogs strongly suggest comparable effects in humans. And though it is not justifiable to conduct similarly controlled experiments on humans, the evidence from studies of deprived malnourished populations is highly indicative, though not incontrovertible, that early malnutrition may have long-term effects on the capacity to process information.

Winick distinguishes two types of intrauterine growth retardation that can be produced experimentally in laboratory animals. These types are clinically distinguishable and are the result of distinct procedures. In one, the uterine artery is ligated, causing insufficient delivery of nutrients to the developing fetus; in the other, the fetus is affected by undernutrition of the pregnant animal. The first mechanism results in an asymmetrical growth failure that spares the brain. In the second type, in which the mother was malnourished, the growth failure is symmetric, affecting all systems, including the brain. The number of brain cells has been permanently reduced and the effects on the animal progeny are abiding. These effects on the brain occur when malnutrition is operative during the time that the brain is developing rapidly. There is evidence that similar reduction of brain cells occurs during human intrauterine development when the mother is seriously malnourished. Cell number is not affected when the malnutrition occurs in children after birth, although psychological manifestations have been observed frequently in poorly nourished children.

THE "SMALL-FOR-DATE" NEWBORN

The average birth weight of infants born at term, that is, after 40 weeks gestation, is between seven and eight pounds. An infant born after a full-term pregnancy yet weighing less than five pounds is definitely small for gestational age. Such an infant is designated as "small-for-date." Fetal growth retardation stems from a variety of causes. Women who smoke throughout their pregnancy tend to have small babies and poverty is a factor, since many mothers of low-birth-weight infants live under conditions of deprivation, poor health, and poor nutrition. Several investigators have also confirmed the low birth weights of infants born to heroin-addicted mothers and though it is not clear what the role of the narcotics may be, there can be no doubt that the lifestyle of the addict, lack of prenatal care, and poor nutritional status all conspire to adversely affect growth and development before birth.

Follow-up studies of small-for-date infants in the United States and in England show a higher incidence of educational and behavioral problems than in children of average birth weight. There has been noted a greater risk of mental and educational retardation as birth weights diminish. Katz and Taylor, for example, have reported a greater incidence of mental retardation in children of low birth weight and Wiener has suggested that the risk of intellectual impairment in low-birth-weight children may be related to the likelihood of neurological deficit in small babies. Butler, in England, reporting on an investigation of seven-year-olds, found a lag in reading ability among those whose birth weights were in the fifth percentile and under. Rosado and Metcoff found the placentas of growth-retarded newborns to be smaller than those of full-term infants. Whatever the cause, intrauterine malnutrition accounts for the newborn's retarded growth though maternal malnutrition is not a consistent finding.

NUTRITION AND BRAIN FUNCTION IN CHILDREN

As reports of follow-up studies become available, the evidence tends to confirm the view that malnutrition adversely affects the developing brain. The timing of nutritional insufficiency seems to be a crucial factor in determining the degree of impairment, its effects being more pronounced when deprivation occurs during the period of most active growth of the brain, that is, during prenatal development. Urrusti and Metcoff have found symmetric reduction of body length, head circumference, and weight, all below the 10th percentile for gestational age, when intrauterine malnutrition occurred before the 28th week of pregnancy. These physical findings are generally associated with corresponding delay in behavioral development in the five areas explored by the Gesell Developmental Examination, namely, gross and fine motor, adaptive, language, and personal-social fields. Since the infants are not premature but small-for-date, no correction is made of the chronological age as would be necessary if the delayed growth and development were due to prematurity.

After reviewing a large number of studies conducted on children in western industrial cities and in developing countries, Scrimshaw concludes that genetic factors alone do not account for the differences in intellectual performance between the privileged and underprivileged and that other adverse factors besides malnutrition (infection, sensory deprivation, and social factors) act synergistically to impair physical and mental growth. Among these factors, Scrimshaw attaches high priority to the elimination of malnutrition in young children in what should be a world-wide program for the welfare of children.

A Ten-State Nutrition Survey of American children showed that retarded growth and iron deficiency anemia were widespread among children from low-income families.

The effect of malnutrition during the preschool years was the focus of a carefully controlled investigation conducted in a Guatemalan village by Cravioto, DeLicardie, and Birch. Apart from the obvious effect of protein-calorie malnutrition on stature and weight, attention was directed to impairment of adaptive function and learning ability. Techniques were developed to evaluate the children's ability to integrate input from separate sensory systems. Tests of intersensory integration assessed the following relationships: visual-kinesthetic, and visual-haptic. Comparisons were made with upper class urban preschool children. Height was used as an indicator of antecedent malnutrition. Intersensory organization is an expression of neurointegrative functioning, and this an indicator of maturation and integrity of the central nervous system. Adverse effects on that system would, in turn, affect its integrating function and find expression in learning disabilities. And indeed, such was the case in the population studied. One of the questions remaining unanswered is how much of the impairment is the result of protein-calorie malnutrition and how much is due to the cultural improverishment that is associated with it. Proof as to the abiding effects of early malnutrition must await conclusion of prospective longitudinal studies in progress.

NUTRITIONAL DISORDERS MAY BE DUE TO CAUSES OTHER THAN INADEQUATE QUANTITATIVE OR QUALITATIVE INTAKE

In the malabsorption syndromes, malnutrition results from faulty absorption and assimilation of nutrients. Typical of this type is the caeliac syndrome in which growth is stunted as a result of the body's failure to absorb complex sugars and fats. A more serious disorder of this type is cystic fibrosis of the pancreas, for which there is no cure at present.

The inborn errors of metabolism are inherited as recessive traits from two parents who are carriers but who do not exhibit this defect. They are heterozygous, but one of four children runs the risk of manifesting the defect because of having inherited the defective tendency from both parents. This child would be homozygous for the trait. Many of the inherited metabolic defects can be detected soon after birth, and treatment will then be started promptly to forestall damage to the developing brain. Phenylketonuria (PKU) and maple syrup urine disease (so called because of the characteristic odor of the newborn's urine) are disorders of protein metabolism. The inherited defect is an enzyme deficiency which blocks the conversion of amino acids so that intermediate products which accumulate in the blood affect the developing brain and often result in mental retardation and neurological dysfunction. Early detection followed by prompt dietary treatment has been highly successful in preventing brain damage in phenylketonuria. Progress has also been made in the treatment of maple syrup urine disease, a more serious defect in which three or perhaps four amino acids cannot be fully metabolized. Tay-Sachs disease is the most serious of the inherited metabolic disorders affecting lipid metabolism; it results in progressive, uncontrollable deterioration of the brain, blindness, and death.

Of the non-genetic metabolic disorders that are associated with mental retardation, the most common is cretinism. Here there is a lack of thyroxine, the hormone produced by the thyroid gland. The result is stunted physical growth and mental development. Early diagnosis and treatment with the lacking hormone are effective in reducing the impairment of growth and intellect. In some areas that are distant from the sea, cretinism may be endemic because of lack of iodine. Without small quantities of this element in the diet the thyroid gland cannot produce its hormone. Mental retardation can be prevented in these regions by adding iodine to the salt and by treating with the deficient hormone when necessary.

Comparative studies of large groups of children consistently show the adverse effect of protein-calorie malnutrition on somatic growth. In a significant number, stunted growth is associated with impaired learning ability. Cultural deprivation typically accompanies malnutrition in deprived families though even the most carefully controlled studies may fail to differentiate among the roles played by inadequate stimulation, ignorance, poverty, and concomitant malnutrition. These Four Horsemen are typically inseparable. Regardless of whether convincing proof may or may not be forthcoming, there can be little doubt that good prenatal care, adequate nutrition, and a sensible hygienic regime, with freedom from excessive stress, are all conducive to better maternal and child growth and development.

While retardation in somatric growth has been shown to affect the child's ultimate stature, it is not clear whether the impairment of intellectual functioning is comparably abiding or irreversible. This is the object of a number of long-term longitudinal studies. In the meantime, efforts should be directed at eliminating malnutrition from all strata of society and at all ages, but especially during adolescence, pregnancy, and early childhood. At the individual level, special educators can work at raising the functional level of those children who were handicapped from the start, and there is abundant evidence to show that impressive gains can be achieved by many children whose earlier behavioral and cognitive development was significantly delayed. The concept of hopelessness is always prejudicial to the welfare of the deprived.

REFERENCES

American Academy Pediatrics—Committee Statement Jan. 1973. The ten-state nutrition survey—a pediatric perspective.

Butler, N. Symposium on Nutrition and Fetal Development. (Reported in Hospital Tribune, Jan. 1, 1973.

Cravioto, J. DeLicardie, E.R., & Birch, H.G. Nutrition, growth and neurointegrative development: an experimental and ecologic study. PEDIATRICS, 1966, vol. 38, No. 2, Part II, Supplement, 319-372.

Drillien, C.M. The Growth and Development of the Prematurely Born Infant. Williams and Wilkins, Baltimore, 1964.

Frisch, R.E. Does malnutrition cause permanent mental retardation in human beings? Psychiatria, Neurologia, Neutochirurgia, 74, 1971. 463-479, Amsterdam.

Katz, C. M. & Taylor, P.M. The incidence of low birthweight in children with severe mental retardation. Amer. J. Dis. Childr. 114:80-88, (Jul) 1967.

Rosado, A. & Metcoff, J. Human fetal growth retardation. PEDIATRICS, 50:568-577 (Oct) 1972.

Scrimshaw, N.S. Early malnutrition and central nervous system function. Merrill-Palmer Quarterly of Behavior and Development, Vol. 15:375-383.

Winick, M. Nutrition and cell growth. Nutr. Rev., 1968, 26:195-197.

4

EARLY CHILDHOOD DEVELOPMENT

Robert E. Weber, Ph.D. *
Special Consultant
New Jersey Association for
Children With Learning Disabilities

*With thanks to my colleagues, especially Richard Weeks, of the Educational Improvement Center, who participated with me in New Jersey's Early Childhood Development Study.

INTRODUCTION

There has been growing pressure in the United States for early childhood development programs, with a particular focus on day care. The impetus for this movement was provided by the research of many investigators over the past two decades. Their findings cluster in several areas: the pre-school years are years of very rapid growth for the human organism, and these years are the optimal time for many different kinds of learning; some groups in our country, because they live in dysgenic environments, encounter developmental lags and achievement deficits—and unless these lags and deficits are remedied early, the children of these groups are subject to cumulative damage and may suffer irreversible harm. Many more of our children have learning disabilities than had previously been realized (in many cases multiple handicaps which seriously impede successful learning) and the optimal intervention for these children lies in early diagnosis, followed by prescriptive teaching and training. Additional urgency was, of course, provided by millions of mothers who felt intuitively that their children needed a head start, or who were working or who wanted to work. The rage for early childhood development programs probably peaked in the White House Conference on Children in December of 1970, where several national groups promulgated the concept of day care as a basic right.

The response to this movement by many private organizations was a frenetic effort to secure contracts and begin programs overnight. Most of these early programs were characterized by ill-conceived curricula or no curricula at all, poorly-trained personnel, and facilities that were hastily improvised. The result was that the programs that came into being were more custodial than developmental and thus did not meet the real needs of children.

That, in brief, is the recent historical perspective. Let us now turn to what we mean by early childhood and by development. The age group under discussion consists, basically, of all children ages 0 to 5. However, recognizing the high effectiveness payoff of preventive programs, certain programs dealing with the "pre-lives" of children, such as maternal nutrition, prenatal care, and most important, genetic counseling, should also be given serious consideration.

Now the question of what is meant by development. All children, except the most terribly damaged, have the ability to learn—how much they learn being determined by the potential of the individual and the quality of the environment. Therefore, any consciously designed intervention in the early life of children, which manipulates and changes the environment to the benefit of their learning, which provides them with increased stimulation and enrichment, we construe to be development. The physical settings for these developmental activities include: the home, infant and toddler centers, nursery schools, day care centers, and pre-schools. The three levels of individual development addressed by the manipulated, structured, or what Montessori would call the "prepared" or "preparing" environment, are the cognitive, the affective and the conative (i.e., thinking, feeling, behaving).   .

The basic ingredients of the cognitive domain have been delineated[1] as follows:

- Perception (dealing with information)

---

[1] S. Shirley Feldman and Susan Crockenberg, "A Profile of Cognitive Development in Children," San Mateo County Board of Education, San Mateo, Calif., Sept., 1969, pp. 1-4.

- Motor Development (specifically perceptual-motor development which influences later cognitive development)
- Language
- Conceptual Activity
- Learning, Memory and Problem Solving

On the feeling level, it is necessary to develop ways of teaching and *relating* to children so that ego strengths get built, resulting in children capable of more autonomy and self-sufficiency, who have better self-images and who are emotionally sound.

On the behavioral level, largely through play, games, and environmental management, the objective is to increase the socialization of children; that is, to increase the self-control of children; to develop good inter-personal relationships, and such behavioral attributes as cooperation, the ability to share, and so forth.

Lastly, special attempts should be made in programs of early childhood development to involve the home, an important point that is virtually ignored by the public schools and both the non-profit and the proprietary programs. By concentrating in this area, a multiplier effect can be obtained in the sense that parents can be taught to provide additional stimulation and to reinforce the activities that take place in a developmental center.

Typical objectives in early childhood development are those formulated by the Task Force on Early Childhood Development of the Education Commission of the States. These are summarized as follows:

1. To develop ways to reach the families of young children and to strengthen their capacities for parenting.

2. To involve parents in the formal education of their children directly and through the decision-making process.

3. To provide for the health, safety and psychological needs of young children.

4. To start the educational process that will contribute to the development of individuals who will be able to solve a variety of problems and are willing to try to solve them.

5. To lay a foundation for improvements that should take

place in the early years of schooling to make it more responsive to the needs of children.[2]

PHILOSOPHY OF EARLY CHILDHOOD DEVELOPMENT

Ideally, the philosophy of programs for early childhood development should be preventive, comprehensive and developmental: developmental, because this approach to foreseeable problems of human welfare always is cheaper and more effective than remedial and crisis intervention; comprehensive, because piecemeal or hit-and-miss programs for early childhood development can only be ineffective and frustrating; and preventive so as to attain the benefits of early intervention, to take advantage of lower costs, and to forestall irreversible damage.

It should be stated clearly and emphatically that the average public school cannot and should not serve as a model for programs of early childhood development. Many of the practices of the public schools are contra-indicated for young learners in preschool programs. In the public schools a number of horrifying assumptions have crept into prevailing practice. Our schools in general are operated as though we believed that: kids learn better when they are lectured to and when teachers talk incessantly; when kids are taught as a group, with little provision for individual attention; when kids are grouped arbitrarily; when kids are seated geometrically; when rewards are extrinsic and with negative reinforcement; when grades are given, producing a "star system" which rewards a few; when rote learning and the digestion of trivia is encouraged over discovery; when irrelevancy is the rule rather than the exception; when education is coerced; when learning is paced according to the "dictates" of mass production; when parental involvement and cross-peer learning are kept at a minimum; and when the environment, including physical design, interferes with learning. All of this adds up to a cruel and relentless dyspedagogia that, in terms of its lifetime effects, is dysgenic for the students.

Learning in the early years, and perhaps through the first

---

[2] Task Force on Early Childhood Education, "Early Childhood Development," Education Commission of the States, Denver, Col., 1971, p. 5.

couple of years of public school, is *inevitable*—how much one learns and how efficiently one learns is limited only by the potential of the individual and the quality of the environment. Young learners—the crib learners and crawling and toddler learners—all learn beautifully and prodigiously, even the retarded ones—except, of course, those in institutions and in other iatrogenic settings. They master that incredible feat called the attainment of speech (which some have called the work-equivalent of a Ph.D.). They are master builders, creating, to fill a void, such tremendous edifices as memory and personality. They learn without benefit of a formal school program, with rewards that for the most part are intrinsic, and in some cases developing where learning is a by-product of exercising a perceptual or motor system.

At this point it is worth spending some time to discuss this autonomous infant who learns so prodigiously on his own terms and at his own pace, choosing, rejecting, exploring, discovering, using what he has learned, or storing learning for future use. Language is a good example. If the linguists are correct, a 90-day-old infant, in his "babbling," will produce most of the sounds found in most of the languages of mankind (some eighty sounds). He will then, at 180 days, restrict his use of sound units to only those he will use in his mother tongue (forget, for the moment, about bilingual infants) and then store these sounds for use at some 300 or 400 days.[3] Has that infant learned! He has also learned how to unlearn (not taught in schools) and he has learned how to store for future use (who *really* determines readiness?). What happens to this autonomous learner—this master self-teacher who attempts so sublimely to approximate the Socratic imperative—when he encounters the prohibiting and toxic environment of the public school system, with its cataclysmic mindlessness and bureaucratic inhumanity? What happens to him is educational alienation. And this alienation is so pervasive that it goes beyond the classroom and reaches into such privacies of his life as soul and spirit.

---

[3] Dr. Harold G. Shane, "Stenographic Transcript of Hearings Before the Labor and Education," House of Representatives, April 22, 1971 (Washington, D.C.: Government Printing Office) pp. 1246-1247.

It is probable that *all* students, for varying periods of time, feel some degree of educational alienation, since, by definition, they are all ex-infants who were, at one time, free to explore, discover, and learn on their own terms. When they encounter the heteronomy of the school system, they discover that they are now not only subject to someone else's rules and regulations, but that there are now arbitrarily superimposed "laws" regarding the acquisition of knowledge. Moreover, they become quickly, and sometimes painfully, aware that this authority does not stop with the acquisition of knowledge, but that it includes the development of a behavioral repertoire whose chief characteristics are obedience, passivity, conformity, and a restricted range of creativity. Unless there is significant compensation for the loss of the autonomy that the students once had as "infant learners," educational alienation will have a telling impact on the bulk of learners engaged in formal education.

But what of the significant numbers of learners who do not fit the mass production mold of the American Educational Establishment—those who appear to be maladaptive because of differences in life and learning styles, such as members of bilingual minority groups, and most of all, those attending slum schools whose brains and personalities have become ghettoized? For them the problem is not one of inability to learn, because the majority have average or above average I.Q.'s. Their problem is one of increasingly intense alienation, as a result of educational maladaptiveness which is often school-induced. They perceive themselves as regimented and manipulated. They see the school as entity-centered and its offerings to be largely irrelevant and lacking in choice for them. They see themselves as victims of one-way labeling and the educational process as a one-sided transaction. They see their individual interests replaced by teacher and administrator interests. They see themselves as reduced to mere instruments of futile production which is periodically assessed with one-way measurement instruments.

Once their perceptions are articulated, an internecine warfare of reactions, counteractions, counter-counteractions, and so forth takes place. Learners react to teacher behavior and attitudes, and teachers react to learner behavior and attitudes. For example, teachers tend to perceive "underachievers," potential dropouts, or maladaptive students as: lazy, unmotivated, stupid, disobedient, disruptive, delinquent, deviant, surly and hostile, suspicious of authority, animalistic, and as failing to even try. In turn, the attitude of the students is that: school is a drag, teachers don't give a damn, school is a place to put in time until you are 16, classwork and homework are boring and irrelevant; they feel that they are unduly demeaned and punished; that they are socially promoted and haven't learned anything; that the school's main function is constantly to criticize them; and that even when they try they still can't make it. The internal manifestations of this conflict are as follows: student phobia on the part of teachers and school phobia on the part of students, with discouragement, depression, frustration and, in some cases, anxiety and emotional upset.

These insidious and totally unnecessary processes begin early in the game. We can record, with a camera, the smiling faces of eager learners, including those from the worst slums, as they enter first grade. In a few short years thereafter we can record the sullen and resentful faces of these same youngsters. Their records match their faces in reflecting the damage inflicted—many are lagging in age-grade status, many are seriously retarded in reading, many have undergone substantial I.Q. losses, and for many, the early and glowing educational expectations have been lost, perhaps forever.

Given the distributive function of education[4] (assigning students' futures or specific levels in the socio-economic pecking order), the school system may be society's most effective regulatory and discriminatory device. The process begins very early, is pervasive, especially for so-called maladaptive students (although this category includes numbers of white, middle-class students), and it plagues most alienated youths for most of their lives.

Another major point requiring emphasis is that the majority of both the non-public/non-profit, and the profit-making proprietary early childhood "development" programs (nursery schools, day care centers) are also grossly inadequate as models for a new

[4] E. B. Sheldon and R. Z. Glazier, *Pupils and the Schools in New York City* (New York: The Russell Sage Foundation, 1965).

universal program of early childhood development. While it is true that many of the profit and non-profit programs are free of the rigidities of the public school system, they are afflicted with the same kind of mindlessness about the needs of kids and how they best develop. What we see when we look at most of these programs can be characterized as "trappings" or semblances with little inherent value. The best that can be said for many of these programs is that, unlike the public system, they don't do much damage to kids. The point here is that *development must be consciously and explicitly designed for*—based on developmental profiles/schedules and sound learning principles.

Most of the activities which take place in these traditional programs are unconscious—one does this or that "tried and true" thing in the hope that, somehow, development will occur. There is a lack of pedagogical engineering—what McVicker Hunt and Katrina de Hirsch call "the problem of match," that is, ascertaining the developmental level (where the child is in terms of skill and concept mastery), and finding the requisite kind of stimulation for him at that point in time. Development in these programs is helter skelter; it is precarious and random. As in the public system, countless opportunities for teaching/learning are lost (e.g., snack time to teach responsibility and hygiene, or the eating of an ice cream cone to teach chemistry, physics, and geometry). There is also often a failure to measure accomplishment, thereby denying the children a sense of proprietorship of knowledge and of increased control over their environment.

It should be clear from the foregoing that we must use different practices in programs of early childhood development, and develop antidotes to the public education toxins and non-public ineffectualities that have spread throughout society. Fortunately, there exist numerous healthy curriculums, with a developmental rather that a custodial focus, that have been designed by early childhood development practitioners, both proprietary, public, and private-non-profit. These are available and provide an eclectic option for new early childhood program designs. If any solution can ever be contained in a single word, it is probably "openness." What we are talking about here is:

    . . . confronting the child with a range of educational experiences and helping the child select from these. The role of the teacher, then, is to be able to observe children and identify learning needs and capacities as well as to be able to extend the child's development by using learning experiences to stretch his capacities.

A number of early childhood educators have recently become convinced of the promise of a form of education that has been called "open education," "informal education" or the "integrated day." The roots of this system are to be found in English infant schools as well as in some American approaches to early childhood education.[5]

"Openness" also means the free ingress and egress of parents and other community adults, the participation of teenagers and geriatric residents, the extensive use of paraprofessionals as a buffer against bureaucratism, built-in provision for cross-peer learning, the use of the community as curriculum, the implementation of an accountability system, etc. "Openness"[*] means a different way of doing business, of providing openings for the winds of change and the free exchange of ideas, the creating of a more receptive environment and of more options within that environment.

We are talking about a system in which no adult is called "principal" (he may be called educational manager or some such thing), but in which all kids are conceived of as "principals."

In addition to the notion of "openness," and no less crucial to the minimization of the custodial and the optimization of the developmental, is the use of behavioral objectives.

To be sure, there are several other models for new early childhood development programs, most of them housed in universities, which we can use as resources in addition to the few nonpublic ones. One thinks immediately of Dr. Martin Deutsch's Institute of Developmental Studies at New York University, Dr.

---

[5] Bernard Spodek, "Stenographic Transcript of Hearings Before the Committee on Education and Labor," House of Representatives, Washington, D.C., April 22, 1971, p. 1250.

[*] For more detailed descriptions of the open school, the British Infant School, and the informal school, see Joseph Featherstone, *Schools Where Children Learn* (New York: Liveright, 1971); Charles Silberman, *Crisis in the Classroom* (New York: Random House, 1970); and Lillian Weber, *The English Infant School and Informal Education* (Englewood Cliffs, N.J.: Prentice-Hall, 1971).

Bettye Caldwell's program at the University of Arkansas, Dr.
Merle Karnes' pre-school in Champaign, Illinois, the laboratory
school of Dr. Doreen Steg at Drexel Institute of Technology, the
programs of Dr. Susan Gray and her colleagues at Peabody College, and many others. It will be the option of those implementing
early childhood development programs to either select a specific
model or build an eclectic model.

RATIONALE FOR EARLY INTERVENTION

General

The rationale for early learning is now widely known and
need only be summarized here. Dozens of investigators over the
past several decades have amassed impressive evidence that very
young children have an enormous capacity for learning and that
this process can be significantly enhanced by improving the quality of the environment. The years from 0 to 4 are years of very
rapid growth for the human organism. As we will note in our discussion on health (later in the chapter), the human brain reaches
90 percent of its growth by age 4. There is a similar large spurt in
the individual's intellectual development, reaching, according to a
number of investigators, about the 50 percent mark by age 4.

It appears that at no other point in his life is the child,
through age 5, so tractable, so responsive to the totality of his environment and its richness and stimulation. We tend, in essence,
to see all endeavors for his nurture as positive. However, we need
to remind ourselves that this very openness to environmental stimuli puts him also in the position of being acutely vulnerable. The
very fact that he is so impressionable must alert us to the fact that
he is just as capable of being hurt and permanently damaged by
negative or destructive experiences as he is of responding positively
to constructive nurturance.

Pre-school intervention programming has been widely hailed
as an effective technique for preventing the academic and intellectual deficits agreed to be common among children. The basis for
the interest in pre-school intervention programming is that early
childhood seems to be the most promising time for effecting de-

sired improvement in intellectual development patterns. Bloom[6] has pointed out, in his summary of the research on child development, that before the age of 4 is the time of greatest intellectual growth and is therefore the optimal time for intervention. Pasamanick and Knoblock[7] have documented the impact of deprivation most vividly in their study of infant development. There is proof from the extensive work of Skeels,[6] Skodak,[6] and others at the Iowa Child Welfare station, and from Kirk,[6] that youngsters described as culturally deprived may be directly and permanently aided by pre-school experience.

Also on the positive side, to make an observation in passing, Suzuki has produced a generation of Japanese violin prodigies merely by exposing them to good music and beginning instruction at an early age.[8]

It may very well be that the general inability of present preschool programs, such as Head Start, to cure the deficits present in deprived children stems from the failure to start early enough to alter the child's environment. As the essential framework and basis for intellectual growth is apparently complete by age 4, intervention after that age can effect only mild changes of a temporary nature; thus far, relatively late interventions have neither been long-term nor have they produced dramatic shifts in performance. In addition, it is likely that a good deal of Head Start failure, including its failure to maintain long-term gains, stems from the use of traditionally trained personnel in the public school system.

Numerous projects are currently exploring the area of early intervention. Most extensive was the program under the direction of Caldwell[9] at Syracuse University. Work in infant stimulation begins as early as possible and extends through pre-school. A day

---

[6] Jerome Hellmuth, ed., *Disadvantaged Child: Head Start and Early Intervention* (New York: Bruner-Mazel Publishers, 1968).

[7] R. T. Anderson and H. G. Shane, *As the Twig Is Bent* (Boston: Houghton Mifflin Co., 1971).

[8] Clifford A. Cook, *Suzuki Education in Action: A Study of Talent From Japan* (New York: Exposition Press, 1971).

[9] Bettye M. Caldwell, "The Rationale for Early Intervention," *Exceptional Children*, Summer 1970.

care center accepts children of working mothers and a developmental program is initiated. Early results indicate that the intervention program can successfully increase the intellectual level of the child and compensate for deprived environments to some extent. White[9] has explored the impact of early visual stimulation on institutionalized infants under 6 months of age. His results suggest that visual-motor development can be accelerated with generally beneficial results to the child's total well being. These programs, then, are efforts at early intervention before the child reaches four years of age. The Skeels[9] 30-year follow-up report of an early Iowa study clearly shows the extensive and positive impact that may be anticipated from these projects when the children involved are in a state of severe deprivation, such as in an institutional setting.

Work (research, experimentation, and demonstration) is proceeding on many fronts, both in this country and abroad, and new knowledge is emerging which may add even more to the rationale for early intervention. At this point in time, however, we can summarize the main argumentation for early intervention as follows:

- There is an optimum time for growth, development, and learning in the very early life of the child, and this period requires a "prepared" and stimulating environment.

- There are normative developmental schedules governing the various aspects of human development; however, because of different kinds of deficits in many families, schedules are not met; children lag behind in development, resulting in unachieved potential, failure, and cumulative failure.

- A trivial intervention can result in gains way out of proportion to the magnitude of the intervention. When Denis,[10] in the orphanage in Teheran, picked infants up from their cribs and held them and smiled at them for *minutes* a day, he got IQ gains; and when Skeels[6] *merely* transferred normal infants from an orphanage to a home for *retarded girls*, he also got impressive gains.*

---

[10] W. Denis, "Causes of Retardation Among Institutional Children," *Journal of Genetic Psychology*, 1960.

* The control infants who stayed in the orphanage, on the other hand, steadily declined in IQ.

- Many families lack the resources and skill necessary to overcome deficits that stem from a debilitating family life and environment.

- There is an enormous amount to be gained through the early identification and diagnosis of learning disabilities; corrective and prescriptive measures can be taken early, thus avoiding or alleviating the problem of treating worsened conditions less effectively at a later time and at a greater cost.

Health

The most successful programs of early childhood intervention are those that are the most comprehensive. They are programs which go beyond mere custodial care and limited cognitive stimulation of young children, and take into consideration the child's total development. These programs, in addition to dealing with the learning and social needs of children, also deal with their medical, dental, nutritional, and mental health.

One point which deserves major emphasis in the area of health is that the most effective comprehensive programs are either of a preventive or early-diagnostic nature. Furthermore, the costs of preventive or early-diagnostic program components are relatively trivial compared with the costs of not maintaining such a basic health program. As we shall see, the cost of not implementing basic health programs can be catastrophic in both dollar and social consequences.

Examples showing the differential costs between preventive and "penalty payments" illustrate the wisdom of prophylactic expenditures. A dramatic example can be seen in the problem of iodine imbalance. The preventive costs for goiter, which used to be a multimillion dollar problem in this country, now amount to one quarter of one penny per person per year (the iodized salt program). Milk fortified with vitamin D is another example of very high benefits/cost ratio.

The cost of iron deficiency anemia, which is prevalent in about 30 percent of the poverty and marginal income population,[11] has been reckoned at about $1000 a case to cure (hospitalization costs of $100 per day x 10);[12] the cost of preventing this potentially debilitating disease, which can influence the achievement rate and quotient, is in the neighborhood of $10/child/year.

Another example is the screening for phenylketoneuria (PKU), a metabolic disorder which, if not checked in time, can cause severe mental retardation. The cost of the screening program for *all* newborns in New Jersey (at present only about 94,000 are screened) each year would amount to $78,000. This is equal to about one quarter of the lifetime maintenance costs of only one child afflicted with that disorder (the incidence in New Jersey, for the population screened, ranges from 4 to 15 children per year). The treatment for this disorder, which is a dietary program, is not expensive.

Maternal nutrition is another program which has a very favorable costs/benefits ratio. The minimal treatment program for malnourished expectant mothers with low incomes is a diet supplement program (multiple vitamins and minerals). These undernourished expectant mothers, some of whom have geophagia (the eating of clay and boxes of starch, which impedes the utilization of some nutrients, such as iron),[13] have a higher incidence of premature infants (infants at risk). The data for these mothers shows increased infant mortality and morbidity, staggering maternal dental costs, a higher incidence of mentally retarded children and children with learning disabilities (neurological impairment, eye and hearing disorders and emotional disturbance). Without the benefit of a prenatal nutrition program, some of the children born to malnourished mothers would require lifetime residential care ($300 thousand/child), sporadic residential treatment ($5000/

---

[11] Margaret F. Gutelius, "The Problem of Iron Deficiency Anemia in Pre-School Negro Children," *American Journal of Public Health*, 59, #1, Jan., 1969, p. 291.

[12] Dr. Robert E. Cooks, "Hearings on Employment, Manpower, and Poverty," Committee on Labor and Public Welfare, U.S. Senate, Aug. 4, 5, 6, 1969 (Washington, D.C.: Government Printing Office, 1970) p. 148.

[13] *Hunger—U.S.A.*, a Report by the Citizens' Board of Inquiry into Hunger and Malnutrition in the United States, (Boston, Mass.: Beacon Press, 1968).

child/year), and special education costs of between $1300 and $3400/child/year (the present average schooling costs for normal children in New Jersey are under $1,000/child/year; the costs for special education last year in New Jersey—excluding the institutional population—were over $62 million). The cost of maintaining this program would be on the order of $15 for each woman involved. Until new census figures are available we will not know how many women such a program might involve (i.e., the percentage of poor women of child-bearing age). In any event, the prophylactic cost of $15 per woman at risk is far more attractive than the increased likelihood of costs in the $1300 to $300,000 range for the children involved.

Lastly, an example in the area of immunization. The vaccination for German measles costs $.65 a shot. While the true costs of the 1964 rubella epidemic have not yet been computed, the evidence of this damaging disease is very apparent, as the afflicted children have now entered the schools. The damage we now have to cope with includes blindness, deafness, chronic heart disease, metabolic malfunction, orthopedic handicaps and mental retardation. These children are often multiply handicapped and emotionally disturbed as well. The annual cost of the immunization program is amortized if we prevent only one severe case of prenatal rubella (the cost of the rubella immunization last year in New Jersey, for example, was $236,746).

The costs discussed above are dollar costs and, while these are important, the social and psychological costs, though incalculable, must also figure in all the equations dealing with human underdevelopment—the costs of premature death, trauma, stigma, pain, and the drastic limiting of an individual's potential.

From the point of view of cost alone—though this should not be our most important consideration—a comprehensive health program is requisite for all early childhood development programs and it should begin as early as possible (i.e., before conception) and continue, if only on a monitoring basis, until all children are thriving and healthful. Thus, the program should begin with genetic counseling—an easily amortized program and one which can significantly lessen the incidence of the most grotesque crippling and other damage to our children, damage which too often results

in long-term institutionalization, profound parent and child suffering, and catastrophic medical costs. Next should come a maternal
prenatal care program and, where needed (i.e., for the population
at risk), a maternal nutrition program. In addition, every child
should have an annual *pediatric* examination (through the age of
six), with special screening for learning disabilities and, where indicated, appropriate follow-up treatments (e.g., visual motor training, visual and audio perceptual training, special medication, etc.).
A program of adequate dental care should be provided for all
children from low-income families, since it is estimated that between 80 percent and 90 percent of such children have never
been seen by a dentist. Lastly, all children from low-income families should be the beneficiaries of a child feeding program so that
the nutritional standards for sound growth and learning can be
met.

At this point we need to give added emphasis to the role of a
child nutrition program in the rationale for early childhood intervention. There are several reasons for this: (1) the traditional
neglect by the medical profession of the field of nutrition, (2) the
emergence of new knowledge, both about the extent of malnutrition in our country and the relationship between undernourishment and learning, and (3) the folly of permitting the existence of
undernourishment in an affluent society which has huge annual
agricultural surpluses.

1. Substantial numbers of our newborn infants who manage
   to survive the hazards of birth and live through the first
   month, die between the second month and second year
   from causes which can be traced directly and primarily
   to malnutrition.

2. Protein deprivation between age 6 and 18 months causes
   permanent and irreversible brain damage to some infants
   in our land.

3. Nutritional anemia, stemming primarily from protein and
   iron deficiency, is common in 30 to 70 percent of our children from poverty backgrounds.

4. Teachers report children who come to school without
   breakfast, and who are too hungry to learn.

5. Doctors testify to seeing case after case of premature and

infant deaths which were attributed to, or indicative of, malnutrition.[14]

Of all the effects of malnourishment, central nervous system (CNS) damage in the early life of the infant appears to be the most serious. As Cameron points out, "The human brain grows very rapidly in the first few months and years of life, and reaches 80 percent of its growth by age 3 and 90 percent by age 4."[15] The critical nutritional period, in terms of the severity of damage which is irreversible, extends from the fetal stage through the early years of life. In cases of malnutrition in this critical period, numerous investigators have found reduction in head size, brain weight, and number of cells, and degeneration within brain cells. While a higher incidence of functional and mental retardation, both in human and animal studies, is associated with malnutrition, several investigators caution, at least at this point, against imputing the cause to malnutrition. On the other hand, some studies have shown that a food supplement program for pregnant, low-income women will result in offspring with higher I.Q.'s. Of these studies, the one by Harrell, *et al* succeeded in producing the largest I.Q. gains, 8.1 above the placebo (control) group as measured by form L of the Terman-Merrill Revised Stanford-Binet Scale.[16]

Another effect of malnutrition is in the area of feeling and behavior. Cravioto and Robles, for example, point out that "One of the first effects of malnutrition is a reduction of the child's responsiveness to stimulation and the emergence of varying degrees of apathy. Apathetic behavior in its turn can function to reduce the value of the child as a stimulus and to diminish the adult's responsiveness to him. Thus apathy can provoke apathy and so contribute to a cumulative pattern of reduced adult-child interaction."[17]

---

[14] Janet L. Cameron, "Malnutrition and Its Social Implications," *School Lunch Journal*, Vol. 24, 1970, p. 46.

[15] Janet L. Cameron, "Brain Development and the Effect of Malnutrition." School Lunch Journal, October, 1969, p. 15.

[16] Ruth F. Farrell, et al., "The Influence of Vitamin Supplementation of the Diets of Pregnant and Lactating Women on the Intelligence of their Offspring," *Metabolism*, Vol. 5, Sept., 1956, pp. 559-560.

[17] Dravioto and B. Robles, "Evaluation of Adaptive and Motor Behavior During Rehabilitation from Kwashiorkor," *American Journal of Orthopsychiatry*, April, 1965, p. 449.

Other studies, some of them dealing with wartime child nutrition, elaborate on these neurologic abnormalities such as irritability, lethargy, and apathy.

School performance, particularly in the area of reading retardation, which is a crucial problem in American education today, may be, in part, traced to poor nutrition. Bokan, citing the work of Cravioto and his colleagues, maintains that "Evidence already exists that the lag in the development of certain varieties of intrasensory integration has a high correlation with backwardness in learning to read."[18]

Another important area of human growth and development, socialization, is also apparently affected by undernutrition. Congressman Mikva, in a speech entitled "Hunger and Poor Performance Linked," cites the finding of the Woodlawn Mental Health Center (Chicago) survey of 2,300 mothers with children attending public schools, that: "The results of these systematic studies show that hunger is important in influencing how well the child socializes in the first grade classroom."[19]

Poor school performance is probably also linked to the fact that undernourishment results in sickly children who are either illness prone or chronically ill and who suffer a high incidence of infectious and chronic diseases. It is also strongly suspected that poorly fed children are less able to stand stress, which leads to anomalous or maladaptive behavior. The irony, of course, is that the poorly fed child often lives in a ghetto, and ghetto life is often characterized by a higher incidence of crises and stressfulness. It should also be pointed out here that "poorly fed" may mean malnourishment, missing meals, or it may refer to a diet lacking in proteins, vitamins, and minerals, but abnormally high in sugars, fats, and starches, which may produce a debilitating chemical imbalance. Note, for example, the following comments on the nutritional status of black Americans:

> While the calorie requirements are generally covered for all
> members of the family, the protein intake of the chidren tends

---

[18] Rita Bokan, "Malnutrition and Learning" *Phi Delta Kappan*, 51, No. 10, June, 1970, p. 528.

[19] Abner J. Mikva, "Hunger and Poor Performance Linked," *Congressional Record*, Dec. 5, 1969, p. E 10389.

to be only borderline. Calcium intakes are low in at least 25 percent of the population, perhaps as much as 35 percent, and iron intake is low in a substantial number of cases, again perhaps as much as a third or more of the population. Of the vitamins, intakes of Thiamine, riboflavin and nicotinic acid are low in 12 to 15 percent of the population; vitamin A requirements are not adequately covered in perhaps as much as 50 percent; vitamin C intake is inadequate for much of the population, particularly the urban group, for several months each year.[20]

Another, longer range effect of malnutrition—the beyond-the-generation effect—is the cyclical pattern which results not only in costs for today's starving or poorly fed children, but also for their malnourished children. Cravioto and his colleagues comment as follows:

> . . . one is led to be concerned with what in an ecological sense could be called a "spiral" effect. A low level of adaptive capacity, ignorance, social custom, infection of environmental paucity of food stuffs appear to result in malnutrition which may produce a large pool of individuals who come to function in suboptional ways. Such persons are themselves more ready to be victims of ignorance and less effective than otherwise would be the case in their social adaptions. In turn they may rear children under conditions and in a fashion designed to produce a new generation of malnourished individuals.[21]

The ancients, in their pre-scientific wisdom, labeled famine as one of the Four Horsemen of the Apocalypse and, as such, a profound evolutionary barrier. In contemporary terms, in a land of plenty, the prevalence of poorly fed and malnourished children bodes ill for their evolution into healthy, proficient, and productive members of society. So we should heed the recommendations of those knowledgeable about health and nutrition, even if for the lamentable reason that the costs of not heeding them could be far

---

[20] "The Nutritional Status of American Negroes," *Nutrition Review*, Vol. 23, No. 6, June, 1965.

[21] J. C. Dravioto, et al., "Nutrition, Growth and Neurointegrative Development," *Pediatrics Supplement*, Vol. 38, No. 2 Part #1966 pp. 319-320.

greater than those involved in implementing what they prescribe.

In summary, very few children in this category are adequately served; too many are institutionalized; too many are educationally at risk; and too few are adaptable.

LEARNING DISABLED PRE-SCHOOL CHILDREN

Handicapped youngsters, like all other children, must be intellectually stimulated, and depriving a child of this opportunity can often magnify an impairment and can seriously reduce the effects of future educational experiences.

The development of a healthy self-image and, concommitantly, the avoidance or reduction of emotional disturbance which seriously complicates the initial handicap, can be achieved by the sustained efforts of aware parents and specialists in early childhood development.

One of the basic tenets imparting this positive outlook is to avoid mislabeling and pigeon holing these children, and whenever possible to broaden their educational experiences by including them in classes with normal youngsters. This would provide a developmental as opposed to a remedial course, affording them a challenge. This is especially true of the physically handicapped child whose mind is as alert or more so than that of the normal child.

Unfortunately, few state legislative mandates exist which provide educational services for youngsters under six years of age. The tight budgetary situation which most school districts must cope with further discourages pre-school programs, to the extent that some local districts have even had to discontinue kindergarten classes.

It has been variously estimated by different groups that from 10 percent to 20 percent or more of the pre-school population have handicaps/learning disabilities.

Estimates of the numbers of children with handicaps vary widely because of definitional problems, measurement difficulties, lack of comprehensive diagnosis (particularly among the poor), and overlapping categories. Nevertheless, conservative estimates, synthesized from a variety of sources, of the number of children with handicaps are as follows:

Category	Incidence Rate (%) (diagnosed and undiagnosed)
Speech Impaired	3.5
Emotionally Disturbed	2.0-5.0
Mentally Retarded	3.0
Neurologically Impaired	8.0-15.0
Hard of Hearing	0.5-1.0
Deaf	0.075-1.5
Crippled or Other Health Impaired	0.5
Visually Impaired	5.0
Dyslexia	13.0

To summarize, at present we have a potential early childhood development special education population of 20-40 percent and a large mother-in-need population.

The term "learning disabled" has some forty synonyms such as minimal cerebral dysfunction, mild central nervous system insult, perceptual handicap, minimal brain injury, neurological impairment, hyperkinetic behavior syndrome, developmental disability, and so forth. While some of these synonyms translate into particular forms of dysfunction (e.g., developmental dyslexia) by and large we are talking about impaired functions of central nervous system (CNS) sensor/receptors, the failure of CNS expressors/drive mechanisms, or the failure of the CNS to integrate the sensors and expressors. All of this adds up to functional deficits. A short list of these dysfunctions will illustrate the extraordinary difficulties—academic, behavioral, affective, social, and psychological—that the learning disabled child carries with him and presents to those of us who are trying to help him. These deficits are in the following areas.

- visual perception
- audio perception
- conceptualization
- gross and fine motor coordination
- hand/eye coordination
- speech
- short attention span
- hyper distractibility
- dyslexia
- memory
- visual recall

- audio recall
- form perception
- visual discrimination
- spatial relationships
- temporal relationships
- computational skills
- balance

As a result of these and other impairments, the learning disabled child is maladept at coping with change, stress, and new stimuli and experiences, and suffers a variety of psychological problems—poor adaptation, unpredictable mood swings, inappropriate emotional responses, poor self-image, poor sense of positive expectancy—due to a combination of factors: the way he is perceived and treated by others in his environment, the accumulation of failure experiences, the perception that he is different, and a sense of self-worth based on normative standards.

The learning disabled child's problems can be conveniently thought of as encompassing the mechanical, the biochemical, and the emotional. On the biochemical level there are a number of helpful procedures: pharmacologic control of convulsive disorders and hyperkinetic disorders, and diet and food supplements. On the emotional level, there are such available measures as 1:1 psychiatric care, group therapy, treating the significant others (e.g., parents, sibs, etc.), and behavior modification. In addition, a program to sensitize normal children and their teachers to the problems of learning disabled children would help immeasurably. On the horizon there are bio-feedback devices, trancendental meditation, and the "sentic cycle," which may also be of enormous benefit.

On the mechanical level—we are talking now of education, training, exercise, and recreation—a great deal can be done to close the deficit gap between so-called normal children and the learning disabled child. All the items displayed earlier—from visual perceptual problems to dyslexia—are amenable to treatment procedures of special education teachers and such support personnel as school social workers and psychologists, remedial reading teachers, adapted physical education teachers, learning disabilities specialists, and so forth. In turn, all of these can be abetted by special programs in scouting, residential camping, special Little League, and a variety of home repertoires which exercise systems, instill confidence, build skills, and strengthen inner resilience.

To be sure, the obstacles presented by the learning disabled child are large. On the other hand, the state-of-the-art is such that our interventions can make a significant difference. Early childhood development programs, we think, are the place to begin. If, after all our efforts, the battle is lost here, it won't be because we haven't tried. And in the final analysis, trying but not achieving great measurable gains will have a higher payoff than merely doing nothing. All the current evidence, however, suggests that early childhood development programs do help—and in ways that are inversely proportionate to the time and effort we expend.

5

EMOTIONAL AND SOCIAL PROBLEMS OF CHILDREN WITH DEVELOPMENTAL DISABILITIES

Larry B. Silver, M.D.
Associate Professor of Psychiatry,
Chief of the Division of Child
and Adolescent Psychiatry,
Rutgers Medical School, of the
College of Medicine and Dentistry
of New Jersey

INTRODUCTION

The special educators point out that Billy has visual perceptual or visual motor problems and focuses on how these learning disabilities interfere with his mastering reading or written language skills. We are used to focusing on this, but what about Billy on the playground who misses the ball because his eyes cannot tell his hands what to do? How will other kids react to Billy's apparent clumsiness and poor performance? How will Billy feel if he is not chosen when the kids pick sides?

So it is with Mary. The educational and language evaluations identified her auditory perceptual and expressive language problems; and, based on this information, a specific educational prescription is developed for her. But is that enough? What about Mary when she is with her friends? She misunderstands what they are saying and responds incorrectly in a game. Someone asks her a question and she can't quite answer. What does this do to Mary? How does this shape her friend's relationship with her? Someone may have explained her auditory language difficulties to her teacher, but her parents never knew. They may even get angry with her for "not paying attention."

Children with learning disabilities pay a price in school. With appropriate help they compensate for or overcome their handicaps. But they also pay an emotional price; their family is affected; their entire social interactions are affected. With appropriate help these complications can be minimized. Without such help, the child might overcome his learning disabilities but still be unavailable for learning or be an emotional cripple.

It is the purpose of this Chapter to discuss the emotional problems of children with developmental disabilities. The problems of the family with a child who has a developmental disability will be discussed in a later chapter. Before discussing problems with these children it would be useful to briefly discuss models for observing behavior and normal development.

MODELS FOR OBSERVING BEHAVIOR

There are three general ways of observing behavior. One can try to understand what is going on within the individual's mind: the *intrapsychic* approach. One can observe how an individual relates and interacts with others: the *interactional* approach. Or, one can observe how an individual relates in the many functional groups he interacts with and how the influences of one group (e.g., family) influence his behavior in another group (e.g., school): the *systems* approach.

In the *intrapsychic* approach we use psychoanalytic concepts. The child has certain basic drives that influence his behavior, an aggressive drive and a drive to be loved or to love (referred to as the sexual drive). He learns that all drives cannot be impulsively responded to and he learns to delay or modify these drives into socially acceptable releases by using defense mechanisms. By about age six the child has a built-in value system that tells him what is right or wrong or what he should or should not do. He feels guilt or shame if he does not respond as this "voice" of his conscience tells him to. The child must also be aware of his outside world and must learn what is acceptable or unacceptable behavior in different settings. He can behave one way in school, another way at home, another way in Sunday School, and still another way on the back lot with the gang.

In the intrapsychic model we try to understand what drives are influencing behavior and whether the child has developed acceptable techniques for modifying and coping with his drives. If the drives are not under control he will experience anxiety and may reflect this in inappropriate behavior. We also try to understand the role of his value system and whether the demands are too great, appropriate, or inappropriate, helpful, or hindering. We also concern ourselves with his ability to perceive the outside world and whether he responds in a socially-acceptable manner or not.

In the intrapsychic approach we observe the interactions of the drives (the Id), the value system (the Superego), and the outside world on the part of the mind that has to put all of these influences together and produce a behavior (the Ego). When a child has an emotional problem we try to see where the relationship between these parts of the psyche are dysfunctional. Individual psychotherapy might be suggested.

In the interactional approach, we observe how the individual relates to others, his parents and other adults, his siblings and peers. Does he relate in a positive, constructive manner? Is his level of interactions appropriate for his age, immature, or precocious? Does he encourage people to interact with him, or does he provoke and chase them away? In this model all aspects of relating would be observed. Some might use an intrapsychic model to try to understand the interactions. Others might look at the acceptable and unacceptable behaviors and not concern themselves with an intrapsychic process. If a child were dysfunctional in any aspect of interacting, group therapy might be suggested.

The newest model of observing behavior is the systems approach. At any point in time in anyone's life he is functioning within a system. A system has boundaries; for example, a family or a classroom. A system has members and each member has a role or roles to play within the system. There are rules governing acceptable and unacceptable behavior. The goal of any system is to maintain a comfortable equilibrium.

We develop roles to play in a system. Usually our roles

evolved in our original family. We enter other systems with our established role but can modify it in a new system. In the systems approach we can make several generalizations. The more important a system is to the person (e.g., the family for a child) the more that system shapes his style or role. One also carries this role to other groups. A change in equilibrium, thus roles, within one system may result in a change in other systems. Conversely, if one tries to help a person change his group style or role in one system, this change will alter the equilibrium in other systems, and thus affect the other members of a system. For example, two parents might have marital difficulties. They have handled these problems by displacing them onto a specific child. Each focuses his anger and frustration on this "bad child" who continued to misbehave. Through therapeutic intervention the child improves. At this point often the parents' marital problems surface, another sibling is picked and starts to act up, or the therapy is sabotaged.

Whether one prefers the intrapsychic, the interactional, or the systems approach—and ideally one would look from all three views—the basic theme is that you must look at the total child in his total environment to understand his behavior.

NORMAL EMOTIONAL DEVELOPMENT

I would like now to briefly review development in an observational manner, refraining from developing specific views. The age norms given will vary with different families, cultures, or socio-economic groups.

Let us start with birth. The child is basically a physiological being, unrelated to anyone, undefined from his environment. All he knows is that his stomach hurts; he cries; something goes in his mouth; the discomfort fades; and, he goes back to sleep. Or, his rear is uncomfortable; he screams; something warm and dry replaces the discomfort; and, he goes back to sleep. To illustrate this stage of development let a small circle represent the child and a bigger circle represent the mothering person or people (mother, father, live-in maid, etc.).

By about three months the child begins to recognize parts of the people in his environment. He responds with a smile, the social smile. That is, with maturation of the eye retina and optic pathways he sees pieces of his world and begins to relate them to pleasurable memories. By 6-9 months the child has firmed up his boundaries and can distinguish himself from the outside world. He begins to recognize whole people and begins to associate specific people with pleasurable experiences; thus, he becomes concerned about unfamiliar people. He establishes a fixed mothering person and forms *basic trust* with her, forming a totally dependent, symbiotic relationship. (The child may do this with several important, consistently present mothering people.) This step of forming basic trust is the first critical step in psychological development. We recognize its arrival by the child's sudden fear of strangers. I sometimes call it the "Grandmother Syndrome" because prior to this time when Grandma came to visit and picked up the child, he smiled. On this visit she picks up the child and he screams and she is convinced that her daughter-in-law has said something about her.

The second major step in development is mastered between 9 months and 3½ years, learning to survive without this key person. Mastery of *separation* leading to Autonomy takes place in stages.

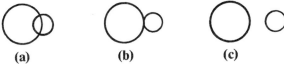

| (a) | (b) | (c) |

At first (a) he can separate as long as he has some type of perceptual hook-up (auditory, visual, tactile). The toddler lies in bed crying; he hears his mother's footsteps coming down the hall and he stops crying. The child crawls behind a chair and does not see his mother; he cries; she walks in view and he stops. The child cries at night; mother comes in and holds him, and he stops. Gradually he may substitute another object for this key person (a transitional object). Thus, with his favorite blanket or stuffed animal he can move out further from mother.

Later (b) he can move out for long periods of time, as long as he can return and tag up at home base every once in a while. The child plays outside but periodically comes in to give mommy a hug or to get a cookie. Finally (c) he learns that he can pull away from this all-important person and survive. He has mastered the second major step in development, separation, achieving autonomy.

Negativism starts about age two and helps the child master separation. His "No, I do myself" is his beginning to say that he has a mind of his own and can begin to function independently. Negativism is seen as a positive sign in development.

Toilet training also takes place at 2½ to 3 years. This process also forces the child to separate and function independently. Toilet training introduces a whole new set of issues for the child to learn to master; for the first time in his life he has to do something to please someone else. No longer is the world simply there to please him. He also discovers that he has an active weapon; if he wants to please mother he makes in potty; if not he squats in front of her with a smile and makes in his pants.

Now that the child has mastered Basic Trust and Separation he faces a third step in development. "Now that I've separated and become a person, who am I?" This task of Individuation usually takes place between 3½ and 6 years.

In the beginning he explores all roles to decide what he will be. Will he be like mother, father, sister, brother, the cat, the dog? Will he be big, little, active, passive? To learn, he tries everything on for size. Listen to pre-schoolers play. They play school or house or doctor or anything they want. They have no reality boundaries. One day they are mommy; the next day they are daddy or teen-age brother, or the dog next door. Whenever he tries to "be" someone in the family, like mother or father, he has to compete with that parent or any siblings who might want to also be this person, and he has to win the attention of the opposite parent. Thus, characteristic of this age period is fighting, dividing, splitting, tension, and sibling rivalry. One day the child is lovey-dovey; the next day the parent feels like bashing him.

This thinking is still at an immature level and he has trouble distinguishing between feelings, thoughts, and actions. His thoughts scare him. He worries that others, like parents, will know what he is thinking and retaliate. Thus, he becomes worried about bodily injury.

For the first time in diagramming we have to identify both parents.

If he wants to "be mother" he has to push mother out of the family as well as any siblings who might also want to compete.

If he wants to "be father" he has to push farther out of the family as well as any siblings who might also want to compete.

By about age six the child answers the question and decides to be like the parent of the same sex. He gives up trying to replace him, or her, and settles for being "just like him or her." With this decision peace settles into the family. The child also builds in his value systems at about age 6. This inside "voice" helps him control his fantasy and aids him in giving up role playing. The presence of this value system is a landmark suggesting that the child has begun to master this stage.

Finally, after the mastery of the first step in development (Basic Trust), the second (Separation), and the third (Individuation), the child is ready to move out of the family into the world (neighborhood, school). All stages must be mastered before he can comfortably move out and be successful.

From 6 until about 12 years the child has no additional psychological tasks to master. He has a "rest period." If he has been successful in development, then he can concentrate on the work of school and the world. He will acquire more new concepts, skills, and knowledge during these years than at any other time in his life.

Then at 12-13 years development picks up again. Everything breaks loose with adolescence. As for the Circle Game we simply repeat the stanza. The adolescent has to remaster each stage again.

Puberty is the onset of the physiological changes. Adolescence is the onset of the psychological changes. The rapid growth in height and weight creates an unfamiliarity with his body. The developing physical sexual changes in height, weight, body contour, voice, as well as the onset of menstruation with the girl, not only add to this unfamiliarity but also force "adulthood" on the adolescent. The newly-found masculinity or femininity is both welcomed and feared. For example, a 15-year-old girl who enjoyed being referred to as "stacked" described to me feeling certain that, as she walked down the street, every male eye was appraising and mentally undressing her. While one part of her was proud, another part wanted to slouch over and hide. She told me, "I don't really know how I should be feeling." The adolescent who matures earlier or later than his or her peers has additional stresses to deal with which make the adjustment of growing up most difficult.

Because of this loss of confidence or mastery of one's body, the adolescent retreats back to a dependent position. The 10 to 12-year-old Little League star is now a tall, gauky, awkward adolescent. The ballerina is now a klutz. Each initially prefers to stay home and withdraw.

In *early adolescence* (12-15 years) the adolescent must again master moving from a dependent to an independent position. We again see negativism: "I can do it myself, ma." The internalized value systems from parents have to be rejected in order to free oneself up: "You can't trust anyone over 30." To further emphasize his independence from "the establishment," he will dress and groom himself differently from his parents. He may choose "the wrong kind" of peers or adopt a value system opposite to that of his parents. He may demand freedom, then become frightened by such freedoms and "force" his parents to take them away. He may, at times, enjoy retreating back to a dependent state; later, when he realizes what he has done, he will become angry at the person who treated him (i.e., allowed him to act) in this way. Becoming dependent on her now takes on an upsetting meaning. For the boy, it is easy to shift from this dependent involvement in mother to an adult type of male-female relationship. The girl has a harder task, for she has to struggle to break away from mother (the dependent figure), and shift to father (the adult male-female figure). As he or she gains his independence from the family, he will shift investments and allegiance to the peer group; this group may become the most important relationship in his life.

Once he or she again masters separation, the adolescent must struggle anew with, "Who am I?" This major task of *middle adolescence* (15-18 years) differs from that of the 3½ to 6-year-old in that he will not necessarily become "just like" someone else but will take bits and pieces from many different important people, mix these bits and pieces with his own developing self-concepts, and blend them all into something uniquely his: his Identity. Identity crises are normal during this time. The resurging 3½ to 6-year-old conflicts become too stressful if focused, as before, on parents; this the adolescent must shift to figures outside the family. The girl will have "mad crushes" on other men (usually older); the boy will have conflicts with authority figures such as teachers, principals, police, etc. Sexual acting out may become a reality for the girl; acting out against authority figures may become a reality for the boy. By the end of high school the issues of role and career become additional critical issues to deal with.

Having mastered independence and identity issues, the *late adolescent* (18 years on) takes the final task leading to adulthood: *intimacy*. Intimacy is the adult form of relating. It is the ability to become intradependent on another yet maintain one's own boundaries and identity, unlike the child who can only become dependent by blending into the other. This ability to blend and share a life with someone, and yet clearly know his own boundaries and life roles, is referred to as *Intimacy*. The final processes of firming up one's identity and of establishing one's roles in life overlap into this period. Dating and courtship lead to marriage and a family. The man becomes comfortable with his career and his role as husband and father; the girl becomes comfortable with her role as wife, mother, and perhaps careerist.

If all has gone well with the "circle game" the individual is ready to have a child and repeat the cycle.

THE CHILD WITH DEVELOPMENTAL DISABILITIES

Perhaps as you were reading the discussion on normal development you were thinking of the many problems children with developmental disabilities might have. Before discussing specific emotional problems I'd like to review normal development again, but this time reflecting on how learning and language disabilities might create problems.

For the sake of this discussion I would like to think of learning disabilities in a cybernetics model:

Input Difficulties:

Visual Perceptual Disabilities	(The brain incorrectly translating incoming light waves)
Auditory Perceptual Disabilities	(The brain incorrectly translating incoming sound waves)
Tactile Perceptual Disabilities	(The brain incorrectly translating incoming touch information)

Integration Difficulties:

Problems with taking all of the many pieces of information coming in from the eyes, ears, touch and past memory and integrating them into meaningful concept.

Memory Difficulties:

Problems with storing and later retrieving information.

Output Difficulties:

Language Disabilities	(Problem finding and organizing words to express what the mind is thinking, especially in a demand rather than a spontaneous situation)
Motor Disabilities	(Problem integrating groups of muscles to work as a team in expressing what the mind is thinking; e.g., writing)

Establishing Basic Trust: (child from birth to nine months)

If a child has Input problems he might have difficulty perceiving and organizing his outside world and firming up his boundaries. At the most serious end of the spectrum, he may never be able to firm up where he leaves off and the outside world begins and he is considered Autistic. At the other end of the spectrum he might simply take longer to master this step. Integrative problems would create the same difficulty in organizing the outside world. In the case of memory problems, the child may not be able to store past experiences to later base safety and trust on. Output problems might interfere with communicating with the outside world, so necessary in establishing a close relationship with the mothering person.

Mastering Separation: (the 9 month to 3 1/2-year-old)

Input problems might cause the child to misunderstand his mother, teacher, peers. Visual problems create eye-hand difficulties; auditory problems create language difficulties. If he cannot integrate his inputs, he might have problems organizing the concept that he can survive without mother. He might have difficulty comprehending his peers at play. The outside world is not inviting and he might hesitate moving away from mother. Memory problems would limit his storage of positive experiences which would provide a base for feeling secure in moving out and knowing that the outside world is safe. Language difficulties interfere with establishing relationships; he feels unsure and prefers to stay close to home. Difficulties with motor (muscle) functions might delay mastery of locomotion, so needed to separate. Again, inability to master the activities and games of the "outside world" might cause the child to think twice about moving out.

At the other end of this "umbilical cord" is mother. The child might be hesitant to cut the cord, but so is she. Sensing his difficulties and seeing his problems, she is more likely to protect longer, to delay separation.

Establishing Identification: (3 1/2 to 6 years)

Input problems continue to interfere with correctly perceiving his interactions with his parents. His incorrect responses have often led to negative experiences and a negative self-image. The integrative problems might make it more difficult for him to handle his magical thinking or organize his feelings and thoughts, and the result might be an impulsive child who cannot handle his behavior. The competitiveness and role playing may get out of hand. The negative relationship might prevent him from resolving the conflicts by becoming just like the opposite parent. The developing conscience takes on the child's perception of his parents' value systems; thus, the child might begin to criticize and belittle himself. His motor or language difficulties make it harder to reach out or communicate his frustrations and concerns in a socially acceptable way.

Latency: (age 6 - 12 years)

Because issues of trust, separation, and identification have not been fully resolved and because of playground failures and academic difficulties, the child usually does not have the luxury of a "rest period." Though he struggles, he continues to do poorly.

Early Adolescence

As when he was a child, he has major difficulty mastering separation. Some young people might give up, becoming dependent, clingy, and fearful of moving out with peers. Others may rebel or become delinquent in an effort to deny their concerns.

Middle Adolescence

Mixed in with the many images he will use to finalize his identity are the years of frustration, failure, and inadequacy. Poor academic performance may close the door to college or to any meaningful training. Identity crises are frequent.

Late Adolescence

All of the above compound into a young adult who may have trouble relating to others. His self-image interferes with his confidence and ability to relate with another in a healthy way. The result may be a lonely, unhappy, angry adult.

Thus, mastering normal developmental tasks is not easy if the child has developmental disabilities. I have not mentioned the additional stresses created if the child is also hyperactive or distractible. These problems often produce havoc for the child and his family.

Think for a moment what skills are needed for a child to hold a conversation with a friend. He must understand the friend, organize the words he needs to express his thoughts, then express his thoughts through language. How about watching TV or visiting a friend's house to play? *His disabilities do not just interfere with school.*

Think what skills are needed to play baseball or football, chase, or hide and seek, cops and robbers, table games like cards or checkers, bike riding, or flying a kite.

Think through the sequence of getting up, getting dressed, combing hair, coming to breakfast, eating, gathering his coat, lunch and books, and walking to the school bus. Then interacting on the school bus, finding his classroom, and getting organized for the day. School has not yet started, yet the child with developmental disabilities has been working many times harder than the normal child to try to compensate for or cope with his difficulties.

THE EMOTIONAL ASPECTS OF HAVING A DEVELOPMENTAL DISABILITY

Children quickly become aware that something is wrong. They are not reading like the others or their script is poor. They are told that they are smart, yet they fail their assignments. One 12-year-old reminisced with me about kindergarten. He was now in a regular class, having had good help and having overcome his disabilities. He recalled, "I remember I used to want to draw a red wagon and I could see that red wagon, but it always came out looking like a hurricane." His mother would comment, "What a nice storm. But why do you always do a storm?" He would mumble that it wasn't really a storm, that it started out to be a red wagon.

I once evaluated a 9-year-old boy with learning disabilities who had been in regular classes. I commented that school must be hard for him. With tears in his eyes he said, "My mother and father always say I don't do it well." I asked him to give me examples of his problems. He showed me on paper how he gets "m" and "n" or "d" and "b" mixed up. He went on to explain. how he could learn better with his ears than with his eyes. He had never seen his educational evaluation but explained every area of his learning disability.

A 14-year-old who had received minimal, if any, help explained, "I have trouble with reading; I just can't read as fast or understand as well. . .Whenever there is classroom reading I fall behind, then the teacher makes me stay after to make up. . .If we have a written assignment in class I just about give up. Either I go slow so she can read my writing but don't finish, or I go fast and finish but get an F because she can't read my paper." Later she told me, "What's so frustrating is that it's all up in my head but I just can't get my hands to put it on the piece of paper. . . Do you know what it is like to be on page 2 when everyone else is finished on page 15. . .I get mad and feel like giving up."

An 8-year-old expressed similar awareness. "Sometimes I just can't get my hand to do what my head is thinking. . .I don't like English because I can't get the work done fast enough. Then I have to do it as homework. . .I get so mad with myself when I don't finish."

I asked one 6-year-old hyperactive child with multiple learning disabilities to describe himself. "I'm a boy who runs around, makes noise, knocks things down and can't do anything right. . . I think mommy is right, I'm just no good."

A defeated-looking 11-year-old told me of his school experiences. "I worry a lot about school. I don't do well and worry that I'll mess up and get yelled at. In first, second, and third grade I really tried and worked hard; only, I still didn't do well; so I began to give up and not try so hard. . .When you try and don't do well it hurts more than when you don't try and fail." Later he told me of his problem with writing; "I really get mad with my teacher. . .Once I wrote a real good paper on bridges. I spent hours at the library and really had good ideas on the paper . . .She didn't even read it but gave me an F because of my penmanship . . . I just gave up; what's the use of trying."

What are the options open to a child experiencing daily frustrations and failures? He could turn his angry feelings inward, getting angry at himself and belittling himself. If he does this he will feel depressed and anxious. He might try to avoid his feelings and thoughts by displacing them to others. "It's not my fault; it's the teacher's." "I couldn't help it; this kid kept teasing me."

Some children select the option of building defensive shells to protect themselves from the hurt. They develop passive styles and avoid potentially frustrating situations. Others might cover up their feelings and concerns by clowning. Some learn how to get adults to like them and continually succeed in getting extra help. Others develop a provocative style that chases adults away. Let's look at several frequent patterns of coping found with these children.

SPECIFIC EMOTIONAL PROBLEMS

Intrapsychic Problems:

The Withdrawal Reaction: The child avoids fears, failures, rejections, and depression by reverting to a fantasy life and self-play. He avoids any potentially frustrating or uncertain situation by withdrawing and becoming passive. He is unavailable for learning. I once asked an 8-year-old girl who was of superior intelligence but, because of unrecognized learning disabilities, had failed several grades and was currently in second grade, what she did in school when she couldn't do her work. "When I was younger I used to crumble up my paper and cry. . .Then they teased me and called me a crybaby. . .so. . .I decided that since school was no fun I had to get away. . . I couldn't leave so I sat and pretended that I was home in my room with my dolls. . .I made up stories and had a good time." The teacher complained that this girl would "daydream the day away if I let her."

The Regressive Reaction: Not able to cope with his frustrations and feelings, a child might regress back to an early stage of emotional or social development, resulting in immature or infantile behavior. The parents of Debbie, a 7½-year-old girl, complained to me that their daughter had been happy and normal until she entered kindergarten. Mother explained, "She had a change in personality. She had trouble keeping up with her work. In first grade she just didn't learn much and is now repeating first." Father added, "Home life is terrible, we yell at her all the time. Since school began this year, she's gone backwards, acting like a baby, talking like a baby. . .It's impossible. . .She won't listen and tunes us out. . .She's begun to wet her bed for the first time since she was 3. . .She even eats with her fingers." At a later session Debbie talked of school: "I have trouble because I don't understand the work, especially reading and math. . .It's hard and I can't do it. . .the teacher yells at me all the time. . .maybe I'm just not as smart as the other kids."

Using the Diagnosis as a Defense: Some children use their understanding of their disability or a label they have heard as a rationalization for their inabilities. A child might say, "I'm brain-damaged so I can't do that." He might generalize his disability and feel totally worthless. "I'm just no good; I can't read." Once, while observing in a special educational class, I heard the teacher comment to one of his fourth-grade students that he should re-do a math problem. The boy answered, "I can't do that; I'm a retard." A 12-year-old boy explained why he didn't have friends: "I'm brain-damaged so I can't catch a ball too good. . .all the kids play ball; so, since I can't play, I don't have friends."

Poor Self-Image Reaction: The child sees himself as an inadequate, bad, worthless person who just can't do anything right. Perhaps this self-image is based on outside feedback. One markedly depressed 10-year-old boy with such feelings had been hyperactive since birth. His mother reported that he was always all over the place. "All he ever heard from me was 'no' or 'don't' or 'bad boy'." He was kicked out of nursery school for being a "monster." Kindergarten was a disaster, as was first and second grade. Still undiagnosed, he repeated second, started third, and was now suspended from school. He has never known other than that he was bad, inadequate, or stupid. The fact that he was hyperactive, distractible, and had multiple areas of learning disabilities, but was very bright, helped me understand what had happened, but it didn't change his self-image.

Usually these children cannot be talked out of their image; the self-image improves when they get the appropriate help and begin to master learning and behavioral tasks. Mike, now 12 years old, was diagnosed at age 5 and received several years of intensive special educational therapy. Because of major secondary emotional complications he and his family also worked with me for several years. He is now in a regular class and doing very well. Recently he reminisced with me: "Remember when I was at the special school and you kept telling me how smart I was. . .I thought you just wanted to make me feel good because I couldn't read or do anything. . .I almost gave up and felt that I would just never make it. . .then one day it clicked and I started to read. . .I really read. . .then I started to do math. . .boy I could really learn just like you told me. . .I must have grown five years that first week I started to read."

The Depressive Reaction: Because of the failures, feelings of inadequacy, and negative feedback, the child becomes frustrated and angry. As noted earlier, he might turn these feelings inward, becoming depressed. In children below about age 8, this ability to turn the feelings inward is usually not developed; so, a depressed younger child might reflect it by being irritable and aggressive toward everyone. An older child might be withdrawn and sad. Some adolescents, in turning the frustration and anger inward, begin to attack themselves, belittle themselves, and a few

even try to injure or kill themselves. Juan, an 11-year-old learning disabled child with a long history of failures, was referred to
me because of his overly polite, passive manner, which made him
unavailable for learning. At one point in my work with him he
began to describe himself as a "bad troublemaker who was stupid
and couldn't do anything right." He added, "I get so mad with
myself when I make a mistake I send myself to my room. . .some-
times I punish myself by making myself go to bed early or by
picking my favorite TV show and then not letting myself see it. . .
once I got so mad I slapped myself."

The Paranoid Reaction: As noted earlier, some children cope
by displacing or projecting their feelings and thoughts onto others,
thus avoiding dealing with them. Teachers, classmates, books,
desks, all get blamed. For some, they begin to believe their concepts and become paranoid, feeling that everyone is out to get
them or to show them up. John, a 10-year-old in a special class,
had frequent episodes of explosive behavior resulting in his hitting
someone, yelling out, or throwing things. His usual explanation
was that someone was talking about him or making a face or trying to get him into trouble. At home he refused to go out and
play because the neighborhood kids were always talking about
him. John was not psychotic. A review of his school history revealed that two years earlier he was a withdrawn, sad boy. One
year ago he was described as an angry child who continually
criticized himself. Now we see his latest attempt to cope: displacement, projection, and paranoia.

Fear Reactions: Generalized feelings of anxiety, anger, and
depression are difficult to handle. Some children focus their conflicts on one or a few issues. By doing this, their feelings take on
meaning. It's not a general feeling of depression or despair he
feels whenever he is in school; it's a specific fear of a particular
kid on the school bus who always teases him. Now his feelings
when he wakes up to go to school make sense. Now he does not
have to relate the feelings to school failures. Steven, age 10, had
the typical history of unrecognized learning disabilities and repeated failures. Shortly after beginning the fourth grade for the
second time he began to have sleep problems. He complained that

he was afraid to go to sleep because he would have nightmares. He would stay up until 2-3 a.m. In the morning he was exhausted and either couldn't go to school or went complaining that he was just too tired to be expected to work.

The Impulse Disorder Reaction: One of the abilities a child develops as he gets older is the ability to delay longer and longer between the initial impulse to do something and the actual act of doing something. The longer the delay the more time he has to think of the consequences of the potential act or to think of possible alternative behaviors. Perhaps because of hyperactivity and distractability, perhaps because of the learning disabilities, some handicapped children do not develop this ability to delay; they are impulisve; they may be explosive or aggressive; they may have temper tantrums or catastrophic reactions. They may be emotionally labile, crying or yelling at the slightest frustration. Sometimes they break things or hurt people unintentionally, simply because they moved or acted too quickly and without thinking. Such impulse disorder children often show other evidences of this problem: stealing, bedwetting, firesetting, hoarding food, or excessive eating. Eight-year-old Mary was hyperactive. She continually broke things and had one tantrum after another. She was still a bedwetter, hid food at home, stole money from her mother's pocketbook, and set fires. When asked about the firesetting, she reflected her own concern with impulsivity and impulse control as she explained that what she enjoyed the most was, "letting the fire get big and almost out of control. . .then I would put it out before it exploded all over the place."

The Somatic Sympton Reaction: Some children reflect their anxiety through bodily functions. They may develop stomach aches, lower abdominal cramps, headaches, diarrhea or frequency of urination or bowel movements. The complaints often are present in the morning of school days but not on weekends, holidays, or summers. They have to leave class to go to the school nurse or to go home. Although it is possible for a child to fake many similar symptoms, it has been my experience that their discomforts are real. Though the stomach ache may be because of his anxiety, his stomach still hurts. A 7-year-old girl once explained, "sometimes I get into trouble because I forget to do what the teacher said or I erase too much. . .the teacher yells at me and I get scared. . .then my stomach starts to hurt and I have to go to the nurse." Eight-year-old Joe woke each school day morning with major stomach cramps and vomiting. His mother kept him home from school and the pains disappeared about noon. Complete medical studies were done and he was found to be normal. Joe must have guessed why I was to see him. He greeted me in my waiting room with, "I know my stomach trouble is because I'm afraid of school. . .only it really does hurt, I'm not faking."

The Hypochondrical Reaction: There are children who become overly aware of their bodies and who begin to complain of multiple bodily miseries. "My back hurts" or "My head aches" or "My knee feels funny." These children are often concerned about body integrity and have a fear of bodily injury. Perhaps their feeling different or "damaged" adds to these fears, with the resulting preoccupation with their body. Sometimes these complaints become rationalizations for their failures. The teacher comments that a child did something incorrectly and he responds, "I can't help it. I feel sick today and my arm hurts."

Healthy Intrapsychic Reaction: For handicapped children certain patterns are necessary to overcome their disabilities. Work must become fun. Compulsive characteristics like insisting on organization, neatness, accuracy, structure, and self-discipline are useful and, within limits, might be reinforced.

Interactional Problems:

The Passive-Aggressive Reaction: The child experiences frustrations and angers, but he does not feel that he can safely express his feelings directly; thus, he chooses a passive pattern. His behavior in and of itself is not aggressive; yet, one finds himself getting angry. Ann, age 9, was a professional at dawdling. She just played with her clothes until her mother was furious and screaming at her. She would look up in bewilderment and say, "Why are you so mad? I didn't do anything." A special education teacher once tried to describe a child in his class, "He's so cooperative and helpful and sweet that I feel like bashing him in the teeth."

The Passive-Dependent Reaction: One way to avoid failure and unpleasant feelings is to avoid situations that might result in failure. This passivity might expand into a lifestyle of relating. The child never takes the initiative, hesitates getting involved in anything, and just sits. When pushed he almost lays there waiting for you to do something for him. Sometimes the danger in public school is that this child's disability is not picked up because he doesn't bother anyone.

Healthy Interactional Reaction: Children with disabilities need all the help they can get, especially from adults. Some of these children become skilled at interpersonal relationships. People enjoy being around them and are willing to help or even do the work for them. To become successful in developing such positive interactions is a great asset.

System Problems:

The Clowning Reaction: The child under stress might resort to clowning. Clowning serves several functions. Frequently it wins peer acceptances. Suddenly the boy everyone teased is the class hero. He might clown to cover his feelings of inadequacy and depression. With some, clowning is a way of controlling feelings of inadequacy. By playing the role of clown or freak, it is as if he were saying, "They call me a clown or freak. It's not because I have chosen to be one. I really can turn it off if I wanted to, but it's too much fun this way." If the child is successful at clowning he will disrupt the lesson plan or be asked to leave the group, thus avoiding the academic work that perhaps produced the stress in the first place. *Clowning then gets reinforced.* In some schools being sent to the principal's office is rewarded by no school work or maybe talking to the secretary, delivering messages or playing with the typewriter.

Mark, at age 13, and after four years of educational and psychiatric help, was now back in public school and doing very well. We had met just to see how things were going and I asked him to describe what he remembered about his old school problems. At one point he said, "Boy were those teachers stupid. Anytime it was my turn to read or do anything I had trouble with, I would tease another boy or clown around. . .it worked great. I got sent out of the room." He went on later to add, "Only you and the teachers got me to see that I was the stupid one. . .you can't get help if you're not in class and I sure didn't want to spend the rest of my life in a special school."

The Pseudo-Maturity Reaction: Faced with all of the feelings and thoughts related to being inadequate and different and fearful that no one will take care of him, a child might decide to grow up quickly. Often, he needs to be in control and becomes upset if he cannot control all situations. He looks, acts, and relates like a serious young man. Sometimes this behavior pays off in that adults compliment him, but psychologically he is covering up issues that are frequently not far under the surface and these conflicts might cause difficulties in other areas or in the future. Seven-year-old Johnny didn't need anyone to take care of him. He was totally independent; in fact, he took care of everyone else in his class. He enjoyed most having discussions with his teacher. He had no sense of humor. His parents described him as a perfect little man who was completely self-sufficient. In a playroom diagnostic session, his fantasy reflected great concerns about dependency needs and a fear that they would not be met unless he took care of himself. All of his emotional energies were being used to maintain his protective facade.

WHAT TO DO

Over the past five years I have evaluated over 600 children, either directly or as part of a team. Many were followed closely or were in therapy after the evaluation. The above descriptions are based on these records. *Almost uniformly I found that when a developmentally disabled child has emotional problems, the emotional problems are a result of the frustrations and stress created by his disabilities and not the cause of the disabilities.* I say this not to minimize the seriousness of the emotional problems, but to emphasize the sequence of events.

Thus, I feel that after a full evaluation the treatment of

choice is special education. I cannot help a child change his behavior by seeing him one or two hours a week when he is experiencing frustrations and failures 25 hours a week in school. Once he is receiving the appropriate educational therapy, the emotional problems frequently disappear. Family counseling to help the parents and siblings understand the child's areas of problems and strengths so that they can refocus their relationships is also essential.

If the problems persist and interfere with his availability for learning or his relationships, therapy might be indicated. At this point it is important to assess the area or type of difficulty. For intrapsychic difficulties, individual therapy may be best. Group therapy might best resolve interactional problems. Family therapy is often indicated for systems-type difficulties. For some, medication is indicated. For others, a behavioral modification program is effective.

Ideally, a team effort between the educational, medical, and mental health team proves most successful. I feel that I've seen more of these children helped in the classroom by a trained, intuitive teacher consulting with a clinician than I've ever helped in individual therapy. Team this effort with educational family counseling and progress is often made.

CONCLUSIONS

Our usual approach to children with disabilities is to focus on their weaknesses and problems. Parents and teachers can quickly tell you what a child can't do or what he does that is "bad" or "wrong." Yet, ask the same parent or teacher to list what he can do well or what behavioral characteristic they like and they pause or have no answer.

In education we are becoming more familiar with the concept of building on the child's strengths while helping him overcome or compensate for his weaknesses.

Behaviorally we need to do the same. If a child fails third grade, hopefully we are beyond the point of simply making him repeat third grade rather than exploring the question, "Why did he not learn." So too, if a child has a behavioral problem we get nowhere by saying he's horrible or sick or impossible. We should be thinking, "Why does he need to behave in that way."

No one likes pain or unpleasant feelings or thoughts. We all try to avoid such experiences. A child will not give up his protective shield until his experiences with failure, frustration, and inadequacy are decreased. We must relate to the behavior but we must also find the fire rather than just continually blow away the smoke.

It is not hard to understand why developmental disability children develop "protective" emotional problems. I can empathize because in a similar situation I would probably do the same. It follows that we cannot treat the emotional problems in isolation. The treatment of choice is a total approach centered around special education.

6

EMOTIONAL AND SOCIAL PROBLEMS OF THE FAMILY WITH A CHILD WHO HAS DEVELOPMENTAL DISABILITIES

Larry B. Silver, M.D.
Associate Professor of Psychiatry,
Chief of the Division of Child
and Adolescent Psychiatry,
Rutgers Medical School, of the
College of Medicine and Dentistry
of New Jersey

INTRODUCTION

Sir Isaac Newton once described the characteristics of physical motion in his historic Three Laws of Motion:

First Law of Motion: "Every body continues in its state of rest or of uniform motion in a straight line, unless it is compelled by some external force to change that state." This law is also known as the Law of Inertia; that is, a body in motion tends to keep in motion and a body at rest tends to stay at rest.

Second Law of Motion: "The rate of change of momentum is proportional to the force acting, and takes place in the direction in which the force acts." This law is also known as the Law of Momentum. For example, if a boy bats a ball with a certain force, and at another time bats it twice as hard, the ball will have twice the speed the second time as it had the first time.

Third Law of Motion: "To every action there is always an equal and opposite reaction." This law is also known as the Law of Reaction.

In the preceding chapter I discussed the systems view of observing behavior. When working with families, the systems approach is essential, since the family is a functional social system with boundaries, members, relationships, rules, and roles. Each family needs to achieve a level of comfortable functioning (homeostasis) and members of a family help to maintain this balance overtly and covertly. Families usually develop repetitious, circular, and predictable communication patterns and acceptable (vs. unacceptable) roles to maintain this balance. When the family homeostasis is precarious, members exert effort to maintain it.

The activities and movements within a family might be considered in an analagous way with Newton's Laws of Physical Motion. We might paraphrase:

First Law of Family Motion: Family members establish roles and patterns of interacting and communicating. Once all family members establish patterns that blend together to establish homeostasis, they continue in this state unless compelled by some external force to change that state.

Second Law of Family Motion: When forced to change its roles and patterns of interacting and communicating, the rate of family change is proportional to the force acting on it and takes place in the direction in which the external force shifts it.

Third Law of Family Motion: For every attempt by a member of the family system to change his role or pattern of interacting and communicating, thus altering the equilibrium, there is an equal and opposite reaction by the other members of the family system to either return to the former level of equilibrium or to establish a new homeostasis.

Thus, we cannot just look at the child with developmental disabilities in isolation; we must understand his family and family dynamics. When one person in a family is in pain, all family members feel the pain and react in some way. The symptomatic member of the family (the "patient") may have unique problems causing the pain but may also be serving a function for the family in maintaining homeostasis, even if this is dysfunctional homeostasis.

External attempts at change will be reacted to by all members of the family. In fact, it is very difficult to change one part of the family system (the patient) without working with the total system.

With this orientation, I would like to first discuss the effect the child with a developmental disability has on individual members of a family—siblings and parents—and then discuss the effect this child has on the family as a functional unit.

THE SIBLINGS

When parents become concerned about their child, they take him to one or more specialists until someone explains to them what the problem is and what needs to be done. Perhaps at some point someone will sit down with the parents and "interpret" the findings. Occasionally, but not often enough, someone sits down with the child and explains to him what his problems are and why certain things will be happening. Almost never does someone explain these issues to the child's brothers and sisters. Yet, they are part of the family and need to know. When one member of a family is hurting everyone feels pain. How might the siblings react?

Some become very worried and feel *anxious*. This is especially true in families where little is said. They ask, "What's wrong with Jimmie?" Their parents say, "Oh nothing special. . . it's o.k." Yet, they see the parents busing him from one place to another and they hear the parents talking. Occasionally they hear words like "brain damage" or "where are we going to get the money for all of this?" They see mother upset, maybe in tears. With lack of facts and aware that something is wrong, their fantasy takes over. Frequently they fantasize worse situations than what exists in reality. Then they worry. I've heard brothers and sisters say, "will he live?," "is he going to die?," "will it happen to me?," "if it's not so serious, then why all the whispers and hush-

hush?" They need clear information at the level they can understand and to the degree that they need to know.

Other siblings may become *angry* and fight with the child
who has problems or with their parents. They get angry at the
double standards. "How come I've got to fix my bed and she
doesn't?" or "He broke my toy and you did nothing." Or, they
may get angry with the amount of time and energy parents spend
with the disabled child. Between taking him to the special tutor-
ing, special programs, and doctors, there is little time for anyone
else. The handicapped child might use up so much money that
everyone has to do without or vacations may have to be compromised, and the siblings complain. Children at school might tease
a brother or sister at school, "Hey, how's your retarded brother?"
or "Your sister sure acts funny. . .what's wrong with her. . .is she
a mental case?" They are embarrassed by the comments or the
behavior and get angry. This can happen at home also; a sibling
might stop bringing friends home because he is embarrassed by his
brother's or sister's behavior.

A sibling may feel *guilty* and, especially, he may feel guilty
for his anger, particularly when the verbal or non-verbal message
from his parent is, "He can't help it" or "It's not his fault." A
brother or sister might think to hinself, "I'm glad it's not me,"
then feel guilt or shame for thinking such thoughts.

Because of these feelings of anger or guilt, a brother or sister
might *act out* against their sibling with the disability. They might
provoke or scapegoat this child to encourage his misbehavior and
as the handicapped child gets punished by his parents, the sibling
feels revenged. Sometimes normal siblings will set the handicapped child up to look or act bad because they perceive that the
worse he looks, the better they look.

There is one circumstance where a normal sibling negatively
affects the child with disabilities. It seems to be the plight of handicapped children that a younger brother or sister is not only super-
normal and delightful but precocious, quickly passing him academically and socially. It hurts.

THE PARENTS

In addition to being mothers and fathers, parents are also human. They have feelings and thoughts. They are also spouses and have a marriage to relate to. Having a child with a disability stirs up feelings and thoughts, fears and hopes. These reactions affect both the individual parents and the marriage itself. At no point is the stress greater than when the diagnosis is made, for it is at this point that parents feel anguish, fear, helplessness, anger, guilt, shame—all at once. Nothing can describe the feelings and thoughts going through a parent's head as he or she rides home from the doctor's office after that conference.

A sensitive professional, aware of this reaction, will never describe a problem without acknowledging these feelings and ending with a positive move, such as, "and this is what we will do about it." Unfortunately, all professionals are not this sensitive. Some play what I call the "Ha Ha you have Leprosy" game. They bang a parent over the head with, "Your child is retarded" or "handicapped" and they say good-bye. Out the parents go, overwhelmed, with no direction to take and little hope.

Though there are normal initial reactions parents will have on learning of their child's difficulties, some of these reactions may become chronic or pathologic.

THE INITIAL REACTIONS

The Denial Reaction: "It can't be true. . .he must be mistaken. . .he only saw him for half an hour. . .I don't believe it." A parent may doubt the professional's competence or castigate him. Frequently, another opinion is sought, but, while getting other opinions is often useful, "doctor shopping" for someone who will tell the parent what he or she wants to hear is not.

The Cover-Up Reaction: One parent, usually the mother, will want to "protect" the other parent by not sharing the results of the studies or by minimizing the problems. Some may successfully cover up the special programs for years. Sadly, the unknowing parent builds up unrealistic expectations or demands things of his child that the child cannot respond to. The child often sees through this cover-up. He is also likely to see through the true reason: "They can't accept me as I am; they have to deny and pretend I'm different." He may feel anger or sadness and will have difficulty accepting himself if he does not feel that the parents accept him.

The Overprotective Reaction: The most normal thing to do when your child is hurting is to reach out and protect him. This is necessary and helpful. But, the goal is to protect him where he needs protecting and to encourage his growth where he does not need protecting. A blanket of overprotection covers the weaknesses but also blunts the strengths. Not only does this behavior keep the child immature or delay areas of growth, but it also makes the child feel inadequate. He knows what's happening. When everyone else has a chore to do and he doesn't, when everyone takes turns clearing the table but he never has to, he might conclude, "see, they agree with me. . .I am inadequate."

These children need love. They need protection for areas of weakness. They also need encouragement and a loving push to develop and capitalize on their areas of strength. If a child has fine motor and eye-hand coordination difficulties, a parent may need to cut his meat for him, but he shouldn't dress him. If he cannot button, parents should buy slipover clothes; if he can't tie, he should have loafers. If he can't play ball well, he should not be kept at home and entertained. Attempts should be made to get him involved in swimming or another group interaction type of activity that does not require fine motor and eye-hand skills. Help with the weaknesses but build on the strengths!

The Anger Reactions: On learning of a child's disability it is normal to feel anger and such sentiments as, "Why me?" "How could God do this to me?" This initial reaction often reflects feelings of helplessness and frustration. The anger is almost like going through a brief grief reaction of losing a part of this child, or the wished-for future that the parent senses may never be. If not dealt with, the anger might be displaced to someone else or so preoccupy one's thinking that effective action is blocked.

The Depressive Reaction: The initial anger may be turned inward, attacking oneself and creating the feeling of depression. Associated with this reaction is a feeling of guilt—"It's all my fault." The parent might berate himself or herself with "God is punishing me because. . .," or "I didn't follow my doctor's advice," or "I've been given this extra burden to prove my worthiness."

If the depression is allowed to continue, the parent might withdraw from the child or the other parent at just the time that the child or the other parent needs him or her the most. With some parents the guilt feeling might be an attempt at having control over a situation considered to be hopeless. By attributing the cause to himself, the parent puts into his own hands the power to control and understand the situation. The "logic" is that if he does not again practice the transgressions it will not happen again.

The Blame Reaction: The initial anger might be displaced outward by attributing the fault to someone else. Like the guilt reaction, it places responsibility in the hands of mankind and protects one against feelings of helplessness. The parent might blame the physician because "He didn't get to the hospital fast enough," or, "I told him I was in labor but he wouldn't believe me and I almost delivered in the car," or, "If the pediatrician had come out to see him rather than prescribe over the phone he wouldn't have had that high fever," etc. This reaction might generalize to all professionals who are then considered bunglers, incompetents, charlatans: "It's the school's fault," or "She's just a young, inexperienced teacher," or "She's just an old, rigid teacher."

The professional may never hear of the parents' gripes, but the child may never be able to forget them. Such reactions may undermine the child's faith in or respect for the professionals he must rely on for help and for hope.

The Social Action Reaction: Another outlet for the initial anger is to channel this energy into a socially useful activity. The irritation of parents with a "poor school system that does nothing" might lead to becoming active in the PTA or attending school board meetings. They might organize groups to "fight" the system and, in doing so, perhaps improve the system. Such efforts have helped to create and develop organizations that have had great positive impact. Through pressuring and lobbying from without or running for office and changing from within, legislation gets passed and programs developed. Many special educators, it should be noted, began as concerned parents who wanted to learn more about their child.

The "Others' Reaction": After learning of their child's problems, the parents may be faced with the question of what to tell people. "How much do I tell the child or his brother or sister?" is a frequent question. As discussed earlier, they need to know, too. What do I tell his grandparents? "They will never believe anything could be wrong with their grandchild." What about other relatives or neighbors? Sometimes a parent might appear to be more understanding or accepting only to find that, instead, she rejects the disabled child and stops her children from playing with him.

These initial reactions of parents are all normal and real. Parent organizations that provide a forum for discussion, mixed with facts and shared experience from parents who have "been there too," can be of great help. Hope and seeing something being done such as a special program also help the parents regroup and say, "We have work to do; let's get started."

THE PROLONGED REACTION

The Denial Reaction: Some parents cannot give up their denial. They must continue to "doctor shop" in a continuing search for someone who will say that nothing is wrong with their child or for the doctor with the magic cure. Such parents greet the newest professional with flattery and praise, depreciating the numerous professionals who have preceded him. Ultimately, he too is rejected and attacked. As the frustration grows, the parents hop from one promised cure to another, often becoming the victims of people who capitalize on such people.

During all of this shopping, the child may be deprived of the valuable programs and therapy that he needs. There are two other serious consequences of chronic denial. Because each professional must be criticized and downgraded as the parent moves on to the next, the child picks up the message that he cannot trust or have faith in professionals. He needs this trust and faith to have hope and to work toward overcoming his handicap. The child also picks up another subtle but clear message from his parents: "We can't accept you as you are. . . we must find someone who will tell us that you are not the way you are." He hears and reacts with feelings of anger, shame, and inadequacy.

The Overly Dedicated Reaction: This parent totally dedicates his or her life to helping this child. And he's furious about it. What comes across overtly is the dedication. No task, no trip, no expense is too great to help "my child." What comes across covertly is the anger at having to do these things. Occasionally, a parent will become a professional martyr, and never let anyone forget it. The surface behavior is to be admired, but somehow the child picks up a parallel message: "Look how much I do for you, you ungrateful good-for-nothing child; you show no appreciation."

Part of being the martyr may be being a masochist, enjoying the suffering. "How noble I am to be able to endure what others cannot. . .people will admire me when they see or hear of my courage and suffering." He seeks pity and evokes guilt or anger.

The Prolonged Anger Reaction: Unresolved, the anger may continue to be felt or displaced. Nothing can go well. Someone is always doing something wrong in the parent's mind: "After all this time and money you haven't helped my child. . .how come?" Such parents become miserable and difficult to live or work with.

The Continuing Overprotective Reaction: That normal initial reaction of overprotecting the child becomes a lifestyle, preventing growth and increasing the child's feelings of worthlessness. In some cases this reaction is an attempted coverup for feelings of inadequacy as a parent. A parent with a low self-esteem and feelings of worthlessness may attain a feeling of being needed and wanted by deluding himself into believing that he is "all the child has in the world."

The child's immaturity and feelings of inadequacy lead to failure and retreating back to the home. An overprotecting parent will see this and feel even more justified in moving in and protecting. A repetitive cycle continues, the child continually realizing that he is helpless without his parent and the parent reinforcing the notion that the child cannot survive without him.

The Withdrawal Reaction: A parent might totally dedicate himself or herself to the child with problems to the point where there is no energy left for further relationships with the other children or the other parent. Taking care of the child's needs are so demanding and tiring that she is too weary for social or sexual relations with her husband, or for accepting the responsibility to the siblings. The result is a dysfunctional family. Often the anger is not expressed between the parents; instead it is being displaced onto the child.

CONCLUSIONS

The family is a relating system. The feelings, thoughts, and actions of one member are perceived and responded to by all other members. If any member is hurting all feel the hurt. When a family learns that one of its members has a disability everyone is affected and responds. A new level of homeostasis is necessary.

With open and honest communication between professionals and family and within a family, a new healthy level of functioning is possible. The handicapped child needs this accepting, understanding, empathetic environment to have a maximal chance at overcoming his disabilities. Continuous overprotection, sympathy, unexpressed or misdirected feelings only add to his burden, sometimes overwhelming him.

If parents do not understand their children's problems they need to keep after professionals involved until they do understand. They need to relate this understanding to the whole family. If they need help they might ask the professionals to participate in these discussions. Sometimes two or three family sessions with the professional or team involved can result in adequate understanding and can open up communication. A clear message is expressed in the family; "We can talk about this. . .we need to understand and work together." With this family effort the child will feel accepted for who he is, not what he and everyone else wishes he could be. To fully attain this feeling of being accepted, it is necessary for him to be able to accept himself. For a good prognosis this feeling of family support is essential if he is to overcome or learn to compensate for his handicaps.

7

PHYSICAL EDUCATION FOR THE HANDICAPPED: A NEGLECTED APPROACH

Thomas M. Vodola, Ed.D.
*Director of Health, Physical
Education and Driver Education
Township of Ocean School District,
Oakhurst, New Jersey*

INTRODUCTION

Educational theorists generally agree that learning involves progression through the following developmental levels: motor patterning, perceptualization, matching motor and perceptual responses, and conceptualization. They, further, contend that the school curricula should be structured so that each child is guided through a variety of learning experiences which will enhance optimum development at each level.

Until recent years, physical education has been viewed as having little educational value. Its justification for inclusion in the school curriculum was to provide children with a "release" from the rigors of the academic program, with a by-product value of developing some physical fitness. However, during the last decade research has refuted the theory that the mind and body follow dichotomous developmental paths. Although there are disagreements regarding the interrelationship (and how learning best takes place), intradisciplinary and interdisciplinary leaders generally support the viewpoint that a well-organized physical education

131

program is conducive to the development of the "total child."

Taking the cue from the research of other behavioral scientists, physical educators started to conduct studies related to the effects of motor activity on academic achievement. Ishmail and Gruber[1] conducted two studies that supported the hypothesis that academic achievement could be enhanced via physical activity that required the child to utilize his cognitive abilities. Cratty[2] has prepared an excellent paperback, *Active Learning: Games to Enhance Academic Abilities*. The text provides a variety of games and activities that can be utilized by the physical educator or classroom teacher. Interspersed, one will find research he conducted to substantiate his findings.

Based on the aforementioned studies and others of a similar nature, there is a perceptible movement in the field of physical education to restructure the curriculum. Where traditional programs focused almost exclusively on the development of physical fitness and motor competencies, stress is, now, also being placed on the development of the mental and socio-emotional qualities. The new curriculum is viewed by the author as being "child-centered" rather than "subject-centered." Curriculum design is predicated on the basis of the developmental needs of children rather than the teaching of a conglomerate of skills, games and activities. In conjunction with the curriculum modifications, we have a change in the role of the teacher. Teaching methods have been drastically modified to totally involve the child in the learning process. The teacher has become a diagnostician; an assessor of behavior; one who prescribes activities and evaluates performance; a guider of the learning process; a resource person—not a dispenser of knowledge. (Refer to the author's text, *Individualized Physical Education Program for the Handicapped Child* for the new role requirements of the teacher and the student.[3])

One might well ask, "What does a review of current trends

[1] A. H. Ishmail and J. J. Gruber, *Motor Intellectual Performance*, (Columbus: Charles E. Merrill Books, Inc., 1967), p. 199.

[2] Bryant J. Cratty, *Active Learning: Games to Enhance Academic Abilities*, (Englewood Cliffs: Prentice-Hall, Inc., 1971), p. 157.

[3] Thomas M. Vodola, *Individualized Physical Education Program for the Handicapped Child*, (Englewood Cliffs: Prentice Hall, Inc., 1972), p. 305.

and research have to do with providing a physical education program for children with learning disabilities?" The new physical education provides an excellent medium for meeting the needs of the child with learning problems. While we realize that one cannot generalize as to behavior manifested by these children, I believe it is safe to assume that they will display some of the following problems: low physical vitality; poor motor performance; a negative self-image; hyperactivity; distractibility; a short attention span; perseveration; impaired perceptual and perceptual-motor responses, ad infinitum. (See the article by Spears and Weber[4] for a detailed description of the neurologically-impaired child.) Physical activity, *if structured properly,* can eliminate or ameliorate many of the problems listed.

The "key" to providing a physical education program for the learning disabled is to design personalized activities commensurate with the needs of each child—that in essence is the definition of adapted physical education. Many teachers and parents have queried the writer as to the values of adapted physical education. Unquestionably, the greatest value derived is the enhancement of the child's self-image. Experience has indicated that most children with learning disabilities become frustrated due to their inability to compete favorably with their peer group. The resultant effect is a manifestation of introvertish tendencies or a seemingly defiant attitude—in either case, the facade is indicative of the child's inability to develop a healthy image of himself. Three reasons why adapted physical education can change the child's self-image are: (1) the constant use of positive reinforcement by the teacher; (2) the use of personalized instruction to establish maximum teacher-student rapport; and (3) the structuring of all tasks/activities so that regardless of a child's ability level he can achieve success. (The writer is currently conducting a research study in conjunction with Widmann and Winterbottom[5] on "The Effects of Individualized Motor-Cognitive Activities on the Self-Image and Academic

---

[4] Catherine E. Spears and Robert E. Weber, *Neurological Impairment—Nomenclature and Consequences,* (East Orange: Association for Children with Learning Disabilities, 1972), p. 33, p. 7 (Mimeographed) [*Editor's note*: Basically, this is chapter one of this volume.]

[5] Alexis Widman, Elizabeth Winterbottom and Thomas M. Vodola, *The Effects of Individualized Motor-Cognitive Activities on the Self-Image and Academic Achievement of Underachieving Students,* (Oakhurst, New Jersey: Township of Ocean School District, 1972).

Achievement of Underachieving Students.") Suggested activities that will benefit the child with a learning disability will be provided in a later section.

THE STATUS OF ADAPTED PHYSICAL EDUCATION IN NEW JERSEY

In 1967, Vodola and Daniel[6] conducted a survey to assess physical education programs for the handicapped in the state of New Jersey. Of the school districts that responded (in excess of fifty percent), less than two percent indicated they provided a comprehensive program that would meet the educational needs of all handicapped children.

Cognizant of the fact that the state law required that *every* child in our public schools receive 150 minutes of health and/or physical education instruction each week, the New Jersey Division of Youth and the New Jersey Association of Health, Physical Education and Recreation conducted a state-wide public relations and inservice program for physical education and special education personnel, administrators, and parents. Further, the Division of Youth published and disseminated several thousand copies of their publications,[7,8] in an effort to inform the public of the need for adapted physical education for all handicapped children.

Simultaneous with the public relations/inservice programs, Senator Alfred N. Beadleston, the Senate Majority Leader, was contacted to solicit his support. (Senator Beadleston is, undoubtedly, the leading proponent of improving the welfare of the handicapped in the state of New Jersey.) Senator Beadleston arranged for a meeting with Dr. Carl L. Marburger, the Commissioner of Education, to discuss what steps had to be taken to insure the statewide implementation of a physical education program for all

[6] Thomas M. Vodola and Alfred Daniel, "The Status of Developmental and Adapted Physical Education in New Jersey Public and Private School Systems," ed. by Robert McCollum (Trenton: New Jersey Youth Commission's Sub-Committee on Youth Fitness, 1967), p. 7.

[7] Thomas M. Vodola, et. al., "Physical Educational for the Exceptional Child" (Trenton: New Jersey Youth Commission, Department of Community Affairs, 1970).

[8] Thomas M. Vodola, et al., "The Pursuit of a Quality Education Program for all Children," (New Jersey: New Jersey Youth Commission, Department of Community Affairs, 1972), p. 4.

handicapped children. As a result of the meeting, the Commissioner of Education forwarded memorandum and survey forms to all county superintendents of schools, superintendents of schools and administrative principals on April 17, 1972. In the memorandum the Commissioner stated[9]:

> Our schools are obligated (18A: 35-5, 7) to provide physical education for every pupil in grades 1-12. The time allocated to this is two and one-half hours in each school week (18A: 35-8). In addition, the State requires that children classified as handicapped shall not be denied because of such handicap, participation in extracurricular, intramural and interscholastic activities as well as health, recreation, and social service activities.
>
> Unfortunately, despite the ever increasing services of personnel working with these children, too little concentrated and coordinated effort has been focused upon ways to expand and enrich opportunities for active participation of the handicapped in physical education.
>
> The growing public concern and interest has dramatized the responsibility of schools and communities to provide comprehensive physical education for all children, which includes all handicapped children.
>
> I am, therefore, recommending that an immediate study of the physical education activities and programs for the handicapped be conducted by the school districts in New Jersey, to ascertain if the activities and programs are commensurate with the handicapped children and student needs.
>
> County Superintendents are requested to have the local district administrators complete the reporting instrument in order that we may have a statewide assessment and evaluation of this most important issue.
>
> I am hopeful that through this statewide study, we can move in the direction of developing pre-training and in-service training programs that will enable us to serve the needs of the handicapped, disadvantaged, and those with special health problems.

It is anticipated that school districts that do not have compre-

---

[9] Carl L. Marburger, "Memorandum" (Trenton: Department of Education, April 17, 1972).

hensive physical education programs for their handicapped will be requested to provide funds in their 1973-74 budgets for program implementation.

An awareness of the need for pre-service and in-service training for physical education teachers of the handicapped prompted Dr. Daniel Ringleheim, Deputy Assistant Commissioner of the Department of Education, to convene the Higher Education Council on Special Education on February 10, 1972. Invited to the meeting were state leaders in the areas of Special Education, Physical Education and Recreation. The Council was asked to identify the major issues and needs as well as ideas and/or plans for model programs in physical education for the handicapped. As a result of the Council's deliberations, the following major issues and needs were identified[10]:

1. After-school recreation programs.
2. Professional preparation in physical education for working with the handicapped.
3. Development of concept of inclusion of all children in physical education and recreation programs.
4. Pre-school and early identification of sensory and motor skills.
5. Changing attitudes toward the handicapped child (the abilities vs. disabilities concept).
6. Camping and summer programs for the handicapped.
7. Activities of daily living—recreation, motor development, body image for low functioning children in community (re: Pennsylvania decision—M.R.).
8. Dual preparation: physical education major and special education minor.
9. Need for institute training for the handicapped for public recreation administrators.
10. Explore how public recreation administrators can enjoin their agency to school-oriented recreation programs.
11. Some training of physical education teachers in areas of exceptionality, including field experiences, seminar with both areas.

[10] Nancy K. Mitchell and Janet L. Koontz, "Minutes of Higher Education Council-Physical Education-Special Education Department Meeting on Physical Education for the Handicapped" (Trenton: Department of Education, April 18, 1972).

12. Recreation experiences via camp programs for the handicapped, using both physical education and special education majors.
13. Innner-city recreational programs for all children (self-concepts).
14. Special education and physical education must respect the goals and objectives of one another by:
    a) defining handicapped children
    b) developing a more interdisciplinary approach
15. Recognition that the idealist approach to general education will never bridge the gap in reaching *all* children; *must* seek a more realist approach.
16. Deal with the apprehension of physical education student in working with the handicapped child because of:
    a) structure of classes
    b) structure of course work
17. Examine the job opportunities.
18. Delineate the needs in terms of our interactions with the children.
19. Examine, for use or a model, the recreation specialist and the educator therapist.
20. Formulate problems (e.g., training of special education experts in physical education) and seek solutions (e.g., offer opportunity for this exposure and special training in undergraduate and/or graduate programs of physical education teacher training programs at the state colleges).
21. Find solutions to other problems, such as the identification of children with learning disabilities in schools by providing exposure for all general educaton students in physical education for handicapped children.
22. Develop the following flow pattern:

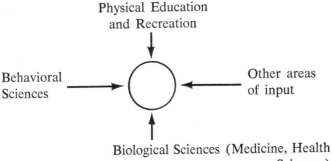

23. Determine the type of graduate and/or undergraduate programs needed to prepare teachers to work with handicapped children. (Adapted physical educators and special educators with background in adapted physical education.)
24. Establish the relative emphasis which should be placed on personnel, program, facilities.
25. Establish interactions:

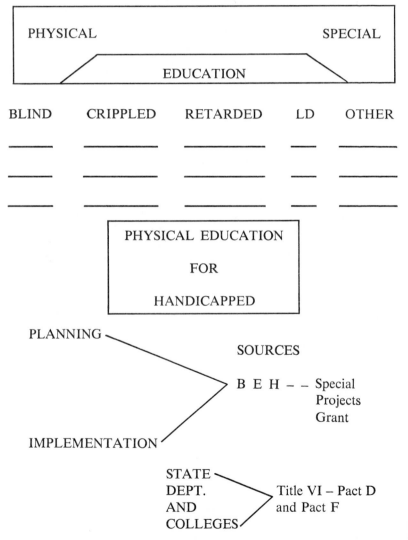

COLLEGES

PHYSICAL   SPECIAL

EDUCATION

BLIND   CRIPPLED   RETARDED   LD   OTHER

PHYSICAL EDUCATION

FOR

HANDICAPPED

PLANNING

SOURCES

B E H – – Special Projects Grant

IMPLEMENTATION

STATE DEPT. AND COLLEGES

Title VI – Pact D and Pact F

PRESERVICE:

> Undergraduate
>
> Graduate

INSERVICE:

> Workshops
>
> Institutes
>
> Other

The unanimity of concern expressed by the Council prompted the State Department of Education to forward a memorandum to all committee members. Members were requested to submit their ideas as to the "direction" the State Department of Education should take. The writer expressed his views as follows:

Possible approaches to the questions posed regarding "Physical Education Programming for the Handicapped:"

1. What is the next step?
   a. Prepare State Guidelines so that we know what we are attempting to do.
   b. Develop two teaching models, one for the utopian situation and the second, a more realistic approach, for those districts that are plagued with staffing and/or facilities limitations.

2. How do we proceed from here? Do we?
   Appoint a steering committee, consisting of twelve members of the first group that met (4 P.F., 4 Recreation, 4 special Education). Appoint three regional committees (north, south, central); the balance of the members of the first committee, plus a few more.
   The Branch of Special Services provides funds for a series of workshops:
   a. Steering committee two-day workshop to prepare working documents related to 1a and 1b.
   b. Working documents to be disseminated to two-day regional workshops so that they can be developed.

      c. Steering committee to convene for a three-day work-
         shop to evaluate/synthesize the three documents and
         produce the final products.
    Expenditures for the total venture should be limited to
room and board and travel.

3. Do we go on as a group? As separate institutions? As indi-
    viduals?
    We should definitely work as a group. To achieve our goal,
    special education, physical education and recreation must
    work together under the auspices of the Branch of Special
    Education and Pupil Personnel Services.

It is evident from the aforementioned that the state leaders and the State Department of Education are aware of the need to provide individualized physical activity for the handicapped children of New Jersey. However, they need the support of every parent. Parents of the handicapped, in particular, can insure program fruition by: writing supportive letters to the State Director of Title VI and legislations showing a concern for special education, contacting school authorities and urging program implementation, and inviting parents of "normal" children to workshops and seminars to apprise them of the needs of the handicapped.

A PERSONAL POINT OF VIEW

At the present time programs for the handicapped are not meeting the *specific* needs of the handicapped child. For example, let us analyze the present situation regarding children with learning disabilities. We repeatedly hear such terms as "minimal brain damage," "slow learner," "mentally retarded," "emotionally disturbed," "minimal brain dysfunction," being used to *categorize* and *stigmatize* children. Such an approach is fraught with problems because educational institutions are striving to establish teacher training programs for each categorical classification. As a result, we are envisioning program fragmentation which has resulted in a duplication of many services which have impeded pre-service and in-service training programs.

---

[11] Correspondence with the Dr. Daniel Ringleheim, Assistant Commissioner of Education, April 25, 1972.

As I view the situation, we, as educators, should not be concerned with or influenced by categorization. Rather, we should be concerned with the behavior manifested by the child. For example, the term "learning disability" is all-inclusive and should be used for all children evidencing learning problems due to cognitive or socio-emotional aberrations.

The medical practitioner, the psychologist and psychiatrist are and should be concerned with etiology; the educator should work closely with the aforementioned and develop instructional programs *based on manifested behavior(s)* rather than on some vague terminology. Thus, each educational discipline should test the learning disabled child, assess his specific needs, prescribe accordingly, and evaluate progress at periodic intervals. The term "minimal brain dysfunction" provides no instructional guidelines for the teacher; on the other hand, a test battery that indicates the child's manifested deficiencies in gross motor patterning and physical fitness will aid the teacher in meeting the child's needs. One of the basic principles of learning is the "identical elements" theory. In essence the theory states that learning will be maximized if instruction is geared to the specific need manifested. Thus, to maximize learning for any handicapped child, we must:

1. identify the behavioral problem(s)
2. prescribe an individualized program that will remedy or ameliorate the situation.

ESSENTIAL INGREDIENTS FOR PROGRAM IMPLEMENTATION

As indicated in the previous section, children with learning disabilities (or any handicapping condition) should be provided an instructional program based on individual needs. To insure successful program implementation each of the following factors must be carefully considered so that policies can be formulated. (Although the following guidelines relate to physical education programming, the same factors can be utilized for providing instructional services in other disciplines.)

Interdisciplinary Steering Committee

The degree of success attained by a physical education program for the handicapped is directly related to the personnel par-ticpating in policy formulation. Thus, the first step that should be taken is to form a steering committee. A committee is needed for two basic reasons—to insure that the "total" needs of each child are met, and to enhance school/community acceptance of the pro-gram as a result of a sound public relations campaign. Members of the committee should include: the school physician, members of the Child Study Team, the school nurse, principals of the schools in the district, a member of the Guidance Department, the physical educators teaching the handicapped, and the Supervisor/Director of the Physical Education Department.

Policies established as a result of the cooperative efforts of the steering committee will do much to eliminate the major deterrent to program implementation—a breakdown in communications. For example, the school physician can keep the local medical society apprised of the program and, more important, solicit their coopera-tion.

Teacher Certification Requirements

One of the questions frequently asked of the writer is, "Would the physical educator who teaches handicapped children be liable in the event of injury?" The answer: physical educators who teach the handicapped cannot be held liable as long as a medical approval form is signed by the parents and family/school physician and the *physician prescribes* the specific activities/tasks and duration.

One must remember that the physical educator possesses ex-pertise in kinesiology (the study of the movements of the body parts) and physiology of exercise (the study of the effects of activ-ity on the body organs). He is thoroughly familiar with gross mo-tor patterning and the components of physical fitness. A marriage whereby the physician or psychologist prescribes and the physical educator supervises is one that will insure the maximum gain for each child.

There are those that advocate the use of a physical therapist in lieu of the physical educator. To do so would negate much of the value of a physical activity program. Probably the greatest value derived from a physical activity program is the enhancement of the child's self-image. While the physical therapist is knowledgeable in terms of anatomy, kinesiology, rehabilitation, etc., he is not an educator. He does not, therefore, have an in-depth knowledge of child growth and development, psychological principles of learning and other foundation courses that aid the teacher in educating the total child.

Teacher-Pupil Ratio

Teacher-pupil ratio should be based on the nature of the handicapping condition and the size of the teaching station. Children with learning disabilities can be provided an effective instructional program if the ratio does not exceed 1-10. The writer has found one exception to the rule—the hyperactive or distractible child. Due to their specific program needs for non-stimulating environment and tasks to decelerate neural impulses, they should be grouped together with a ratio not to exceed 1-7.

It should be noted that it is recommended that children with different handicapping conditions be grouped heterogeneously, except for the aforementioned, for two reasons:

1. The program is individualized so that each child is performing on the basis of his needs.
2. The children learn to interact with and develop a positive attitude toward other children who manifest a variety of handicapping conditions.

Facilities, Supplies, Equipment

A separate teaching station measuring 30′ x 60′ would be ideal. However, a program can be, and should be, started if there is no instructional classroom available. One should pursue the school facilities and utilize any available area such as a team room, stage, large storage room, corridor, etc. The success of the program will elicit administration/board support so that in subsequent years additional teaching stations will be constructed.

The supply and equipment needs for the instructional program are minimal because most items are readily available in the physical education department. Other specific items that are needed can either be constructed by the maintenance department or purchased for a nominal fee.

Individualized Instructional Program

Previously it was mentioned that the instructional program must be designed to meet the specific needs of each child. A physical education program, or any other program, cannot achieve optimum success unless the program is predicated upon the specific needs, interests and abilities of each child. One of the glaring inadequacies of many programs viewed by the author is that *all children are performing the same activities.* Have you not viewed a program where all children walk on a balance beam? The teacher will attempt to justify the program by stating that the children have been grouped homogeneously and thus manifest similar problems. Research, on the other hand, tells us that homogeneous grouping is a misnomer (it implies that all children are of a similar ability). If children are grouped homogeneously, they are equated on the basis of one test; further testing will reveal tremendous intra-individual variability.

To provide a sound instructional program, the physical educator should:

1. Contact the members of the Child Study Team, specifically the school psychologist, or school/family physician for their recommendations (in writing).
2. Test each child for general motor performance and physical fitness.
3. Assess performance.
4. Prescribe activities for each individual.
5. Evaluate performance periodically and modify tasks/activities as necessary.

Each instructional period should be structured so that the first half of the period is devoted to improving *evidenced disabilities*; the second half of the period should focus on the *evidenced abilities*. Once again, be sure to provide time for each child to participate in those activities with members of his peer group.

SUGGESTED ACTIVITIES FOR CHILDREN
WITH LEARNING DISABILITIES

Following the premise that an educational program for the handicapped should be based on the behavior(s) manifested by the students, one has but to identify those disabilities evidenced by children with learning disabilities and plan an instructional program accordingly. A review of the literature will reveal that the learning disabled child may be clumsy, poorly coordinated, and lack physical vitality. Further, he may manifest the following psychological problems:

1. Perseveration—the inability to volitionally cease the performance of the same act repeatedly.
2. Hyperactivity—the constant manifestation of excessive motor activity.
3. Distractibility—the limited ability to concentrate on the task at hand due to distractions caused by external stimuli.
4. Dissociation—the inability to integrate basic data into "meaningful wholes."
5. A negative self-image—a total feeling of personal inadequacy due to the inability to control bizarre patterns of performance, achieve success, and be accepted by the peer group.

While, admittedly, a child with a learning disability may not evidence all of the problems listed, experience has indicated that the display of two or more characteristics necessitates an individualized instructional program. The balance of the section provides some suggestions for activities that may be programmed on a personalized basis. The list provides examples for each problem. The reader may procure a detailed explanation of activities by referring to texts by Golick,[12] Cratty,[13] and Chaney and Kephart.[14]

---

[12] Margaret Golick, *A Parent's Guide to Learning Problems* (Montreal: Quebec Association for Children with Learning Disabilities, 1970) p. 24.

[13] Bryant J. Cratty, *Development Sequences of Perceptual-Motor Tasks: Movement Activities for Neurologically Handicapped Children and Retarded Children and Youth* (*Freeport*: Educational Activities, Inc., 1967) p. 88.

[14] Clara M. Chaney and Newell C. Keyhart, *Motoric Aids to Perceptual Training* (Columbus: Charles E. Merrill Publishing Company, 1968) p. 138.

Low Motor Ability

The child that exhibits low motor ability can be distinguished by his inability to posturally orient his body during movement, to perform gross motor coordination activities, and to perform finite coordination activities.

1. *Suggested activities to enhance postural orientation*

    a) Walking forward, backward, sideward on a balance beam. Vary the width, plane and height of the beam.
    b) Jumping, hopping on an innner tube/trampoline.
    c) Balancing the body in varying positions on one foot, both feet, forearm stand, head stand, hand stand, etc.
    d) Performing a variety of tumbling tasks such as rolling sideward, forward roll, backward roll and shoulder roll.

2. *Teaching cues*

    a) Incorporate a variety of balancing tasks to substain attention and develop overall competence.
    b) Vary the difficulty of each task so that the less gifted child can achieve success and the more skilled individual is challenged.
    c) Motivate creativity by requesting the children to devise original balancing stunts/activities.

3. *Suggested activities to stimulate gross motor coordination*

    a) Hopping on one foot/alternate feet. Vary by having child hop a number of counts on one foot and a different number on the other foot.
    b) Jumping forward, backward, sideward and from different heights.
    c) Skipping
    d) Galloping
    e) Crawling
    f) Climbing up and down stairs.

4. *Teaching cues*

    a) Constantly vary the skill so that efficient gross motor coordination rather than discreet motor skills are learned.
    b) Include "follow the leader" games. Rationale: The *leader*

will reinforce that which he does well (his ability) whereas the *follower* may be improving a deficit (his disability).

5. *Suggested activities to improve finite coordination*

    a) Ocular-pursuit activities to improve eye/hand coordination:

       i) Following a moving whiffleball (suspended on a string) with the eyes.

      ii) Touching a moving whiffleball with the hand/finger.

     iii) Striking a stationary/moving whiffleball with a plastic bat.

    b) Catching a yarnball with one hand/alternate hands.

    c) Catching a yarnball with a partner.

    d) Throwing/batting at targets to improve coordination/accuracy.

    e) Basketball shooting.

    f) Kicking a stationary ball with alternate feet.

    g) Dribbling a soccer ball.

    h) Dropkicking a football.

6. *Teaching cues*

    a) Insure success by structuring tasks from the simple to the complex. For example, with all striking activities start with a stationary object. Similarly, adjust the size, shape and composition of the ball to the child's ability level.

    b) Always stress form and accuracy first, then stress distance.

Low Physical Vitality

To develop reasonable motor skill competencies and to function efficiently in the performance of one's daily tasks requires a minimal level of physical fitness. Low physical vitality is defined as subpar performance in terms of muscular strength, muscular endurance, and cardiorespiratory endurance.

1. *Suggested activities to develop muscular strength/endurance*

    a) Static arm hang from an overhead bar/ladder.

    b) Push-ups/pull-ups.

    c) Hand-walking on overhead ladder/parallel bars.

    d) Climbing on "Jungle Gyms," cargo nets, ladders, suspended ropes, etc.

e) Performing sit-ups.

f) Weight training activities.

2. *Teaching cues*

a) Increase tolerance levels by increasing repetitions, time duration, or level of difficulty.

b) Use magnesium carbonate (powdered chalk) for hand-climbing activities as a safety precaution.

c) Perform sit-ups with knees flexed to avoid lower back injury.

d) Weight training is contraindicated for students evidencing hernia or coronary condition.

3. *Suggested activities to develop cardiorespiratory endurance*

a) Side straddle hops (jumping jacks).

b) Shuttle races, relay games, running in place.

c) Rope skipping.

4. *Teaching cues*

a) Incorporate the competitive element in cardiorespiratory activities to motivate the student. For example: running per se is boring, but running while catching a ball becomes "fun" and thus motivates.

b) Any activity that provokes "breathlessness" improves cardiorespiratory endurance.

Perseveration

It has been theorized that children who tend to "perseverate" do so because they have achieved a degree of success in performing a particular act and are fearful of attempting a different task due to the fear of failure, thus they repeat the same act over and over again.

1. *Suggested activities/teaching cues*

a) Have the child practice those skills that will improve his deficiencies.

b) Varying tasks/activities is essential when working with children who manifest a tendency to perseverate. In order to overcome student reticence to perform, the parent/ teacher must be gentle, patient and yet forceful. Once the child has been assisted through the movement, he will develop confidence and start to perseverate again—thus the need for constant variation.

Hyperactivity

The hyperactive child is done a disservice if he is placed in the unrestricted physical education program because of its focus on constantly stimulating the child through competitive, vigorous activities.

1. *Suggested activities/teaching cues*

   a) Performing relaxation exercises daily. Exercises should include tensing and then gradually relaxing the major muscle groups of the body. (Refer to the author's text,[3] for tension control exercises developed by Edmund Jacobson, M. D.)

   b) Performing regular motor activities with a focus on decelerating neural impulses. For example, have students run as fast as they can, 3/4 speed, 1/2 speed, 1/4 speed, and as slowly as they can.

Distractibility

Many children who are hyperactive also manifest distractible tendencies. Further, the line of demarcation between the two is very fine—the hyperactive child is constantly in motion performing a variety of tasks reasonably well, whereas the distractible child moves from task to task without displaying any skill competencies due to an inability to focus his attention on the task at hand.

1. *Suggested activities/teaching cues*

   a) Structuring the teaching environment so that distracting stimuli are minimized.

   b) Having the group concentrate and work on one task until success is achieved before moving on to the next task.

   c) Increasing the difficulty of a task as soon as success is achieved to constantly sustain attention.

   d) Performing relaxation exercises.

Dissociation

Some children who are learning disabled can perform many discrete tasks very well, but become confused when requested to combine individual tasks into a more complex motor pattern. For example, a child may possess the ability to hop on either his right or left foot but will have extreme difficulty hopping on alternate feet.

1. *Suggested activities/teaching cues*

    a) Stressing the "whole-part-whole method of teaching. Start by having the child see the total pattern of performance desired, then break the skill down into its component parts, and finally constantly demonstrate the "whole."

    b) Using pegboards to develop "closure" perceptual-motor skills.

       Have the child view an incomplete pegboard pattern on one board and attempt to reproduce the completed pattern on a second board. (See Figure 1.)

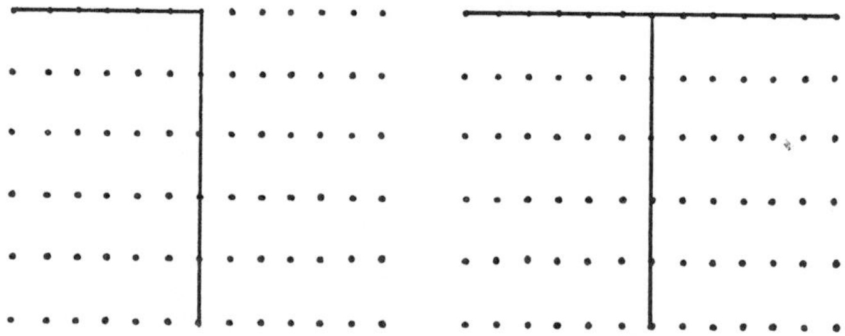

Incomplete Pattern   **Completed Reproduction**

Figure 1. Pegboard Closure Activity

Note: **Pegboard activities can be used to stress color discrimination; concepts of laterality and directionality (awareness of body in relation to space); spelling, reading and mathematical concepts; and creativity.**

Negative Self-Image

The single most common characteristic displayed by children with learning disabilities (in fact, with any handicapping condition) is a definite feeling of inadequancy. The inferiority complex is attributable to a constant frustration caused by an inability to achieve even the simplest of tasks and ostracization/rejection by peer group members.

1. *Suggested activities/teaching cues*

    a) Structuring tasks to insure success regardless of ability level.

    b) Reinforcing *all* behavior patterns immediately in a *positive* manner.

    c) Referring to each child by his or her first name.

    d) Having children record their own scores (if of sufficient age) so that they get concrete evidence of their progress.

    e) Using student aides in the program to dispel many of the misconceptions regarding the handicapped and to engender empathetic relations.

    g) Integrating the learning disabled child in with the normal school population, where educationally sound.

Motor-Cognition

As indicated in an earlier section, the "new" physical education places stress on the development of the "total" child. Such an approach is not meant to disparage motor skill or motor patterning development, but rather to improve overall instructional effectiveness. While motor-cognitive activities have implications for the unrestricted physical education program, they have even greater significance for teaching children with learning disabilities. As a case in point, many special educators have indicated that hyperactive children cannot sit still long enough to inculcate any of the concepts being taught. In these given situations, properly structured physical activity provides a fertile field for providing an adjunctive service for the classroom program.

1. *Suggested activities/teaching cues*

    a) Integrating avenues of information (senses) with motor response. Design all tasks/activities that require the child to use visual, auditory and verbal skills simultaneously. For example, instead of having a child hop at random, have him hop in marked footprints or patterns on the floor, or have him respond motorically to auditory stimuli.

Note: Motor-cognitive activities can always be discerned by the fact that the child must make a decision. As an example, performing jumping jacks is almost a purely motor response when learned whereas having the child replicate demonstrated arm/leg positions is motor-cognitive as he must make a decision.

b) Hopping/jumping on grids to identify symbols, letters, numbers, to spell words, and to add and subtract. Have the child verbalize while performing the task.

c) Playing games with flash cards. For example, having relay races which include identifying and picking a flash card from a deck and returning to the line; the object— to spell a word. (Similar activities can be designed where children write letters, numbers and words on a chalkboard.)

d) Running obstacle courses. Signs are placed at each station informing the children to "jump," "crawl," etc.

e) Performing tasks/patterns sequentially to enhance the concept of serial ordering.

f) A word of caution: Do not integrate cognitive skills with motor skills until the motor skills have been mastered.

A MESSAGE TO PARENTS AND TEACHERS

The "key" to a successful physical education program, or any educational program for children with learning disabilities, is the establishment of a *personalized* relationship. The activities (content) of the program have value and must be individualized, but they will be of little value unless the teaching/learning methods applied engender rapport.

To summarize this chapter, I suggest some "Do's" and "Don'ts" for your careful consideration.

Don't	*Do*
1. Teach all children the same skills	1. Individualize instruction
2. Criticize the child	2. Use positive reinforcement

3. Perform the task for the child

3. Have the child perform the task and assist, where necessary

4. Offer the child sympathy

4. Treat the handicapped child as you would the normal child

5. Assign similar task requirements for each child

5. Vary tasks according to ability level

6. Assign grades on the basis of *achievement*

6. Assign grades on the basis of *improvement*

7. Say, "Hey you"

7. Say, "John," "Mary," etc.

8. Use the lecture method

8. Use demonstration while explaining

9. Incorporate any activity where some children are not involved in learning process

9. Insure that every child is actively involved in the learning process

10. Focus instruction solely on the physical

10. Incorporate the use of all "senses" and cognition (thinking)

8

THE DILEMMA OF THE HANDICAPPED ADOLESCENT

Robert W. Russell, M.A., M.Ed.
Director of Special Pupil Services
Northern Valley Regional High
School District, Closter, New Jersey

When an adolescent boy refers himself to the school psychologist, he really has a problem. Larry was just that kind of young man. When asked about the nature of his problem, he replied, "I need to survive." Larry is in quite a bind. He is age seventeen and in his three years of high school has achieved only twelve and a half credits, which leaves him still a freshman. There is no doubt that Larry is a bright boy. His records indicate that he has consistently achieved intelligence test scores throughout his school years that range between a high average to superior. This apparently got him through elementary school, where his teachers from year to year continued to bet on his good ability to eventually bring him through, and socially promoted him. Larry, however, in casting back over the years, could not express one feeling of satisfaction about his life in school. In recent years, his parents, out of frustration, have been caught up in an accepting-rejecting pattern. Larry apparently does well in his after-school work and tends to behave responsibly on home chores. His parents, who have been told over the years that he is a bright boy, cannot understand why he does so poorly in school. They feel that his problem is "pure laziness."

155

Larry is at the crossroads of making a decision. He will be eighteen in a few months at a time when the State of New Jersey, in which he lives, has given the eighteen-year-olds full rights and responsibilities of citizenship. Larry is appalled at the prospect of being entirely on his own in a world so demanding of competence. His father, in frustration, has avowed that upon achieving eighteen, if Larry is not succeeding in school, he must quit, get a job, and support himself. Larry has thought of the Navy as his only solution, since he has over the span of his school years gradually downgraded his career aspirations from physician to navy deckhand.

It is paradoxical that Larry's superior intelligence has throughout his school life masked a very subtle learning disability which on the continuous scale of developmental disabilities would be on the mildest fringe. Some physicians call Larry's condition "an inefficiency of brain function." In Larry's case, his inefficiencies are found in speed and accuracy of written output. Larry is perfectly capable of understanding advanced mathematical concepts. He made a perfect score on tests of spatial relationships which measured his capacity to visualize the manipulation of objects in space. This is a fundamental requirement for success in higher mathematics. Larry, however, manages the language of mathematics, which is simple arithmetic computation, very poorly, and has throughout school found that, even though he could manage rather complex mathematical formuli, because of minor computational errors (usually by only plus or minus one digit), his answers were consistently marked wrong. He must sometimes check his answer three or four times to be sure it is correct. This consumes time and if he takes the time, he usually doesn't finish his work. If he works rapidly, he makes many simple errors.

Larry's teachers have been consistent in reporting him as a young man with excellent capacity and with high levels of creative potential. His self-image, however, because of his minimal, specific disability, is more consistent with low average intelligence and total personal inadequacy. It is no wonder then that Larry looks forward to the arrival of age eighteen with paralyzing anxiety.

Larry's anxiety is justified when we consider that he is facing a world in which the demand for academic credentials has been increasing almost geometrically. Many of the trade unions now require the completion of a high school education plus other requirements in order to enter their apprenticeship programs. Seventy years ago a young man like Larry could respectably drop out of school, enter the world of work and achieve at maturity the respect of his fellow men based on his occupational success alone. Such a man was Thomas Edison who, according to facts revealed in his biography, had a rather poor school experience and failed to complete first grade. He is, however, highly admired for what he was capable of producing without a completed education.

Young men like Larry, however, are well aware that because of an incompleted education, they may not even get the chance to show what they are capable of doing. In the past few years, a campaign supposedly to discourage dropping out has been mounted that has placed a considerable stigma on the dropout. There has been a tendency to treat the young people who drop out of school statistically like highway fatalities.[1] They have been reported perhaps erroneously as earning less over their life span than high school graduates. They have been listed also as significant contributors to the ranks of the drug abusers and the juvenile delinquents. This serves to put young men like Larry under a considerably greater bind. He cannot leave the source of his greatest dissatisfaction, which is school, and attempt to obtain greater self-respect in the work-a-day world of the community where he is already experiencing his only successful endeavor. In spite of his condition, however, the prospect of Larry achieving successful independence is great. The tragedy is that he may not achieve a level of success commensurate with his intellectual capacity.

If Larry's case represents a minimal learning disability, what is the prospect for the adolescent who experiences a moderate to severe learning disability? The problem here is that these young people may not achieve the ultimate goal of successful independence.

---

[1] Jerald Bachman, Swayzer Green and Ilona Wirtanen, "Dropping Out is a Symptom," *The Educational Digest*, April 1972, pp. 1-5.

Such a young person is Sally, who at age twenty has graduated from high school but is unemployed and still living with her parents. There is no doubt that Sally is verbally adequate. Frequent psychological examinations over the years have indicated superior vocabulary scores, and her general verbal intelligence measures consistently at the high average range. Her non-language intelligence, specifically her perceptual motor functioning, has always been at the level of retardation. This wide discrepancy has produced a young woman who can talk a good job but can't perform. Her very poor spatial adequacy limits her in the concepts of time and quantity. The result is that she is not functionally adequate in matters mathematical. She has, however, always been a good reader from the beginning of her school experience and although her handwriting is very poor, she communicates easily by letter, which is one of her chief occupations during the lonely hours she spends at home.

Sally is a loner. During her high school years she was seen as "odd" and at times her behavior was described as bizarre. She was seen as a "freak" even by her classmates in her special class. What seemed to Sally to be appropriate behavior in her high school classes was seen by her classmates as "way out" and treated with smirking contempt. It seemed to Sally that when her gym class was in the next to the last period of the school day it was sensible not to get dressed but to go to her final class in her gym suit. She could be counted upon to say the right thing at the wrong time or vice versa, such as openly discussing her menstrual problems in her health class, unconsciously revealing many of her secrets to the total student body or answering rhetorical questions, much to the annoyance of her teachers. Sally could relate socially only on a level consistent with a child in the mid-elementary school years, and what few social acquaintances she had were all much younger than she. She was, however, well liked by younger children.

An inventory of Sally's occupational skills reveals that she is not verbally adequate enough to succeed in any of the occupations that require high verbal performance. There were, however, many tasks on which she could perform. The problem was that she could not sustain these tasks to completion. This was particularly true when the work assignment required speed and accuracy or attention to routine detail. From a personal standpoint, over the years, Sally has learned that if she did something badly enough, people would discontinue making demands upon her. Consequently, Sally frustrated her teachers in arithmetic instruction, whereupon they turned to her competency in reading and further reinforced that area until reading became almost her sole occupation. This did little, however, to improve her reservoir of basic knowledge, because Sally became an encyclopedia of superficial information and can bore her listeners to death discussing Lipizzaner horses and Scottish castles. This perseveration in conversation bores her co-workers to exasperation and is the main reason why she has been unable to hold a job successfully.

In spite of the range of development between Larry and Sally as it pertains to learning disabilities, they have much in common. Over the years they have suffered considerable ego damage and their self-esteem is at the nadir. They have accumulated feelings of frustration and inner rage that are oftentimes directed toward the authorities in their world as either passive or active aggression. They face all aspects of their identity crisis with feelings of inadequacy and see the onset of adulthood with little or no place in the world for them. In many instances they have alienated their family, on whom they are still vastly dependent, and it will not be long before they begin to alienate the authorities outside the home. Dr. William Glasser, a nationally noted psychiatrist and school consultant, in an article which appeared in the *U.S. News and World Report* in April 1970[2], blames much of the rebelliousness of youth on accumulated failure, and he lists school as the main contributor to these feelings of failure. Dr. Glasser says in his article:

> The average youngster senses very early, usually in the first grade, that he is worth just about whatever grade he gets from his teachers. If he gets low grades, and we hand out low grades liberally to little kids—he gives up early. This means that if he learns the right skills and enough of the right answers he is a success. If he doesn't, he is a failure and is

---

[2] William Glasser, "Youth in Rebellion—Why," *U.S. News and World Report*, April 27, 1970, p. 42.

labeled as such. When you are nine or ten years old and you believe you are a failure, you may never try again in school. The rest of your school years are like being in jail.

It would appear that the majority of the problems faced by the adolescent with the developmental disability could be eliminated by early and appropriate school management. However, these young people will be arriving at the doors of our high schools in sufficient numbers to require strategies of management that accept them where they are, and *managed by adults who do not complain about what they are not.* It is very simple for the professional person dealing with youth of high school age to project blame on the elementary schools for the problems of young people so inadequately equipped to achieve. Programs of early identification and early treatment are certainly fundamental and the hope is that in years to come, fewer and fewer young people will enter our high schools so ill equipped. However, in the foreseeable future high school educators will be called upon to contend with nearly 20 percent of the high school population that range from Sally to Larry. It is a certainty then that educational strategies are needed for the management of these young people based on their unique personal, social, and educational needs.

In planning appropriate strategies for the handicapped adolescent, certain facts must be considered. *First, the program must not isolate him from his normal peers.* By the time the youth with the learning disability has reached the adolescent years, he has become so highly sensitive to failure that he will tend to see most attempts on the part of the school and family to help him as a "put-down."[3] These young people are well aware that certain strategies have an association that is socially stigmatizing, particularly those that isolate him from the mainstream of his school and social life. On the face of things, special class placement seems appropriate and humane because it removes the youth from the experience of academic failure and theoretically allows him to begin at his level of achieved performance. Research, however, has shown that the segregated special class has for the most part been no more successful than the results obtained by handicapped

---

[3] William Glasser, *Schools Without Failure* (New York: Harper and Row, 1969) pp. 82-85.

young people who have been given no special help at all but who have been left to contend with the usual school curriculum.[4] Placement in the special class oftentimes removes the adolescent from the stimulation of normal companionship, which is a fundamental adolescent need. Over several years the author has experienced a wide range of reactions on the part of the youth with learning disabilities to segregated special class management. In one instance, when they were compelled to ride a school bus labeled, "Department of Special Education," dozens of ploys were used to avoid being seen by their normal peers while on this bus. Most of them rode on the floor, others sneaked off at the first stop. Oftentimes the youth with the learning disability in the special classroom will demand to be seated near the wall so that he cannot be seen by his normal peers from the hallway of the school. There is enough intellectual integrity remaining in the youth with the learning disability to permit him to fully understand what special class or special school placement means, but it is most difficult to convince him that this is really for his best interests.

Recently a teenage boy phoned the educational writer of his local paper.[5] He was described by this writer as furious. His voice from the telephone bristled with bitterness and hurt. It seemed that the writer had written an article describing the opening of a new special needs vocational school that was located near the county hospital. It was described as a school for fourteen- to twenty-year-olds who are educable mentally retarded, neurologically impaired or emotionally disturbed. The boy took exception to that paragraph, saying, "I'm in that school and there ain't any, I mean, there aren't any kids like that in there. We can't take it no more, the papers are always writing that. It's not right. We were told it was strictly a trade school." He asked, "Why did you write that about us in the paper? With some self-respect we got to get in a rebuttal. It's bad enough when we get off that bus every day; everybody looks at us; people say 'look at the freaks.' We wouldn't mind it if it was a regular school bus but why do

[4] Lloyd M. Dunn, "Special Education for the Mildly Retarded—Is Much of it Necessary," *Exceptional Children,* September 1968, pp. 5-21.

[5] Alice Olick, "They Treat us Like Little Kids," *Bergen Record,* February 16, 1972, pp. A-21.

they put us in a van? It's hard enough in that school. Why did you write that?"

The boy also took exception to the fact that it was near the county hospital (read county mental institution) and he also complained about the curriculum materials saying, "They treat us like little kids. The reading they give you is like first grade. 'Charlie got a goat named Sam.' " The boy went on to explain the needs of the normal adolescent and complained bitterly that these were not being met. He put in words better than most young people the feelings of the youth with learning disabilities in an isolated setting segregated from his normal peers.

If the special class is used, it should only be for purposes of providing a sheltering environment for the adolescent who is learning disabled and also vastly socially inadequate until he makes the adjustment to high school. To be effective in this respect the classroom must be located in a high school building. If successfully used, most of these young people will outgrow the need for such a special class placement by the end of the sophomore year, and at that time will be capable of taking advantage of other strategies of educational management that integrate him with his normal peers. When an adolescent is placed in the special class, the school authorities should already be making plans to move him out of it and into the mainstream of school life.

Sally, described above, began her school experience in a special class. She needed much sheltering by her teacher, who intervened on her behalf in many difficult situations. It took Sally three months to learn the plan of the school so that she could move from her special classroom to other classes on time. It took her just as long to learn the complexities of the combination lock on her locker. In all these instances, she was supported by her teacher as she learned to contend with the demands of high school outside of her special classroom. Sally spent her last year in high school rarely in the special class and although she has not yet achieved independence, the blame could not be projected onto the school but rather on the unavailability of resources within the community to intervene in Sally's case after the school had done what it could.

Second, *any program planned for the high school youth with learning disabilities should be made as invisible among the other offerings as possible.* As previously mentioned, these young people are highly sensitive to failure. They very quickly pick up such things as special grades on report cards and instructional materials prepared for the elementary grades. Many of these young people may be incapable of managing material beyond the fourth or fifth grade level but if forced to contend with materials written for the elementary school child, rebelliousness can be expected. Fortunately, there is a growing reservoir of materials written for the illiterate adult for use in prisons, the armed forces, job corps, and adult general educational development programs that can very appropriately be used at the high school level.

Glasser, in his book *Schools Without Failure,*[6] has recommended the development of courses for young people who are failing that could be passed by them with appropriate effort. Such a program was instituted in Northern Valley Regional High School at Old Tappan, New Jersey. The young person with a learning disability who is socially adequate and intellectually average is given a choice of fourteen courses throughout his four years in high school where he can achieve at his level using adult-oriented materials. These fourteen courses are taught by two teachers certified in the area of the education of the handicapped. These students attend regular home room, participate in all minor and extra-curricular activities, and are admitted to these courses *only* in their area of academic deficit. If an area of strength suggests that the young person can contend with mainstream courses, he is guided into those. The results over three years have shown that the greatest effort is made during the freshman year, when anywhere from fifteen to twenty students will be enrolled. The number feathers out usually to only two seniors still in need of the program. This program allows also for early work study or for placement in a satellite vocational school. These young people are also graded according to the standard letter grades and receive a standard report card. The grade is based on individual progress on their own prescriptive program rather than against course require-

---

[6] William Glasser, *Schools Without Failure* (New York: Harper and Row, 1969), pp. 82-85.

ments. They are also eligible for the honor role if they achieve all A's and B's in their special courses.

The third necessary characteristic of strategies used for managing the youth with learning disabilities in school is *flexibility*. Most of these young people, although they have experienced a lifetime of school difficulties, are highly successful in pursuits of all kinds outside of school.[7] Many of them are successful in school only in minor subject areas. The reference, "minor subject," in this instance is very inappropriate. Oftentimes the girl with the learning disability is a fine student in home economics, if she can be relieved of the responsibility of term papers and written tests. The boy is oftentimes a fine shop student but may have difficulties managing job sheets, keeping notebooks and, again, passing written examinations. Many do well in physical education but fail health courses, again primarily because of the demand for written output. Most of these young people can comprehend the material under discussion in most of their regular classrooms. Again, their chief difficulty appears to be in written output. Many of them can understand mathematical concepts but do poorly in computation. If the school is flexible enough to make allowances for what amounts to merely clerical inefficiencies, many of these youngsters could reveal their excellent levels of thought by being given oral examinations based on what they have been capable of learning from what was seen or heard in the classroom discussions. In short, many young people, if given the status of an auditor, can profit greatly by the high level of language stimulation in the academic classroom. Many of them in an interview situation will reveal excellent conceptual thinking and a good grasp of the subject matter.

In New Jersey the child study team has been given unusual powers to make specific prescriptive recommendations for high school youths. This is a prerogative not often used. Specific recommendations by the child study team can tip the balance in the direction of flexible prescriptive management. In many instances all that is needed is a conference conducted by the child study team with the teachers who are managing any one youth with a

---

[7] Vera C. Perrella, "Working Teenagers," *Children Today*, May-June 1972, pp. 14-17.

learning disability, informing them of his unique personal and educational needs, together with a description of his unique learning style, and then making suggestions for appropriate action.

Fourth, any program designed for the learning disabled high school youth must have *high expectancy* for normal achievement. In many instances, the labels "handicapped, slow learner, learning disabled, neurologically impaired, educable retarded," tend to put the young person in a position where little will be required of him mainly because it is expected that he has an overall incompetency. The child with the learning disability is characterized by wide discrepancies between his best capacities and his poorest. As in Sally's case, where her vocabulary was superior and her numbers concepts were preschool, her teachers gave up on her because they didn't expect that functional competency was possible in the mathematical area. The result is that she is a young woman age 20, who cannot tell time or count change. Any program that is set up for the adolescent youth with a learning problem must go on the assumption that the child is essentially normal and can be expected to make a normal life adjustment. This involves focusing primarily on the areas of integrity and using these to compensate for areas of deficit or inefficiency. Of primary importance is the recognition that the young person's inefficiencies or deficiencies may relate only to academic subject matter.

Many educators become frustrated as they overemphasize highly language-oriented academic subject matter, which is, in reality, irrelevant to the youngster's future career goal. It is not unusual in the average vocational school to see many young people failing their academic subjects while they make very respectable grades in their vocational program. *Oftentimes the teachers who manage the youth in the area of failure are completely oblivious of his success in the other areas of his life.* Certainly one area of success alone should communicate to the educators that success is possible. It *is* a fundamental requirement then that all adults managing a youth with learning disability feel that achievement of independence is possible. In the experience of the author, all youth will reveal an area of success and interest if the adult searches long enough for it. In the failure-oriented, ego-damaged youth, this will be difficult to find and it will be necessary almost always to search somewhere beyond the youth's life in school. In one instance several youths with learning disabilities were taken on a four-day camping experience sponsored by the special services of their local school district. During this experience the psychologist, learning specialist, social worker, special class teachers, and many other contributing regular class teachers discovered competencies in these young people as they left the walls of the school that could never have been discovered had they dealt only with the sample of classroom behavior that was available to them.

A fifth characteristic of educational strategies is that the program must be reality bound and relevant to the youth's immediate needs. Recently a young man who had achieved an A in his vocational auto mechanics shop defended his failure in English by explaining, "Who needs Silas Marner to fix an engine." Certainly something can be done in almost any subject area to make it relevant to the life the young person will lead at maturity and since legal maturity is so close at hand in the latter high school years, it is now a mandatory requirement. Many young people have already been successful in many occupational pursuits in the after school and weekend periods, and this aspect of their life has much meaning for them. Working for an employer produces a greater consistency in the management of behavior than can be found in any other aspect of their life, including family or school. Grades certainly do not have the reinforcing effect on appropriate behavior that a paycheck does. Many young people who are not successful in a vocational program are highly successful in work-study programs for this reason. They see their occupational life much more realistically, and the addition of the paycheck adds to this realism. In many instances the youth in a vocational program, where he is learning only basic tool processes, oftentimes is appalled by the complexities of the production-oriented industrial shop. One of the recommendations of the White House Conference on Youth stresses the need for finding alternate forms of education.[8]

Certainly there are wide choices in any community for children to learn outside of school, in industrial plants, business estab-

---

[8] *Report of the White House Conference on Youth*, Estes Park, Colorado, April 18-22, 1971, U.S. Government Printing Office, 1971, p. 87.

lishments, professional offices, libraries and museums. There is a great need for an extension of the kinds of programs, such as the Parkway Project in Philadelphia, where young people are assigned to educational experiences and required to make contact with the school only once a week to report what they have learned or to receive a new assignment. The Ridgewood, New Jersey high school staff has just instituted what is called a "Ten O'clock Scholar Program." This permits the young person to be given credit for his job throughout the day and to receive his necessary instruction in English, history and physical education in the evening hours, conducted by specially selected teachers in the evening adult program. The program terminates with graduation and a diploma. Such a step certainly makes education more realistic because of actual participation in a life experience. Much of our school programs conducted rigidly within the walls of the school frequently attempt to *describe* again in the various forms of language what life will be like after schooling is finished. The success stories of the youth with learning disabilities on work experience programs is well documented and would satisfy all of the requirements listed above.

Much focus has been directed to the youth in his contest with school. This is highly important since it is "his place of business" and also the primary scene of his failure. However, whether the young person achieves successful independence is going to depend also on his personal and social adjustment. Sally is a case in point. Sally could do many things but couldn't sustain effort. She bored her fellow workers to exasperation. Sally had developed a role in life where she learned to make incompetency pay off, which envolved into a role that passively defeated authority whether at home, school, or on the job. Sally is a very difficult young person to like. As a result she is living a life of almost total social isolation. There seems to be a profusion of programs established for the recreation and socialization of young people with learning disabilities that again focus on segregation, accepting the premise that young people are cruel and treat handicapped youth inhumanely. This results in therapy groups, recreation groups, socialization groups staffed by humanistically motivated professionals, and volunteers who tend to reinforce segregation and isolation.

Recently a program called "Triangle Club" was organized

by a group of parents of handicapped young people and was sponsored by the Passaic-Clifton, New Jersey YMCA. In this program a handicapped adolescent is matched with a normal adolescent approximately a year older. This group of normal and handicapped adolescents participated in many activities together under the leadership of a college-age volunteer. No professional or parent intervention is permitted or necessary. The young people are treated with the same restrictions as any normal group of young people going out on their own. They attend the theater and concerts in New York City, go on hay rides, sponsor dances and engage in other normal adolescent activities. The parents demanded only that they know where the young people were going and that they return at an appropriate hour. One of the most important insights that came out of this program was that normal adolescents, rather than being cruel, are frankly honest and realistic in their relationship with the handicapped. One young man who exhibited very bizarre and socially inappropriate behavior was told very directly and without malice by his teen pal to "quit behaving like a nut." This young person stopped the bizarre behavior immediately. Most professional people would not have handled him that directly and would have disapproved highly at the suggestion that such a thing be done. Here again, many of the principles enumerated as necessary ingredients in school programs become also highly important in the out-of-school socialization. They are: that it should be focused on reality, flexible in its application and scene of operation, and should provide for interaction with normal peers.

The foregoing enumeration of options available to the young adult with a learning disability within his home, school and the community is of no avail if the disabled young person is contending with insensitive, uncommitted or disinterested adults. The young person will not succeed if merely presented with the option of special help, no matter how well-planned the program is or how appropriately it has been chosen for him. As mentioned previously, the chances are the adolescent will reject the help, seeing it as another "put-down" that further reinforces his sense of failure. Only committed adults can inspire him with the courage to try again and perhaps again and again. Only an inspired, committed and sensitive adult can emphatically feel the vast feelings of inadequacy that many of these youngsters experience constantly.

Most of the success stories have resulted in well-chosen programs that match the needs of the disabled young person, coupled with a teacher who is sensitive enough to see what was possible and inspired enough to stay with the young person through many failures until success was achieved.

A review of Dr. Dominic W. Flamini's book, entitled *The Store Front School,*[9] lists certain basic program elements for the educationally maladjusted youth. He included motivation (his students were paid for going to school) and a curriculum focused on developing competency in reading and math. The students participated in the decision-making processes, and the only disciplinary rule established was that no student would physically harm another student. The program was work-oriented and *the teachers were chosen from the most caring, optimistic people available who were successful in their own right and who looked at the failure of their students as partly their own responsibility.* The disabled young person cannot be given a choice of options and then when his choice has been made, told that "It is entirely up to you." There must be the commitment between the youth and his teacher that says, "Now you have decided what you need, it's entirely up to us."

Finally, we must consider another area of conflict—the developmentally disabled youth in his family. As previously stated, these young people frequently bring their frustrations home and displace their accumulated rage on their families in the form of active or passive aggression. They also are experiencing the normal adolescent strivings for independence but with much less capacity to cope with the responsibilities of maturity. The result is often excessive rebelliousness directed toward their parents. All of this may be occurring in a family whose morale has already been badly battered by years of contention with their handicapped youth. Negative cultural factors and attitudes of the general public also make their contribution to the denigration of the parents.

For generations a concept has been evolving that, simply

---

[9] New Jersey Department of Education, Branch of Special Education and Pupil Personnel Services, "The Store Front School, *Bureau Briefs*, Volume 3, Number 4, 1972.

stated, says that a child comes into the world much like a blank slate and what he becomes is what is written on that slate by his parents' management of him. This concept puts the primary responsibility for the child's future success entirely on his parents. If the child develops adequately or achieves a position of prestige, the parents can take pride. If the child fails to develop adequately, then his parents are to blame.

Over the years parents have internalized this concept so completely that they now ask when their children are developing inadequately, "What did we do wrong?" As this concept became more universal, even the children began to blame their parents for their own inadequacies. Later, the mass media communication took up this concept and magnified it so massively that today the first response of the general public toward the parents of an inadequately developing child is, "It must be their fault." Even the schools have been caught up in this erroneous assumption and project the blame for the child's inadequacies in school again on his poor parents. This is a very unfair judgment of the parents of a developmentally disabled child and produces much irrelevant guilt, which begins to erode the parent-child relationship from the very beginning.

Stella Chess and her associates at the Albert Einstein Medical Institute in New York City have shown, after an intensive longitudinal study, that infant temperament can be assessed at the earliest period of infancy and that certain characteristics tend to pervade even into adulthood.[10] They found that a child with a very difficult temperament can be a very potent negative stimulus on a parent. They conclude that at least half of what a child is came into the world with him. This should be very good news for the parent of the developmentally disabled child and should help to relieve some of the self-doubt they experience. The fact is that a parent of a developmentally disabled child is dealing with a much more difficult child to raise than the average and he needs more consistent management, much higher structure and much more clearly defined rules and limits than the average child. Mis-

[10] Alexander Thomas, Stella Chess and Herbert G. Birch, "The Origins of Personality," *Contemporary Psychology*, Readings from Scientific American, San Francisco: W. H. Freeman and Co., 1971, pp. 350-357.

guided parents, whose reactions to the child are fraught with much guilt, will find it very difficult to mobilize the firmness and consistency needed and will tend to behave toward the child with a lack of conviction in their discipline of him. The result will be a massively inconsistent and unpredictable environment for the already poorly developed child. This child, who has stronger dependency needs than the average, will quickly learn that authority can be manipulated and made undependable. Considerable disturbance can result from the anxieties this ambivalence produces.

The first ingredient, then, in any plan of management for the developmentally disabled adolescent, is the establishment and maintenance of a consistent predictable environment with rules well-chosen and enforced. He needs also to be managed by parents who know what they want of him and who are realistically confident that what they require of him is in his best interest. This kind of confidence as it is projected to the youngster proves to him that his parents are dependable and really love him. It helps him thus to gradually establish his independence in appropriately programmed stages. The adolescent who alienates his family and the authorities in his school in his strivings for independence eventually becomes more dependent, and oftentimes turns to drugs and alcohol as a substitute.

The youth with a developmental disability oftentimes has a rather poor social feedback and does not pick up the nuances of emotional expression from people in his environment. As a result many continue to behave inappropriately because they do not get the message of how they are affecting the people around them. It seems to be a trait of human nature not to honestly express the disapproval that many of these young people need. Usually, adults will not react to the inappropriate behavior of the developmentally disabled adolescent, fearing that they will further traumatize him and cause his behavior to deteriorate further. This was true in Sally's case, where the special services team of her high school met with all of her teachers yearly, pointing up her need for them to be completely honest in their appraisal of her. Sally had to be told directly by her teachers, on the spot, not to bring her personal private difficulties into the open in her classes, and arrangements were made to discuss them privately with her afterward. It was also recommended to the teachers managing her that they had to directly intervene in her perseverative conversation and that this needed to be done objectively with neutral emotion. These expressions helped Sally to get some understanding of the impact of her behavior on others. She began to see more directly how inappropriately her behavior was and how it was rejected by the people in her world.

In many instances the adolescent with the developmental disability is like the central character in the mouthwash commercial, where everyone is afraid to tell the boss he has bad breath.

Blatant honesty by the responsible adults in daily contact with the handicapped adolescent becomes a fundamental need and should not be feared if the expression of emotion is neutral and free of ridicule and contempt. This kind of response to the handicapped adolescent does not traumatize, but rather humanely helps him overcome behavior that will eventually lead to social isolation in the adult years.

The support that the youth with a developmental disability needs in the adolescent years oftentimes must be extended into the years of young adulthood because a significant number will not be ready to achieve full citizenship at age eighteen and will be dependent on their families well into the early twenties. These young people tend to become socially isolated, still living at home, completely dependent on their families, and remain in a state of perpetuated adolescence. A break of some kind must be made from the home similar to that of the normal youth leaving for work, the armed services, or college. There is considerable need for young men and young women like Sally to have some means of living separately from their families, with assistance in the form of supportive counseling to help them gradually adjust to living independently. The creation of facilities of this kind should be the highest priority for research and program planning in the field of developmental disabilities.

9

POST SECONDARY PROBLEMS: AN OPTIMISTIC APPROACH

Thomas-Robert H. Ames, F.A.A.M.D.
*Assistant Professor of Community
Mental Health Technology,
Department of Health Service Technologies,
Borough of Manhattan Community College,
City University of New York*

INTRODUCTION

What of those late adolescents and young adults who have been through various developmental, educational and treatment experiences and have arrived at the point when vocational training should begin but are found to be ill-equipped to meet the stress and demands of the social aspects of training and work? In the past, this was a time of great anguish for both the handicapped young people and their families. Frequently a fruitless search for help ended in the handicapped member being designated as "unfeasible for rehabilitation services" by agencies charged with providing those services.

Many of the young people with learning disabilities are multiply-disabled. The severity and complex interaction of disabilities has greatly lessened their opportunities for adequate socialization and full participation in the usual learning experiences of childhood and adolescence. Despite all the professional help and fam-

173

ily love that could be provided, the integrative experiences, which help fashion a healthy self-concept and the maturity essential in preparing young people for their adult roles, have been missed or under-utilized.[1]

This is not to say that they have failed to learn. Much learning may have been inappropriate and did not address the fact that there is heavy stress for an adult, in our modern society, in terms of emotional maturity, acceptable social behaviors, vocational competence, and self-direction. Our culture places a tremendous emphasis on achievement, together with those qualities which make it possible: brightness, conformity, physical attractiveness, sociability and a strong competitive drive.

Development is not evenly achieved and gaps or lags remain which, in turn, retard other areas of growth, development, and learning. Hence, multiply-disabled young people can reach the appropriate age for greater independence without having achieved a state of readiness for the new demands which more adult roles thrust upon them.[2]

Parents will ask how can this be? Why hasn't my child developed to his full potential when others similarly disabled have? Two principle variables affect the probability of the learning disabled developing serious social and emotional problems which complicate the primary disability: first, the severity of the disability; second, the chronicity of the handicap. The more severely disabled will have greater possibility of developing disturbances or maladaptive behaviors. The greater the period of time the person endures the handicapping features of the disability, the more likely social and emotional conflicts will develop and impair functioning. Other variables can also contribute to the development of serious emotional and social problems: the handicapped person's sex,

---

[1] Christopher Connolly, "Social and Emotional Factors in Learning Disabilities," *Progress In Learning Disabilities*, Vol. II, ed. by Helmer R. Mykelbust (New York: Grune and Stratton, 1971), pp. 159-60.

[2] Thomas-Robert H. Ames and Joel M. Levy, "Adult Programs: The Programs in a Hostel for Working Mentally Handicapped Adults" unpublished presentations delivered at the 9th International Conference of the Association for Children with Learning Disabilities, Atlantic City, New Jersey, February 5, 1972, p. 13.

membership in a particular subcultural group, the socioeconomic level of the family, and his level of intelligence. A prime characteristic of the learning disabled is the marked disparity between potential for development and level of performance. This is the most difficult aspect for both the disabled person and his family to accept.[3]

While no single reaction pattern is prevalent in all those who are learning disabled, there are certain traits common to many. Possibly this is because of similar experiences endured by the learning disabled and the parallelism in response shared by parents, teachers, and others in the environment. A vicious cycle, involving the incessant demands by others, repeated failures, and the resulting frustration engendered, produces intense anxiety, fear, and anger. To cope with these powerful emotions, strong neurotic defense patterns are developed such as: rationalization, projection, displacement, denial, and regression. Often the pressures are so great that the handicapped person undergoes cognitive changes which veer from reality and he develops maladaptive behaviors which markedly impair functioning.[4]

While certain select psychotheraputic techniques are used effectively with many of the learning disabled, increasingly professionals are impressed with the failure of traditional psychiatric treatment to produce meaningful results and, in some cases, avoid bringing about increased harm.[5] What they require is a total Life Adjustment program of sufficient comprehension, intensity, and duration to allow them to arm themselves with the multitudinous skills necessary and the facility to function as independent adults.[6] If we recognize that adjustment is a daily effort even for so-called normal people and that it requires their best to meet the challenges of the real world, perhaps we can better appreciate the

---

[3] Connolly, op. cit., pp. 157-60.

[4] *Ibid.*, pp. 161-65.

[5] *Ibid.*, pp. 156.

[6] Bert MacLeech, "A Forward-Looking Concept in Rehabilitation," *Seventh Annual Distinguished Lecture Series in Special Education and Rehabilitation,* ed. by Bert MacLeech, Donald R. Schroder (Los Angeles, California, 1969), p. 24.

magnitude of the problem facing young people handicapped by lifelong disabilities.

LIFE ADJUSTMENT: A NEW HABILITATION APPROACH

Solving the problems stated above requires a change in perspective for many parents, professionals and the community, and a new habilitation approach. To be effective, a Life Adjustment program should be viewed and planned as a continuum of training and support beginning prior to entrance into vocational training and proceeding on into job placement and, in some cases, beyond. All too often the socialization and personal adjustment aspects of training are applied like so many bandaides: a bit of recreation here, a bit of psychotherapy there.[7]

Life Adjustment programming necessarily utilizes and adopts the principles and techniques of special education, psychology and other mental health and rehabilitation disciplines in a process designed to change and modify behavior and develop new skills for living.[8] All services must be viewed and provided within the context of the principle of normalization which is "the utilization of means which are as culturally normative as possible, in order to elicit and/or maintain behaviors which are as culturally normative as possible."[9]

Life Adjustment training enhances the young people's developing self-concept by: assisting them to a state of readiness for learning by providing an environment conducive to the learning process and reinforcement for what is learned, hence facilitating their motivation for further learning; providing whatever is needed in training and supportive services to help them achieve and sustain maximum independence; and never doing for them what they

---

[7] Thomas-Robert H. Ames, "Intensive Life Adjustment Training for Mentally-Disabled Young Adults," *Journal of Rehabilitation* (publication pending), p. 1.

[8] MacLeech, op. cit., pp. 25-6.

[9] Margaret Fritz, Wolf Wolfensberger, and Mel Knowlton, Position paper on "An Apartment Living Plan to Promote Integration and Normalization of Mentally Retarded Adults," Douglas County, Nebraska, 1970, p. 2.

can do for themselves, thus encouraging self-reliance and self-confidence.[10]

Two alternative types of program may be developed to provide Life Adjustment training: an Adjustment Center, and a Group Home.

The Adjustment Center

The Adjustment Center can function separately, but concurrently, with either a special education program, sheltered workshop or other vocational training facility, or as an integral part of an overall program, including academic and vocational training. Generally speaking, small homogenous groups of four to seven lend themselves well to this type of curriculum, with attention given to individual needs in a specific treatment plan. The essential elements of an Adjustment Center are:

1. Adjustment counseling for the development of insight and the resources to handle problem-solving and change. Both individual and group techniques are useful in facilitating change in the young person's feelings about himself as a dependent, inadequate person having experienced a family or institutional environment in which he was seen and treated as a child and where passivity, dependency, submissiveness, low self-esteem and inertia were reinforced consciously or unconsciously by over-protection or even, in some cases, neglect. The counselor or teacher may use socio-drama and role-playing to act out the young person's problems in the supportive atmosphere of the center, with suggestions and encouragement from the other group members.

2. Social skills training to enhance interpersonal relations. The group can work on a multitude of problems such as those associated with: eating in public, table manners, food ordering, figuring the tip, paying the bill, grooming and dating. These are frequently the first opportunities the young people will have had to be away from the supervision and control of their parents or guardians. An effort should be made to extend their social activities to all those experiences normal for their age-group peers.

---

[10] Ames and Levy, op. cit., p. 2.

3. Sex education, a related area of training, to help the young people understand and accept themselves and others as sexual beings and to establish those behavior patterns in dating and relating that can lead to a greater sense of fulfillment. This is still a largely neglected or inadequately attended aspect of Life Adjustment training because of the ambivalent attitudes and conflicting moral standards within society. Without attention to this aspect of adjustment there can be little hope for the handicapped person's attaining maximum independence. Without focusing on his needs and allowing for alternative adjustment patterns not traditionally or universally condoned, additional burdens are heaped upon the shoulders of an already overburdened person with every right to express his sexuality.

4. Communication skills training to increase the young people's ability to relate and receive information productively. Many will need continued attention to their problems related to: adequate feedback and monitoring of what is said, in understanding and remembering what is heard and seen, and in the vocal and motor expression of ideas, as well as in written communication. Frequently, very basic behaviors such as concentration of attention must be relearned or strengthened before complex skills or behaviors are reintroduced.

5. Employment skills training to develop an understanding of work, the complex role of being a worker, and the sense of dignity, fulfillment and independence it imparts. Most of those referred for Life Adjustment training will not yet be in job training programs or, if they are, their behavior is often inappropriate for the training or work setting and they may have a confused idea of what work is. Within this group, the young people can be helped to focus on what is expected of them. Their awareness can be heightened by the use of visual aids, and discussions with their peers who are successfully training or working can help their motivation for this experience.

6. Therapeutic recreation can help them learn to share with others and to be good members of the team. Many need to learn much more about how to use their bodies and to follow rules used in group games. Because of relative isolation and poor motor skills and coordination, many will

not have experienced the pleasure of group athletics and other cooperative and social activities. In this group, they can put into practice what they are learning in the other training groups. In addition, special community events, scheduled periodically and properly utilized, can help broaden their horizons and teach them to use community facilities and resources. Once the young people realize they can participate in such activities as folk dances, concerts, plays or the local skating rink, they can be encouraged to go alone or in small groups.

7. Other elements of training that may be included are: reading, arithmetic, the functional academics such as making change or budgeting, and, in large urban communities particularly, travel by public conveyances.

8. One more element of programming is imperative if success is to be achieved: parent or family counseling. The use of both individual and group experiences is useful in encouraging a change in parental and familial responses to their handicapped young person and their expectations of his behavior as an adult. The difficulties bearing upon parents and siblings of learning disabled children and adolescents are legion, and often neurotic patterns develop in the family in relation to the handicapped member. The family must be helped to break through these patterns and become an effective part of the habilitation team that includes the professionals, paraprofessionals and the handicapped member.[11]

Such an Adjustment Center program was pioneered by the Young Adult Institute and Workshop, Inc. In 1966, a research study supported, in part, by a grant from the Vocational Rehabilitation Administration of the Department of Health, Education and Welfare, studied the adjustment of the first one hundred multiply-disabled clients provided with these services between 1957 and 1963. Some of the findings were:[12]

---

[11] Ames, "Intensive Life Adjustment Training," pp. 2-3.

[12] Herbert Rusalem, Bert MacLeech, Ruth Cummings, and Pearl MacLeech, *"An Exploration of the Advisability of Developing a Research and Demonstration Project Concerned with Elevating the Readiness for Vocational Rehabilitation of Multiply-Disabled Young Adults,"* Young Adult Institute and Workshop, Inc., August, 1966, pp. 73, 78, 110, 111.

Table 68	Table 69
Range of Achievement Attained	Time Spent in the Adjustment Center
1. Achieved success in independent funtioning, productive employment and appropriate social relationships 39%	(One term equals five months)—Mean number of terms: 3.8 terms
2. Achieved significant gains in enhanced vocational readiness, socialization and independence 39%	4.0 terms
3. Achieved limited gains — improvement to a degree but not sufficient to have affected status materially 20%	1.9 terms
4. Achieved no appreciable gains, remaining at the level at which he was upon entrance into the program 2%	1.0 terms

At the time of the study:

> 76 percent held competitive jobs (not sheltered workshops)
>
> 50 percent were fully self-supporting
>
> 10 percent were married

The findings of the study speak eloquently for the Life Adjustment approach.

The Group Home

The group Home is an alternative type of facility for those whose problems are aggravated by living within the family for whatever reason. The opportunity for a residential experience as a fully integrated program of life adjustment, with many facets, including those enumerated above and the additional aspect of environmental or milieu therapy, can often mean the difference between success and failure.[13]

Frequently there are two misconceptions which hinder parental consideration of this type of program:

> The first is that somehow the family, and more particularly the parents, feel that they have failed. Feelings of guilt are not the basis for good decisions. A realistic appraisal of the situation, for both the handicapped member and the family, may clearly demonstrate that the removal of the learning disabled person to a Group Home would be beneficial for all concerned and allow the process of habilitation to proceed to the desired goal of independent functioning.

> The other misconception is that a Group Home is an institution and institutions frequently have had a negative image, often justifiably. On the contrary, ideally a Group Home should be within the community and provide relatively small concentrations of people with similar problems and a very intensive experience in Life Adjustment. Families should not be divorced from the experience but involved in a new way to alter the problem situations and to stimulate and reinforce healthier, happier ways of relating. Parents and families need assistance to plan, accept and utilize this experience for their own and the young person's benefit. Therefore, family counseling is again an integral part of this type of program.

One method for effective training and treatment in a Life Adjustment program that needs to be stressed is that of behavior modification. This is a term which applies "to a number of different behavior change techniques that have the goal of changing human behavior in a beneficial manner."[14]

It is an optimistic approach. The origin of the maladaptive behavior is not sought in deep psychological disturbance or viewed as an unalterable result of brain damage, but rather is

---

[13] Edward L. French, "Principles of Residential Therapy as a Rehabilitation Tool," *Seventh Annual Distinguished Lecture Series in Special Education and Rehabilitation*, ed. by Bert MacLeech and Donald R. Schroder, (Los Angeles, California: The University Press, University of Southern California, 1969) pp. 31-36.

[14] William I. Gardner, *Behavior Modification In Mental Retardation*, (New York: Aldine-Atherton, 1971), p. 61.

seen as resulting from an inappropriate or inadequate learning environment.[15]

Not only can behavior be predicted, but by using systematic procedures, the conditions in the environment can be so arranged as to be utilized in definite operational prescriptions for changing behavior predictably. The systematic procedures necessary for effective behavioral change are:

a) Direct Observation—involving a description of the observed behaviors, the selection of a target behavior, a delineation of the characteristics of the target behavior, and a counting of the frequency of the target behavior over a period of time to determine the rate of occurrence.

b) Continuous Measurement—to facilitate a precise evaluation of the effects of changes in contingencies and reinforcers used.

c) Systematic Changes in Environmental Conditions—to obtain a reliable measure of the degree of influence a particular environmental condition has upon the target behavior.

d) Contingency Management—by specifying a systematic utilization of reinforcing modalities such as praise, privileges and a token economy in relation to the target behavior to facilitate behavioral change or learning.

e) Maximizing Conditions for Learning—by using appropriate instructional materials to elicit the desired response, controlling the consequences for responding so that only the desired behaviors will be reinforced, and sequencing small units or learning steps to permit an accurate and correct response successively approximating the desired effective behaviors.[16]

MAINTENANCE OF MAXIMUM INDEPENDENCE

Ultimately the sustaining reinforcement for desirable behaviors comes from the personal satisfaction derived in engaging in those behaviors and the social approval they elicit. For some

---

[15] Gardner, op. cit., pp. 16, 22, 44.

[16] Norris G. Haring, "Behavior Principles in Special Education," *Seventh Annual Distinguished Lecture Series in Special Education and Rehabilitation*, ed. by Bert MacLeech and Donald R. Schroder, (Los Angeles, California: The University Press, University of Southern California, 1969, pp. 53-67.

learning-disabled people a plateau may be reached in development or a marked slowing down in acquiring additional skills may occur. While a tremendous amount of growth has been accomplished and further learning can be expected, the learning-disabled person may have reached a developmental level allowing for relatively independent functioning, providing certain supportive services are available to lend assistance. It would be foolish to withhold the opportunity for maximum independence merely because there is yet room for improvement. Conversely, it would be unwise to abandon the learning-disabled individual as he launches out to make his way in the world. For a number of these young people a series of transitional services can facilitate a very adequate independent adjustment. For others, there will be a need for ongoing support on an indefinite or permanent basis. Each person's needs will be uniquely his own and will possibly change with time. The selection of services to be provided must take into account his right to continue growing and to be as independent as possible.[17]

The range of services available should provide for the breadth and scope of a variety of lifestyles and for special needs at different times of life.

The Hostel

One such service is the Hostel, "a supervised residential facility for disabled persons on a long-term or indefinite basis."[18] The Hostel differs from the Group-Home in that it is not a treatment facility, although the staff must consider each resident's needs and evaluate his ability to handle self-care needs, personal problems and ancillary problems related to his job and group living. Some remediation in deficient areas may be necessary in order that the individual can function at his optimum level.[19]

---

[17] Ames and Levy, op. cit., p. 2.

[18] New York State Dept. of Mental Hygiene, *Regulations for the Operation of Hostels for the Mentally Disabled*, (Utica, New York: State Hospitals Press, July, 1970), p. 11.

[19] Thomas-Robert H. Ames and Joel M. Levy, "The Hostel: "Problems in Planning and Development", *Journal of Rehabilitation*, (publication pending, p. 11.

The Hostel should provide for a moderate number of residents in order to facilitate a home-like atmosphere and group spirit. A population ranging from ten to thirty would seem ideal.[20]

The choice of area for The Hostel must take into consideration the accessibility of dental and medical services, public transportation, shopping centers, and public recreation facilities, as well as the residents' places of employment. Time and cost factors can't be overlooked.[21]

While a funding supplementation from outside sources may be necessary, direct parental payments of fees is unwise, as it continues the psychological dependence of the residents. Being able to take the responsibility for paying their own way frequently helps to build a more adequate self-concept and improves their awareness of themselves as separate adults, independent of their parents.[22]

A particular word ought to be said about the type of staffing patterns for The Hostel. One pattern which has shown itself effective is the utilization of a young, trained paraprofessional staff who provide supervision under professional direction. Having the staff near the age range of the residents facilitates the establishment of rapport, lessens the residents' feelings of being "mothered," and makes interactions of a peer nature possible because the residents perceive the staff as friends and not merely supervisors. Also, a youthful, energetic, mature, and highly motivated staff, properly trained and supervised, can best cope with the sustained periods of stress and pressure which are manifested in helping a multi-problemed, learning-disabled population and still provide latitude for growth and independence.[23]

As a part of a continuum of services for those living marginally independent lives within the community and as ancillary services for hostel residents, the parent agency or organization may find it advisable to provide one of all of the following programming components:

---

[20] *Ibid.*, p. 4.

[21] *Ibid.*, p. 5.

[22] *Ibid.*, p. 7.

[23] Ames and Levy, "Adult Programs," p. 13.

a) A social club organized and designed to provide members with opportunities to plan and operate their own social and recreational activities with the aid of a professional and para-professional staff. The club's activities might encompass a monthly business meeting, an evening social, and a special event, such as theater party, discotheque, or out-of-town tour. These affairs would be supplementary to the small group activities and of a frequency which the learning disabled arranged for themselves.

b) A current events discussion group designed to facilitate the members' growing awareness of the world around them, to help them to form opinions on important matters and to participate more effectively as citizens.

c) Bi-weekly group counseling may be beneficial for many in helping them resolve new problems arising from the stresses inherent in our complex society.

d) Finally, the development of satellite apartments scattered throughout the community can be arranged for those ready for minimal assistance and greater integration into the fabric of community life. For such people, only occasional assistance from a paraprofessional advocate may be necessary.

For those learning-disabled persons living relatively independent lives in the community, there may be a recurring need to seek assistance, advice, or counseling for specific problems or in developing new plans, such as in moving to another community or changing jobs. Ordinarily, we are all accustomed to seek professional advice when faced with questions in which we lack expertise or familiarity. For the learning disabled, the range of situations requiring assistance will be broader so that additional special attention and opportunities are needed. Agencies concerned with providing on-going services for these handicapped people may want to consider developing and providing Advocates who can be available for such periodic assistance. These are paraprofessionals or technicians whose job it is to facilitate the decision-making process for the learning disabled by: acting as a sounding board in planning; providing suggestions for alternatives; giving guidance on such matters as where to get more information, how to file a correct form, or how to apply for a loan. The advocate's role is to enhance the learning-disabled person's independent functioning, not to be a surrogate parent. It is the learning-disabled person who, recognizing a need for assistance, seeks out the Advocate and asks for specific help or advice. Such behavior on the part of the learning-disabled person strongly suggests that a high level of maturity has been attained. This is a worthwhile life goal for any adult.[24]

Communities are beginning to develop a sensitivity and concern for the special needs of various groups of their citizens. Public money, facilities, and programs are being allocated and fashioned for the senior citizen, the youth, and the disadvantaged. Various segments of the learning disabled can also benefit from such public funds and services. Parent groups and others interested in their welfare can and should continue to push for a greater public recognition and commitment to meeting their needs.

The clergy play an integral role in the overall maintenance of mental health in the community. Through all the phases of development for the learning disabled and their growing participation in the community's life, the clergy can make a positive contribution. The clergy often enjoy relationships with their congregations and with larger communities frequently not available to other professionals. They can speak out on the great and important problems of life and work for their acceptance and remediation of these problems. More particularly, they can contribute in the following ways by.

> Visiting and getting to know the resources for help within the community so that they can advise and refer for the needed services; by helping the learning disabled accept themselves and their appropriate roles in the life of the community; by helping to reduce the sense of isolation of the handicapped through participation within the congregation; by stimulating the parish or congregation to encourage and allow the formation of a nucleus of a group where none exists and to provide space for activities; and by helping to interpret to the congregation and larger community the learning disabled person's presence, potential and need for attention, acceptance, affection, trust, respect and love.[25]

---

[24] *Ibid.*, p. 14.

[25] Thomas-Robert H. Ames, "Ministering to the Mentally Handicapped and Their Families in the Community, *Journal of Pastoral Counseling*, Vol. V, Winter 1970-71, #2 pp. 3, 4.

Adjustment is an on-going process for all of us and this is no less true for the learning disabled; increased maturity brings greater opportunity for the development of long-term emotional and sexual relationships; and middle age, retirement, and old age add new challenges for us in helping enrich the lives of the learning disabled and giving scope and opportunity for their contributions to the welfare of all.

SUMMARY

The transition from childhood to adulthood for many learning-disabled individuals may be a time of crisis, but it is also an occasion for imaginative and effective programming. Enough experience in designing and operating habilitative services for the learning disabled has been gained to allow us an optimism tempered by the realities of the disability. The Life Adjustment approach to training and treatment, drawing upon the full range of skills and techniques which have emerged over the years and which are continually being improved upon, together with the development of a continum of services throughout the life-cycle of the learning disabled, means that we stand ready and able to give new meaning and depth to the ideal of the "good life." We can concur with Emily Greene Balch who said, "the measure of our civilization is the possibility for every individual's development."

10

LEARNING DISABILITIES
AND JUVENILE DELINQUENCY:
A DEMONSTRATED RELATIONSHIP

Frank N. Jacobson, Ph.D.
Arapahoe Mental Health Center
Englewood, Colorado

INTRODUCTION

Scientists clearly agree that there is a relationship between learning problems and delinquent behavior. Precisely how these behaviors are related has not been clear. Do learning disabilities generate delinquency, or is poor learning a result of a delinquent's belligerent attitude toward teacher and school?

Over the last century, scientists and professionals have accumulated scattered evidence which shows that delinquency and learning disabilities are related. Recently the literature has more insistently suggested that learning disabilities lead to delinquency. It is the contention of this writer that incipient delinquent behavior grows from schoolroom frustrations experienced by the child who generally appears normal, but who is handicapped by a learning problem. The specific focus is the teacher impact on the teacher-child relationship. Very often neither recognizes the child's limitations; neither can accept the child's poor performance. Both child and teacher become frustrated and aggressive; their interactions lead to a rebellion by the child which eventually becomes identified as delinquent.

Why this relationship has not been previously recognized and dealt with is a major concern. To understand the current problem it is necessary to understand much relevant historical information. In addition, the pattern generally followed in the school in which the child with a learning problem became delinquent needs to be described and comprehended. Finally, this review will implicate needed research, social action, and remedial programs to combat the current situation.

DEFINITIONS

First of all, *what is a learning disability*? It can be a deficit or a dysfunction. As a deficit it is the difference between estimated ability (tested) and actual performance (schoolroom). As a dysfunction, it is a function which itself is not deficient, but interferes with other functions. One of the most common examples of this is the individual who performs arithmetic problems poorly with his eyes open, but adequately with them closed. His vision, per se, is not deficient, but the incoming visual stimulation interferes with auditory reception of information for arithmetic problems, holding that information in immediate memory, or performing operations upon the information.

The deficits and/or dysfunctions may occur in one or more components of spoken/written language or behavior. These deficits and dysfunctions should not be solely determined by test scores. The most appropriate contexts for assessment are basic academic tasks such as: reading, writing, spelling, computing and oral communication. The rationale for the emphasis on the learning or performance task is due to the limitations of the tests taken by themselves. There are many factors which would result in a child being deficient according to test score, but adequate in classroom performance.

First of all, all tests have a percentage of error; consequently, a certain number of tests will indicate that a child is subnormal when he is not. Second, there are factors in the conditions under which a child is tested which differ from those of the classroom and which may account for failure. For example, a child who may be slow to comprehend oral instructions may not understand the test task and fail the exam. However, in the classroom, where instruction may be repeated or is accompanied by visual information, he may have no difficulty.

Third, all of the sensory-motor channels and psychological processes involved in a class learning task may be unknown or merely not included in a test task. As an example, a child who needs both auditory and visual information in learning to spell may have only auditory information in a testing situation and would therefore do poorly.

Finally, the human learner—especially when highly motivated—may, by means not easily recognized, be able to compensate for natural defects. If for any reason (e.g., competition or relationship with teacher or peer group) the child is more highly motivated to perform in class than in a testing situation, he may pass the former and fail the latter. Therefore, if test scores alone are used as signs of a learning disability, the diagnosis may be erroneous though remediation may be necessary. Unless test signs can be tightly related to a classroom learning task, they have little diagnostic value. On the other hand, if a child does well in testing but poorly in classroom learning tasks, and emotional or motivational factors are ruled out, then the information is diagnostically valuable and may be of remedial value. Of course, it is necessary to establish that the classroom meets criteria of adequacy, i.e., that teacher and local qualities of education are adequate. Assuming that fact is established, then test scores can only give confirming information about the child, while his classroom performance is the ultimate criterion and the basis of final diagnosis and treatment. Ideally, the workup on a child suspected of having a learning disability should include academic and psychological tests, teacher observations, a neurological examination, and an electroencephalograph.

Learning disability deficits or dysfunctions are not due to lack of motivation, mental retardation, sensory deficits or dysfunctions, cultural or instructional factors. (Instructional factors include interference from established habit orders or inappropriate use of the optimal or early critical learning period.) The cause may be disease, accident, development (including heredity), chronic mental disturbance, or unknown. Essentially the process is a disorder of information processing in sensory-motor channels, or a disturbance of psychoneurology at perceptual, integrative or expressive levels.

This definition is convenient for screening purposes. By adding the question of under what conditions does the child fail the learning task and under what conditions does he adequately perform the task, the definition becomes valuable for remediation. That is, this approach identifies deficient or dysfunctional processes which cause failure and specifies effective processes and conditions for learning so that teaching/learning methods may be designated.

A delinquent is here defined as a juvenile whose actions deviate from social norms and is labeled as a "delinquent." He is so labeled when he is detected and then encounters court and law enforcement authorities. Attitudes and interaction between delinquent and justice agents have a primary significance in this labeling process.

LITERATURE REVIEW

Terminology has been one obstruction to recognition of the relationship between delinquency and a learning disability. Wide use of the specific term "learning disability" is recent[1] and overlaps a vast variety of closely related terms.[2] The obvious difficulties in collecting data were reduced to some extent by a 1966 task force for the Department of Health, Education and Welfare, which devised a nomenclature that related the various terms used in the

---

[1] E. Jorgensen; O. Bangsgard; T. Glad, "Adolescent Psychiatry in a Private Danish Institution," *Journal of Learning Disabilities*, I (1968), 38-41. This is the earliest known article (to the writer) to relate delinquency to learning disorders.

[2] Other recent articles utilizing the specific terminology of this article are:

F. Duling; S. Eddy; V. Risko, "Learning Disabilities and Juvenile Delinquency," Unpublished study at the Robert F. Kennedy Youth Center, Morgantown, West Virginia, 1970;

A. Berman, "Learning Disabilities and Juvenile Delinquency; initial results of a neuropsychological approach," Paper presented at the International Conference of the Association for Children with Learning Disabilities, Atlantic City, New Jersey, February 4, 1972; and

E. Walle, "Learning Disabilities and Juvenile Delinquency," Paper presented at the International Conference of the Association for Children with Learning Disabilities, Atlantic City, 1972.

learning disabilities field.[3] Preceding such current literature that related the two phenomena, the National Association for Children with Learning Disabilities has had a committee on delinquency since 1965. Earlier studies implicated the relationship between delinquency and learning disabilities, but as indicated, under many other terms. (See list of articles in notes.)[4]

Professionals in the field have observed traits among delinquents that would indicate a learning disability. Specifically, two things were noted: (a) much and extreme psychophysiological reactivity and hypercondriasis, and (b) they learned readily by observation.[5] This suggested adequate conceptual ability, but poor

---

[3] S. Clements, *Minimal Brain Dysfunction in Children* (Washington, D.C.: U.S. Department of Health, Education and Welfare, 1966).

[4] Some of the early studies linking delinquency and types of learning disorders include:

1. E. Jorgenson, op. cit.

2. R. Keldgord in "Brain Damage and Delinquency: A Question and a Challenge," *Academic Therapy*, IV (1968-9), 93-9, relates it to brain damage.

3. L. Tarnopol in "Delinquency in Minimal Brain Dysfunctions", *Journal of Learning Disabilities*, III (1970), 200-7, relates it to minimal brain damage.

4. C. Rousy and W. Cozad in *Hearing and Speech Disorders Among Delinquent Children* (Topeka, Kansas: Menninger Clinic, 1966) see delinquency related to speech and hearing disorders.

5. M. Harrower in "Who Comes to Court?" Paper presented at the American Orthopsychiatric Conference, 1964, has related reading retardation and delinquency.

W. Mulligan in "A Study of Dyslexia and Delinquency," *Academic Therapy*, IV (1969), 177-87, connects delinquency with dyslexia.

7. H. Hershkovitz; M. Levine; and G. Spivak in "Antisocial Behavior of Adolescents from Higher Socio-economic Groups," *Journal of Nervous and Mental Disease*, CXXV (1959), 467-76, claim intellectual inferiority and delinquency are related.

8. M. Harrington in "The Problem of the Defective Delinquente," *Mental Hygiene*, XIX (1935), 429-38, relates mental deficiency and delinquency.

The literature, especially under reading and intellectual inferiority, is far too extensive to be summarized here. The relationship between learning disabilities and delinquency has been studied in specific detail, for example: A. Petric; R. McCullough; and P. Kazdin in "The Perceptual Characteristics of the Juvenile Delinquent," *Journal of Nervous and Mental Disease*, CXXXIV (1962), 415, found distinct perceptual characteristics in delinquents when compared with non-delinquents. F. Jacobson and C. Ekanger in *The Model School Project* (Englewood, Colorado: Englewood Public School, 1968) found differences in auditory memory between delinquent and out-patient clinic boys.

[5] C. Poremba, Presentation at the International Conference of the Association for Children with Learning Disabilities, Atlantic City, 1972.

perceptual or language processing ability. These behaviors were not explainable on the basis of any psychosocial disorder or retarded development alone.

Studies concerned with the personality of delinquents often give descriptions of delinquents consistent with behavior characteristics of learning disability cases. For example, Glueck described delinquents in contrast with non-delinquents as being less organized in work methods, more concrete, and having less abstract thought processes.[6] Other writers saw additional relationships between minimal brain damage and delinquency.[7]

That delinquency and learning disabilities were related also was suggested by data (most of which remains unpublished) obtained in 1965 at Lookout Mountain School for Boys, Golden, Colorado. Data drawn from WISC (Wechsler Intelligence Scale for Children) indicated concreteness, and the Bender-Gestalt test suggested varied perceptual difficulty, mainly visual and spacial, as well as directional problems, in a majority of cases.

In the last few years, a significant amount of evidence has been published verifying the relationship between learning disabilities and delinquency. In 1972, Anderson reported EEG abnormalities in 50 percent of adult female prisoners.[8] In the same year, Berman found that 60 percent of delinquents have auditory problems which would impair learning,[9] and Walle found speech and hearing problems in 48.3 percent of a delinquent population.[10] Dzik, in an earlier study, found visual perceptual problems in 53 percent of delinquents.[11]

THE HISTORICAL PERSPECTIVE

Since the relationship between learning disabilities and de-

---

[6] S. Glueck, "The Home, the School, and Delinquency," *Harvard Educational Review*, XXIII (1953), 17-32.

[7] C. Anderson, *Society Pays: The High Cost of Minimal Brain Damage in America* (New York: Walker and Company, 1972).

[8] Ibid.

[9] A. Berman, op. cit.

[10] E. Walle, op. cit.

[11] D. Dzik, in "Vision and the Juvenile Delinquent," *Journal of the American Optometric Association*, XXXVII (1966), 461-8, reported visual perceptual problems in delinquents, beyond the usual expected frequencies.

linquency has been indicated repeatedly, why have neither theoretical explanations nor remedial activities followed? Both the areas of delinquency and learning disabilities, separately and conjointly, have been beset with problems which make study and remediation difficult.

Learning disabilities have escaped detection because of the general lack of information, particularly concerning the availability of techniques and methods of diagnosis. Until recent decades, learning disabilities were buried in a high percentage of mediocre performance (i.e., "C" letter grades), school failure, and dropouts, which were tolerated by the education profession and the public. Much failure and mediocrity occurred at times when the normal curve was popularly applied to the distribution of intelligence and ability, i.e., a majority of children were incapable of attaining higher than "C" performance. The concept of normal was replaced by the artificial measure of average.

Delinquency and crime historically arouse emotional and antagonistic reactions in the lay public and professionals. As a result, delinquents have been deprived of objective understanding. The factors in this attitude are numerous and complex. Briefly, research has always been biased to some extent by the attitudes of society, for scientists are people and scientific training is no absolute guarantee of objectivity. Explanations of delinquent behavior, such as a learning problem, have not only been overlooked, but perhaps unconsciously rejected. Traditionally, the social order is not to be questioned but defended. There is a tendency that is deeply written into this culture to punish the violators of law or custom.

Sociological Explanations

Durkleim began a sociological trend which focused upon forces operating in the social system that produced delinquency.[12] While these affected everyone, any handicap made the individual more likely to become a delinquent. However, at this time, sociologists did not cite learning disabilities as handicaps; neither the term, nor closely related ones, were then in wide use.

One important segment of the social order containing pressure factors toward delinquency is the schools. Mead indicated that the character of a general social system is reflected in its educational system.[13] There is ample literature which supports the application of this theory to the United States. For example, the pressures of success and goal achievement expectations pervade the schools just as they do the general society. It follows that any characteristic which may be handicapping—such as a learning disability—will place a child in greater jeopardy of failure. Therefore, he would be under greater pressure (i.e., frustration and aggression) toward becoming delinquent.

The sociological point of view may be too broad to be concerned with such specific factors in the field of delinquency as learning disabilities, although now they are better understood. The compartmentalization of fields has caused some of the difficulties involved in connecting learning disabilities with delinquency and in acting on this relationship. It is now the task of those working in education or with delinquency to detail the role of learning disabilities and to act to prevent or remediate delinquency.

Psychological Explanations

Another trend, that of the individual psychology of the delinquent, has been concerned with understanding the essential nature of the delinquent. This professional view paralleled and tacitly supported the general public viewpoint that the causes of delinquency were to be found within the delinquent himself.

---

[12] E. Durkheim, cited in R. Merton, *Social Theory and Social Structure* (Glencoe, Illinois: The Free Press, 1957) viewed deviations in Western societies as a result of the lack of limitation or "regulation" of expected goal attainment. Merton was more specific. He posited that deviant behavior was a function of the discrepancy between level of aspiration and degree of access to the means to those goals. H. Hyman in "The Value Systems of Different Classes: A Social-Psychological Contribution to the Analysis of Stratification," in *Class, Status and Power*, ed. by R. Bandix and S. Lipset (Glencoe, Illinois: Free Press, 1953,) showed that the disparity between the two levels increased as socio-economic level decreased. R. Cloward and L. Ohlin in *Delinquency and Opportunity* (Glencoe, Illinois: The Free Press, 1960) pointed out that those juveniles excluded from the success system become defined as delinquents as they are deflected into with court and law enforcement agents. The trend from Durkheim to Cloward and Ohlin clearly established the relationship between delinquency and the general social structure for the social scientific community.

[13] M. Mead, *Sex and Temperament in Three Primitive Societies* (New York: W. Morrow and Company, 1935).

Society views the delinquent as rejecting its values and therefore society rejects the delinquent. Strictly speaking, it is the "means," not the "ends" that are rejected (according to Merton[14]), but the antagonistic emotions aroused in this issue do not allow such fine distinctions. Many moral and rational issues, Puritanism and the Protestant ethic, all become involved and are activated by these antagonisms. The result is that the personality as well as the humanity of a delinquent has been impugned by the general public. In addition, it is psychologically necessary for law enforcement agents, who must deal with individuals in a dehumanized way, to think of those people as less than human. The use of force, the application of punishment and the deprivation of freedom are inescapably dehumanizing. Institutions and agencies which do these things to people invariably develop dehumanizing procedures. Therefore, the processes of law and order have almost necessarily resulted in derogatory labels for delinquents. Lombroso promoted the suggestion that the criminal was biologically inferior with his concept of atavism (a reversion to earlier evolutionary form).[15] The study of body-type-determined temperament as a cause of delinquency is seen as another scientific branch of the concept of constitutional inferiority, which was a relatively minor line of inquiry which occurred early in the psychological trend. It produced some literature, some findings, but they were of little practical value in the prevention or correction of delinquency.

Aichorn's application of psychoanalytic theory to delinquency started a new line of inquiry into the intrapsychic factors of the delinquent. The widespread persistence of this trend is reflected in a mass of current literature. Our practical application is the psychotherapeutic approach, which aimed at reducing delinquency. The persistence of this type of treatment for delinquency is aston-

14 R. Merton, *Social Theory and Social Structure* (Glencoe, Illinois: The Free Press, 1957); and

H. Hyman, "The Value Systems of Different Classes: A Social-Psychological Contribution to the Analysis of Stratification," in *Class, Status and Power*, ed. by R. Bendix and S. Lipset (Glencoe, Illinois: Free Press, 1953).

15 C. Lombroso, *Crime, It's Causes and Remedies* (translated by H. Horton) (Boston: Little, Brown and Company, 1912).

16 A. Aichorn, *Wayward Youth* (New York: Viking Press, Inc., 1935).

ishing, for although the approach has had long dominion, it continues despite a lack of evidence that it is effective enough to be practical.

Intelligence and Delinquency

Intellectual inferiority has been another aspect of the concept of constitutional inferiority. The intellectual inferiority of delinquency-oriented school children became apparent early, and there is extensive literature on this particular relationship.[17] Intelligence has been a persistent and seductive correlate of delinquency. It has been found to be inversely related to delinquency regardless of social status.[18] However, the relationship between low intelligence and delinquent behavior is not pronounced, and the promise that intelligence gave for explicating delinquency is not a sufficient cause of delinquency, but is a potentiating and complicating factor.[20]

Intelligence and Learning Disabilities

While intelligence was somewhat misleading as a factor in delinquency, it has been more misleading in learning disabilities.

---

[17] C. Burt, *The Young Delinquent* (New York: Appleton Press, 1935).

H. Goldstein, "Social and Occupational Adjustment," in *Mental Retardation: A Review of Research*, ed. by H. Stevens and R. Heber (Chicago: University of Chicago Press, 1964). noted that estimates of the percentage of delinquents who are mentally retarded vary from 0.5 to 55.0 percent. These discrepancies may be due to variations in tests, definitions and legal processes used with delinquents.

[18] S. Glueck and E. Glueck, *Unraveling Juvenile Delinquency* (New York: Commonwealth Fund, 1950).

H. Hershkovitz, op. cit.

[19] M. Woodward, "The Role of Low Intelligence in Delinquency," *British Journal of Delinquency*, V (1955), 281-303.

A. Blackhurst in "Mental Retardation and Delinquency," *Journal of Special Education*, II (1968), 379-91, cites numerous factors which may account for the relationship between delinquency and intelligence; it is generally similar to the relationship between delinquency and mental retardation, except for the higher incidence of the latter among the disadvantaged as cited in R. Allen's "Toward an Exceptional Offenders Court," *Mental Retardation*, IV (1966), 3-7.

[20] D. Beier, "Behavioral Disturbances in the Mentally Retarded," in *Mental Retardation: a Review of Research*, ed. by H. Stevens and R. Heber (Chicago: University of Chicago Press, 1964).

The wide acceptance of the Intelligence Quotient as an adequate estimate of intellectual functions has significantly clouded the understanding of learning problems. Learning disability examiners still encounter a tendency for parents, teachers, and some colleagues to question how a child who has "normal intelligence," and no sensory impairment, no emotional problems, and adequate teaching, can have problems with learning.

Psychology of Learning

Another unanswered question is why the subject of learning disabilities has not been dealt with by the psychology of learning professionals—traditionally the concern of psychologists. Until the 1960s, most of the voluminous work in the psychology of learning was conducted by experimental psychologists concerned with the general principles of learning theory, not with the nature of learning tasks.[21] Systems for describing tasks in the field of learning theory are recent developments.[22] Consequently, it has been difficult to apply the work on the psychology of learning to practical issues of children's learning and problems in learning school tasks.

Relatively little attention has been given to the psychoneurological abnormalities of human learning (i.e., compared to how extensively general principles of learning or abnormal behavior have been studied). Until recently, when estimates of such problems reached as high as 25 percent, abnormalities in psychoneurological capacities for coping with learning seemed too minimal to attract the thinking of many investigators.[23]

The failure to perceive the causal role of learning disabilities in the early signs of delinquency within the school can be attributed to a limited viewpoint. For example, the early appearance of

---

[21] E. Fleishman, "On the Relation Between Abilities, Learning, and Human Performance," *American Psychologist*, 27:11 (1972) 1017-32.

[22] G. Theologus, T. Romashko, and E. Fleishman, *Development of a Taxonomy of Human Performance: A feasibility study of ability dimensions for classifying human tasks*, (Washington, D.C.: American Institutes for Research, 1970).

[23] N. Kephart, A presentation at Flood Junior High School, Englewood, Colorado, 1966; and

J. McCarthy, A presentation at Loretto Heights College, Denver, Colorado, September 25, 1970.

delinquency in school was correctly observed in the failure and resistance to schoolroom learning. However, these early investigators were either sociologically or psychodynamically oriented, and their observations focused upon status, attitude, and psychosocial variables. At that time it was widely assumed that in the relationship between school performance and attitude, psychosocial factors were causal and academic retardation was a consequence rather than a cause. This misleading assumption led to the misperception of evidence concerning learning disabilites and delinquency; the latter was seen as a precursor of learning problems, not as a result. Another example is Elliott's findings that delinquent behavior occurs more in children while they are in school than out of school.[24] Ignoring the factors of learning disabilities, he concluded that attitudes relative to social status were the cause.

Another factor in the failure to perceive a relationship between learning disabilities and delinquency was that indicators, measures and concepts were relatively unavailable. It was not until 1961 that 14 and 6 spikes in EEG tracings were found in 50-80 percent of behaviorally disturbed children.[25] Although the significance of these phenomena is not yet clearly understood, the findings would suggest some irregularity of brain functioning. Anderson, without specifying the nature or significance, reported 50 percent abnormal tracings in 700 women prisoners, equivocal findings in 11.5 percent more.[26] Tarnopol cites studies which find 70 percent of delinquents with abnormal EEG readings. He also states that some neurologists can identify learning disabilities in 85 percent of the cases from EEG readings.[27]

The standardized psychological tests, widely available for half a century, have been of questionable value in identifying learning disabilities. They permit only norm-referenced or achievement-

---

[24] D. Elliot, "Delinquency, School Attendance and Dropout," *Social Problems*, XIII (1966), 307-14.

[25] J. Hughes; D. Gianturco; and W. Stein, "Electro-Clinical Correlations in the Positive Spike Phenomenon," *Electroencephalography and Clinical Neurophysiology*, XIII (1961), 599-605.

[26] C. Anderson, op. cit.

[27] L. Tarnopol, *Learning Disabilities: Introduction to Educational and Medical Management,* (Springfield, Illinois: Charles C. Thomas, 1969).

level analysis.[28] The examiner can only state how the child compares with others in his peer category. Consequently, no amount of test scores—normal or subnormal—comprise a complete evaluation. Such tests have been inadequate for remediation because they only measure deficiencies, or merely what the child has not achieved or could not perform.[29] In addition, one critic of the tests noted that ". . .neither the required test administration nor the required data analysis are channel-and-system-specific." That is, the results did not yield information about sensory-motor patterns and learning processes.[30] Normative scores at best only confirm what the teacher usually knew, but they do not tell how to teach.

By contrast, early in the trend of searching for the essential problematic nature of delinquents, researchers had the methods and concepts of intelligence, which were more accessible then than the measures and concepts of learning disabilities are now. Reinforced by continually finding correlations, although limited and unproductive, researchers have been reluctant to abandon that particular field for one less developed. Similarly, psychological examiners have been reluctant to shift from the standardized tests, despite their limitations, to more appropriate, informal examinations. Thus, work with learning disabilities has been, and still is, misguided by inappropriate concepts and methods. Progress has been hampered by the lack of terms, tools and information.

Reading and Delinquency

One serious oversight accounting for the delay in associating

---

[28] B. Bateman, "Three Approaches to Diagnosis and Educational Planning for Children With Learning Disabilities," *Academic Therapy*, II (1966-7), 215-22.

[29] F. Jacobson, "Improving Perceptual Motor Integration on the Bender," Paper presented at the convention of the Rocky Mountain Psychological Association, Denver, Colorado, 1972;

R. Venezky, as cited in *Current Trends in Educational Linguistics*, ed. by B. Spolsky (The Hague: Mouton Company, in press) and

D. Weikart, "Early Childhood Special Education for Intellectually Subnormal and/or Culturally Different Children." A presentation at the National Leadership Institute in Early Childhood Development, Washington, D.C., 1971.

[30] H. Mark, "Psychodiagnostics in Patients with Suspected Minimal Brain Dysfunction," in *Minimal Brain Dysfunction in Children*, ed. by H. Haring Washington, D.C.: U.S. Department of Health, Education, and Welfare, 1969).

learning disabilities with delinquency is the failure to fully appreciate the significance of reading retardation in delinquents.[31, 32] The vital role of successful reading to school success is widely recognized, and the documented presence of large percentages of retarded readers (as high as 94 percent prevalence has been reported) among delinquent populations have been clear and available for a long time.[33] However, it has not been clear how much retarded reading was a result of and not a cause of delinquency (i.e., reading being neglected consequent to academic estrangement or interfered with by a delinquent career).

Another oversight was the failure to perceive that certain well-known behaviors of delinquents suggested the presence of learning disabilities. Such behaviors as concreteness, lack of abstract ability, hyperactivity, and a general psychoneurological immaturity have been regarded as frequent symptoms of the delinquent personality. Only recently have behaviors been reputed as indicators of a basic learning disability.

Summary of History

In summarizing the oversight of learning disabilities as a factor in delinquency, generally, two broad trends—sociological and psychological—have divided the field of delinquency and therein created gaps in understanding. Theories have directed and hence limited inquiry to specific concerns. While historical trends

---

[31] P. Blanchard, "Reading Failure," *Mental Hygiene*, XII (1928), 722-88;

E. McCready, "Defects in the Zone of Language," *American Journal of Psychiatry*, VI (1926-7), 267-77;

M. Monroe, *Children Who Cannot Read*, (Chicago: University of Chicago Press, 1932);

A. Gates, "Failure in Reading and Social Maladjustment," *Journal of National Education Association*, XXV (1936), 205-6;

K. Hermann, *Reading Disability* (Copenhagen: Munksgaard, 1959); and

T. Ingram, "The Association of Speech Retardation and Educational Difficulties," *Proceedings of the Royal Social Medicine*, LVI (1963), 199-203.

[32] E. Critchley, "Reading Retardation, Dyslexia and Delinquency," *British Journal of Psychiatry*, CXIV (1968), 1537-1547.

[33] D. Dzik, op. cit.;

L. Tarnopol, "Delinquency in Minimal Brain Dysfunction," *Journal of Learning Disabilities*, III (1970), 200-7;

A. Berman, op. cit.

do have their contributions, eclecticism is perhaps a measure of the maturity of a field. A broad, balanced and integrated view is needed to encompass delinquent behaviors and to ascertain relevant methods of treatment.

The purpose of reviewing this history has been to provide the scientist, the professional, and the concerned layman, with the lessons of history so as to avoid repetition of errors. On the basis of that history, the following can be anticipated:

1) There will be continuing difficulties with definitions and terms used for learning disabilities. The variety of terms will require astuteness on the part of researchers and program implementors to the important difference subsumed under each term and whether or not the related data is appropriate to the term "learning disability."

2) Preliminary work on measurements is probably indicated by the lack of well-developed and appropriate assessment procedures.

3) Certain widespread attitudes may undermine the support for research and programs for the learning disabled delinquent. The negative reactions (societal) against delinquents will probably not provide much interest toward an understanding approach to the situation. Therefore, it will be difficult to establish the much-needed screening and remedial programs in educational, judicial, and correctional agencies. It will be difficult to change the attitudes of society and many of these professionals who regard much school failure as normal and acceptable; this will allow the schools to avoid finding effective methods of coping with either learning disabilities or delinquency. An overview of current professional journals suggests that two theoretical trends still continue and may create conflicts among professionals involved in this area. As a result, those attempting research and programs for learning disabled children or delinquents, with the focus proposed in this chapter, may not receive support from most colleagues.

4) Sociologists, in general, will probably continue their examination of the social system for its contribution to delinquency. Psychotherapists will persist in trying to treat delinquency out of existence. Established testing methods will continue and the shift from normative tests to clinical and educational process assess-

ments—which may be vital to remediation of learning disabilities—will be resisted.

THEORETICAL FRAMEWORK

The lack of a theoretical treatment of the relationship between learning disabilities and delinquency has been one significant factor delaying its awareness. Thus, explanation of this relationship becomes the main task of this chapter. This logically begins with the educational system.

School and Society

Briefly, the purpose of the educational system is to prepare the young for adult roles within society. Toward this end, forces in the school shape a child's experiences so that they closely parallel his experience as an adult in society. Mead demonstrated this relationship in three primitive societies.[34] However, the relationship is also easily observed in complex contemporary societies such as ours. While there may be much irrelevant academic content, the classroom social processes, such as "psyching-out" the teacher to achieve the few available "good" grades and performing routine tasks under an authoritarian structure, are similar to adult occupational roles. Since the school structure closely parallels society, the social forces for delinquent adaptation, which have been identified in general societal terms, function in the school system as well. These forces spring from the competitive success structure, an achievement emphasis, and the increasing disparity between goals and means.

Frustration and Delinquency

In school the child finds himself in a limited success structure at the kindergarten level and as he progresses through the grades, success becomes more difficult to attain (i.e., the disparity between goals and means increases). For example, those students who achieve the highest academic success in elementary school

---

[34] M. Mead, op. cit.

must, upon entering junior high, begin anew to compete for position with children from other elementary schools who were similarly outstanding. This process is repeated at the high school, college, and graduate school levels. The success structure is partially revealed by one index: e.g., the "B" average, which is generally the turning point of school success. For example, in 1969, five Denver area school districts reported that the percent of "B" averages or better for high school graduating classes ranged from 18-26 percent. Being above average, "B" or "A" grades are commonly regarded as good. We may assume, then, that approximately 80 percent of the children in these areas did not receive "good" grades; that is, they were not successful. This situation threatens a child's emotional adjustment. To be happy and adjusted, according to Rotter, one must be able to perform what others value.[35] To the student, grade-point-average is valued much as salary is valued by the adult in the occupational world.

Not only is the child's happiness and adjustment threatened by his inability to obtain good grades, but also the educational system reacts to his inability with pressures toward delinquency. In 1939 Dollard put forth the formulation now generally accepted by psychologists, that "frustration leads to aggression."[36] Kvaraceus' application of Dollard's theory showed that frustration in school leads to aggression in school. He further deduced that the causes of delinquency would be found in situations that frustrate and that the school was a primary source of frustration.[37] A child's frustration due to unsuccessful performance (grades) may be deflected in various symptomatic or aggressive ways. The child's aggression focuses upon the teacher because the teacher plays a central role in the child's school experience.

An unpublished report by the writer provides some insights into teachers' high expectations, negative perceptions, and sensitive vigilance toward their students. To begin with, teachers tend

[35] J. Rotter, *Social Learning and Clinical Psychology* (Englewood Cliffs, New Jersey: Prentice Hall, 1954).

[36] J. Dollard; L. Doob; N. Miller; O. Mowrer; and R. Sears, *Frustration and Aggression* (New Haven, Connecticut: Yale University Press, 1939).

[37] W. Kvaraceus, "Forecasting Delinquency," *Exceptional Child*, XXVII (1961), 429-35.

to see most children as underachieving. Junior high school teachers, rating a population of 232 students, regarded one-third as
"underachieving somewhat" and another one-third as "definitely
underachieving." The teachers' acute awareness of each child's
performance was revealed by another rating task. Each teacher
estimated the year-end grade-point-average of his 150 (approximately) children. These estimates and the children's actual grade-
point-average were extremely highly related (correlation coefficient
of .918). Of further interest was the finding that compared with
the actual grade-point-average, the estimated grade-point-average
was more highly correlated, and with more measures of attitude
and school performance. Analysis showed that the teachers' high
estimates were associated with student attitudes of maturity, future
time orientation, and self-direction. Where estimates were lower
than actual grades, teachers were responding to the general student under-performance, delinquent and other anti-social attitudes.[38]

The type of interaction and labeling that occurs in the school
is essentially the same type of process as that which defines the
delinquent. Cloward and Ohlin observed that ". . .it is custom-
ary for authorities to distinguish between the behavior of the delinquent and his attitude in relation to the system of social rules
which he has violated" and "the anticipated official response to
deviant action."[39] Like law enforcement personnel, teachers make
crucial, discriminatory decisions about children on the basis of the
child's behavior and attitudes.

The Learning Disabled Child in School

If he has a learning disability, the child becomes a more likely candidate for the negative labeling which can begin a delinquent career. He is obviously more disadvantaged than the normal child in school and the disparity between his goals and means
of achieving them is greater. Consequently, the child experiences

---

[38] F. Jacobson, *The Adjustment of Junior High School Students* (Englewood, Colorado: Englewood Public Schools, 1967).

[39] R. Cloward and L. Ohlin, *Delinquency and Opportunity* (Glencoe, Illinois: The Free Press, 1960).

more frustration. In addition, the teacher is more frustrated by this type of child than the normal child. Without special training, teachers tend to regard learning disabled children as some kind of attitudinal problem—baffling, unmotivated, emotional, and sometimes retarded. They are more clearly aware of performance and attitude than the underlying causes (i.e., the dysfunctions of learning disabilities). The visible discrepancy between the learning disabled child's potential and his academic performance is likely to be greater than the normal child's. Tests frequently show normal intelligence and the appearance of the child is generally normal (not retarded). Consequently, the teacher tends to see the child as an underachiever with an attitudinal problem. In the relationship between the teacher and child, a learning disability will increase the probability of mutual threats, frustrations and aggressions, and the teaching of basic lessons in delinquent orientation. The probability of such behaviors increases as the child's condition continues unrecognized.

Theoretical Statement

Learning and adjustment to the school is the most important task for children. It is a stress-loaded task. Learning disabilities greatly increase the probability of the child's failure and frustration and therefore bring the child into conflict with the teacher in a way that generates delinquency. Other factors may further or cancel out delinquency (e.g., parental attitudes toward the child and school, school assessment of the child's performance, and other individual factors of teacher and child). Also, learning disabilities are not absolutely essential to a delinquency adaptation in or out of school. Familiar, cultural and individual factors may be casual. However, the position the author has postulated is that most frequently delinquency begins in an antagonistic interaction between teacher and student and that the greatest catalyst of that antagonism is learning disabilities.

It has not been established whether learning disabilities in general, or various types of learning disabilities in particular, are cognitive, motivational, or some combination of both. However, this writer's position is that in any learning or behavioral control situation, the learning disabled child has a cognitive, not a motivational problem. For the child to cope with his problem in such a situation, information must be organized and/or processed in a different way, so that its presentation is comprehensible by the child.

RESEARCH AND PROGRAM DEVELOPMENT

The implications for research and program design logically converge upon prevention. Wallin observed in 1924 that it is easier to prevent delinquents than to reform them.[40] The avoidance of human suffering and monetary expense also recommends prevention. The school's preventive responsibility has been repeatedly cited. The rationale is that the school is more easily manipulated than other forces contributing to delinquency and it is more capable of implementing programs.[41] Since the school is where delinquency most frequently begins, it is the logical place for preventive action.[42]

The most sweeping preventive actions would consist of reducing the school's mass production of failure and frustration in children. As Glasser suggests, this could be achieved by a redesign of schools which avoids failure, but that is a social and a political problem.[43] As shown earlier, schools tend to be what the social system needs. For example, the persistence of practices like letter grades may be attributed to powerful social support. Failure and frustration could be reduced by developing teacher understanding of the nature of learning disabilities and the performance limitations of the learning disabled child. (This subject will be discussed in a later section on training.)

---

[40] J. Wallin, *Education of Handicapped Children* (Boston: Houghton-Mifflin Company, 1924).

[41] S. Glueck, and E. Glueck, *One Thousand Juvenile Delinquents* (Cambridge: Harvard University Press, 1934);

W. Kvaraceus "Delinquency, a By-product of the Schools?" *School and Society*, LIX (1944), 350-1.

[42] M. Harrington, "The Problem of the Defective Delinquent," *Mental Hygiene*, XIX (1935), 429-38;

F. Jacobson; and C. Ekanger, *The Model School Project* (Englewood, Colorado: Englewood Public Schools, 1968);

D. Elliot, op. cit.

[43] W. Glasser, *Schools Without Failure* (New York: Harper and Row, 1969).

Another preventive strategy involves early detection of the learning-disabled child. This strategy would require the use of early screening techniques and procedures. Delinquency proneness scales have resulted from investigations into the early signs of delinquency. They have not, however, shown a high degree of predictive validity. However, they have not been used in conjunction with the numerous instruments which are available for the prediction of learning disabilities. If used together, delinquency proneness scales and scales of predicted learning disabilities might prove to have a high degree of forecasting accuracy.

Both treatment and prevention should be based upon an understanding of psychological and social factors. In addition, the psycho-physiology of the person and his learning (especially basic skills learning) have been neglected and need to be involved.[44]

Recently there has been some shift of attention from visual to auditory factors in learning disabilities.[45] Berman's 1972 study is a specific instance in the field of delinquency and learning disabilities, where auditory problems have been highly related to delinquency.[46] Demonstrations of the effectiveness of remedial education with delinquents is inadequate and there has been little application of an approach to the prevention of early or late stages of delinquent development.

The speculation that delinquency is related to dyslexia or reading retardation dates back as far as 1926.[47] Monroe's formulation in 1932 was that dyslexics drift into truancy and then to delinquency.[48] Although this particular sequence has been criticized, there is ample evidence to thoroughly establish the relation-

---

[44] H. Quay and D. Peterson, "Personality Factors in the Study of Delinquency," *Exceptional Child*, XXVI (1960) 472-6.

[45] R. Carpenter, and D. Willis, "Case Study of an Auditory Dyslexic," *Journal of Learning Disabilities*, III (1972), 121-9;
D. Dzik, op. cit., accords vision a critical role in learning to read, however, his own data does not support his contention.

[46] A. Berman, op. cit.

[47] E. McCready, op. cit.

[48] M. Monroe, op. cit.

ship between reading retardation and delinquency.[49] Reading, as a medium for intervening with delinquency, has provided some of the most focused and successful approaches in prevention and remediation. Roman describes a comparison of three experimental group methods of remediation with delinquent boys. He studied a remedial reading group, a therapy (only) group, and a tutorial-therapy group. All three groups showed improvement in reading, intellectual functioning, and social adjustment. However, the tutorial-therapy group was generally productive of the most significant improvement and the therapy-only group of the least improvement.[50] The results of these approaches have not yet, however, been generally applied in program efforts to correct or prevent delinquency.

There is much work in early education which would suggest preventive applications to high risk groups. For example, Irwin found that ten minutes of reading per day to infants, beginning at thirteen months, produced generally advanced linguistic ability by twenty months.[51] Similarly, programmed instructional materials and hardware, as well as some television (e.g., "Sesame Street" and "The Electric Company") might effectively be used with high risk or early-diagnosed learning disability groups. The use of such

---

[49] E. Critchley, op. cit., investigated Monroe's study and reported that it ". . . did not reveal the manner whereby a dyslexic child may drift into delinquency." He did not find any greater truancy among retarted readers. The study is seen to be suffering from a number of methodological errors: retrospective historical procedures, questionable comparability of groups, and questionable concepts and measures of dyslexia. A source of controversial results is the likelihood that dyslexics were also underreported. Of greater importance, it should be noted that Critchley tested the proposition that the three phenomena were linked in sequence: reading retardation leads to truancy and then to delinquency. Truancy will vary according to the teaching of the school, as cited in B. Potter and F. Jacobson in *Reducing Delinquency by Systematic Control of Contingencies* (in press). A factor which Critchley did not consider in the connection between truancy, reading retardation and delinquency is, that there is no necessity to posit the intervening link of truancy between reading retardation and delinquency: ample evidence has shown that there is a definite relationship between reading retardation and delinquency.

[50] M. Roman, *Reaching Delinquents Through Reading* (Springfield, Illinois: Charles C. Thomas, 1957).

[51] O. Irwin, "Infant Speech, Effect of Systematic Reading of Stories," Journal of Speech and Hearing, III (1960), 187-90.

techniques is particularly indicated with the bilingual/bicultural children who live in rural areas where delivery of quality educational programs is rarely practicable.

There are many methods of remediating learning disabilities which might be applied to the prevention of delinquency. One is worthy of mention for reasons of previous inadequate reporting, plus its ease and efficiency of use and its wide applicability. It consists of verbal regulation of behavior for improved performance and learning. This method has been developed by Luria, in working with brain-damaged and normal subjects. However, it has found limited applications for perceptual motor tasks.[52] This procedure is applicable to performance improvement on the Bender-Gestalt test and to the remediation of basic skill learning difficulties in learning disability cases.[53] It would appear to be particularly indicated for many learning disability cases where conceptual ability is intact, but where difficulties exist in perceptual or motor areas.

Another problem for research is the difficulty in determining the role of two factors in the causation and correction of learning-disabled children. Two approaches are involved, neither of which clearly differentiates the cause and process factors. One approach —mainly educational—is that cognitive factors are basically causal and are the primary interventional target. The other approach— therapeutic—assumes motivational factors as primary. The field of learning disabilities is divided in relating to these approaches. In one point of view it is unnecessary to distinguish between the two; for example, the Colorado Department of Education's special education program uses the term "Educationally Handicapped" to include both types: motivational and cognitive.[54] They consider these factors so often interwoven that both are included in remedi-

---

[52] A. Luria, *The Role of Speech in the Regulation of Normal and Abnormal Behavior* (New York: Liverright, 1961);

H. Palkes; M. Stewart; and B. Kabana, "Porteus Maze Performance of Hyperactive Boys After Training in Self-Directed Verbal Commands," *Child Development*, XXXIX (1968), 817-26.

[53] F. Jacobson, 1972, op. cit.

[54] J. Ogden, *Special Education for Handicapped Children* (Denver, Colorado: Colorado Department of Education, 1970).

ation programs. However, Kephart believes that it is necessary at some point of intervention to determine whether one is facing a deficit of response capacity—"cannot"—or a motivational—"will not"—problem.[55] Behavioral approaches largely ignore the issue; they perhaps do not perceive the need to isolate motivational from cognitive variables. In general, special education approaches attend mainly to cognitive factors. However, both approaches can relate to the two factors. In behavioral or other therapeutic methods, while the manipulation of continuencies and reinforcement are related to the influence of motivation, attention, and memory, other aspects of cognition may also be affected. Special education approaches, on the other hand, acknowledge that expectancy, self-fulfilling prophecies, transferences, and other interpersonal variables affecting motivation may also affect remediation.

While the two approaches view the phenomena of learning disabilities differently, the remediation of learning disabilities can be explained from either point of view. A well-known illustration of the ambiguity is the hyperkinetic child, who commonly learns adequately in a one-to-one setting, but performs poorly in the classroom.

Some investigators do not concern themselves with the issues of uncontrolled factors; others intentionally use multivariable approaches and thereby avoid the issue of which type of problem is being treated or which factors are effective (i.e., both therapeutic and remedial educational methods have been employed simultaneously).[56] In any event, experience with the various approaches is equivocal. Until there is evidence for the degree of effectiveness of the various approaches, and factors which are affected in various case types, experience with remediation will not be clear. At this time it is impossible to conclude what the specific effects of each variable are. Therefore, remedial efforts undoubtedly include elements of ineffectiveness and inefficiency. Such elements could probably be eliminated by research.

To research the causal connection between learning disabilities and delinquency, the various types of learning disabilities found

---

[55] N. Kephart, op. cit.

[56] R. Rice, "Educo-therapy: A New Approach to Delinquent Behavior," *Journal of Learning Disabilities*, II (1970), 16-23.

in delinquent populations should be identified. Representative and matched samples of these types should be treated using cognitive, behavioral, and psychotherapeutic approaches and controls. After the first period of experimentation, in which the effectiveness of each single approach has been established for each type of learning disability, combined approaches can then be implemented and evaluated.

It is important to assess the interaction between student and teacher. However, this may indicate some modification of the classroom and school success system, as well as some alteration of the teacher's perceptions and his/her reaction to the learning disabled child. A definitive study could begin with the assumption that the delinquency-producing interaction described in this chapter is true. It would be obvious, then, that the usual consequence of delinquency could be avoided by remediating the learning-disabled child. It could be avoided also, by training and orienting the teacher to avoid the frustrations and aggressions commonly developed in the learning-disabled child. A related demonstration effort is indicated in the field of corrections. Correctional programs need to take account of the fact that there are learning disabilities which have caused delinquency. Evaluating and remediating the learning disabilities is the most efficient and effective way to "rehabilitate" most delinquents. Ordinarily, the educational programs of correctional agencies are simply more of the same type of experiences which initially overwhelmed the learning-disabled child. An analysis of probable learning disabilities could easily be added to the evaluation and testing centers of existing correctional institutions.

The Need for Professional Training

The exhortation to orient professionals to the nature of the problem occurs so regularly in chapters such as this that it becomes quite banal. However, the theoretical framework developed earlier makes it absolutely essential in the case of learning disabilities to urge orientation and training of educational personnel—particularly the teacher, who is the other member of the dyadic relationship in which the learning-disabled child is turned into a delinquent. It is logical to choose the teacher, rather than the child, as the most promising focus for change by instruction in this problem: the teacher is a professional and an adult. (There may also be some profit in orienting the involved parents and children.)

Significant value exists in developing the teacher's ability to recognize learning disabilities. Such recognition would largely avoid the poor image (and self-image) of the student, mutual frustration of student and teacher, and the initiation of delinquent orientations. However, teacher training will need to provide more substance than mere instruction in the use of diagnostic-remedial cookbooks. While these provide the teacher with a few more alternatives for the learning disabled child, they do not enable the teacher to match remedial methods with specific learning disabilities, basic skill deficits, or process and channel specifics.[57]

The need for training applies to administrators and specialists in the schools. Clinically-trained psychologists are ordinarily limited in their capacities of identification of learning disabilities, and any expertise in specifying remediation is ordinarily acquired in an informal or capricious way. It is unfortunate that psychologists who ordinarily are well educated in the psychology of perception, cognition, and learning, lack the critical knowledge of how to apply their education to learning-disabled children.

The Need for Attitudinal Change

Change is necessary, but the lack of current knowledge by court, law enforcement, and correction agencies, and others in the field of delinquency, is serious. A profound change is indicated for the way in which delinquents are viewed and treated. As of now, justice and correctional personnel tend to further the process begun in the schools. What appears needed is a general training program for those currently in the professional fields which see learning-disabled delinquents and for inputs about learning disabilities to be added to formal education programs.

---

[57] A. Bannatyne, "Matching Remedial Methods to Specific Deficits," Paper presented at the International Convocation on Children and Young Adults with Learning Disabilities, 1967;

H. Mark, "Psychodiagnostics in Patients with Suspected Minimal Brain Dysfunctions," in *Minimal Brain Dysfunction in Children*, ed. by H. Haring (Washington, D.C.: U.S. Department of Health, Education, and Welfare, 1969).

As a result of prevailing public attitudes, there has been little support for research, training, and programs based upon the premise that, to control delinquency, it must be understood. The current public viewpoint is that delinquency requires mainly control —not understanding. Generally, such controls have been whatever authority and force the school and law enforcement agencies bring upon the child. Such an approach can only aggravate the delinquent's reaction of frustration and aggression.

Characteristics of Teachers

It is unrealistic to expect broad, general appeals to teachers to achieve understanding. Teachers are very much a part of the system which produces delinquency. Teachers generally learn to tune out the "exhortation of the year" as a matter of their adaptation to the system. Therefore, a more specific system change and teacher education change is indicated. At present, the school system rewards the teacher for moving the greatest number of children through the most achievement levels. It does not reward the teacher for the questionable achievement of moving a learning-disabled child from under-achievement to average achievement. Teachers generally have an authoritarian character, which has been described by numerous investigators.[58] The author has made the following observations about the type of person who becomes a teacher: while a student, they liked their teachers, identified with them and wanted to be like them; they tended to be good at classwork, dutiful and obedient; they did not tend to question or criticize the school system; they tended not to ever get in trouble. In short, they have no personal experience for understanding an underperforming or resistive student. Generally, there are significant differences between teacher attitudes toward school and the attitudes of learning-disabled students, especially if these students are delinquency-oriented.

Perhaps the simplest, most effective thing the school could do for the delinquency-oriented, learning-disabled pupil would be to

---

[58] R. Allen, "Toward an Exceptional Offenders Court," *Mental Retardation,* IV (1966), 3-7;

O. Harvey; D. Hunt; and H. Schroder, *Conceptual Systems and Personality Organization* (New York: Wiley Publishing Company, 1961).

recruit teachers who were formerly learning disabled and/or delinquent. The same suggested staffing practice applies to justice, law enforcement and correction agencies. However, such a decision is likely to occur only under pressure from advocates for the learning-disabled child, such as A.C.L.D. (Association for Children with Learning Disabilities) and A.C.L.U. (American Civil Libeties Union). Institutions act in ways benefiting their own survival and are therefore unlikely to staff themselves, by choice, with those who have been their adversaries. Therefore, before the learning disabled and/or delinquent child receives a fair hearing in court or in school, he will need a powerful outside advocate.

SUMMARY

Only recently have learning disabilities and juvenile delinquency been strongly linked, despite historical evidence of a close relationship. The critical importance of learning disabilities has been eclipsed by greater attention to social, intrapsychic, and intellectual factors. The evidence is now clearer: learning disabilities of various types appear to occur with a high degree of frequency in delinquents. The explanation of the relationship is as follows: schools, like society, are success ladders, with few successes possible and pressure upon all to succeed. Children who have learning disabilities are more handicapped in such an extrusive, competitive system than are non-learning disabled children. Those children with learning disabilities become frustrated by school and interact with it in delinquent behaviors. The teacher, frustrated in return by the child, adds pressures by his/her reaction, which further catalyzes a delinquent orientation.

The implications are clear for research. Practical methods to reduce delinquency necessarily involve orientation of school and related personnel, as well as law enforcement and correctional agencies. The particular problems and consequences for children with learning disabilities need informed treatment. Learning disabilities need to be prevented or diagnosed and remediated early to avoid such effects. In addition, there is a need to alter the environment and to modify the failure-producing structure of the school, which adversely affects not only the learning-disabled child, but also nearly all other children.

11

THE BRAIN-INJURED ADULT: AN OVERLOOKED PROBLEM

Camilla M. Anderson, M.D.
Sidney, Montana

INTRODUCTION

Developmental Brain Damage, a more accurate title than the more commonly used term, Minimal Brain Damage, or MBD, has been increasingly well-recognized since the 1940s, when Alfred Strauss and Laura Lehtinen published their *Psychopathology and Education of the Brain Injured Child.* However, despite the fact that this is a very common handicap in childhood, and despite the fact that it is neither a self-limiting nor lethal malady, there is little or nothing to be found in the literature about MBD symptomatology in adults. It is as though an impassable chasm separates children with MBD from adults with problems, and few clinicians seem to be aware of the obvious continuity between them.

In adults, as among children, there is no rigid or characteristic pattern which is invariably present. There are perhaps even more variations in the symptoms and signs displayed by adults with MBD than there are in children because adults have had a lifetime to develop compensatory or collateral patterns to help them cope with their problems in living. It is not only the wide spectrum of possible symptoms which may occur that has deflected the attention of the behavioral experts from easy recognition of the nature of the basic handicap, but it has been the psychodynamic overlay which commonly exists. It is almost inevitable that the human environment of children with MBD would provide pressures and stresses which occasion the development of the overlay.

Some of the most common situations tending to generate interpersonal tensions are early and prolonged colic, a variety of digestive disturbances, sleep disturbances, hyperkinesis, difficulty in "reaching" the child, failure in communication, overall immaturity, poor coordination, poor comprehension, poor empathic capacity, poor appraisal capacity, and perhaps of major importance, failure to provide parents with significant reciprocal gratification.

It is not strange that clinicians should be aware only of the psychodynamic overlay in their adult patients and should accept them exclusively at that level. Because of the general acceptance of the concept of privacy in the therapeutic relationship, the clinician rarely calls in, for the purpose of clarification, the members of the patient's family, his neighbors, or his school record, but relies instead on the statements and actions of the patient in the sessions to develop a comprehensible picture of the patient's life history. One cannot help wondering, if this type of privacy or secrecy should be discarded, would psychotherapy, as it has traditionally been practiced, not also be largely abandoned. Commonly, a single session with a more normal or healthy family member can bring more light and clarification to the situation than can many times the amount of time spent with the patient alone.

A continuing complication, when one is trying to assess why clinicians have been so tardy in their recognition and research in the area of MBD in adults, is that these patients are highly unreliable in their statements. It is not that they deliberately falsify; they suffer from the same human tendency that all flesh is heir to, namely the need to preserve our pride system intact as best we can. The problem is, rather, that they are endowed with such poor appraisal capacity that they have failed to really perceive what has occurred in their lives. Additionally, they have always had difficulty recognizing what is more and what is less important, so that t is entirely likely that whatever they say will be highly distorted. Then, there is also the probability that they never did have access o pertinent information concerning their developmental experiences and patterns, so they could hardly be expected to provide basic information. Whether it be from lack of information, the need to project blame, problems with appraisal, with priorities, or with integration, whatever they say ought to be suspect. Naturally, the appraisal needs to be done objectively and without moralistic judgment.

There *is* an area of clinical recognition of deviant behavioral symptomatology produced by brain damage, namely documented insult to brain tissue after birth, often later in life, resulting from infection, trauma or toxemia. Kurt Goldstein's *After Effects of Brain Injuries in War* is such a classic presentation which sharply delineates and focuses on the common details of this disability. This is also the same area on which psychology has focused in establishing its criteria for determining the presence or absence of brain damage through psychological testing.

Whereas clinicians in both psychology and psychiatry need to be adept in recognizing and dealing with this extensive area of handicap, the fact remains that a far more important and more prevalent area of disability arises much earlier in life. Because the damage occurs before birth, during the birth process or very early in life, neither Goldstein's conceptual framework nor the standard psychological test criteria suffice to give reliable early diagnostic leadership in this field.

It has been my privilege to have worked closely with several competently trained psychologists during the period of approximately thirty years since I first became involved with trying to understand the nature of the disability. No doubt I was particularly fortunate in my training situation in that I lived with a developmentally damaged child and worked primarily with adult patients, so that the entire life span picture began to emerge. After discovering that the conclusions regarding brain damage reached as a result of psychological testing did not agree with the clinical facts, I began to inquire more specifically into the testing construct, and I learned, for example, that the tests are set up primarily to determine *loss*. Inasmuch as in the developmental damage disabilities there has never been a time before the loss, it seems clear that the tests are only partially applicable. Likewise, there are several segments of test data which have been regarded as essentially pathognomonic of brain damage; when these are not found to be abnormal the assumption has been that brain damage does not exist.

As a result of these many years of scrutiny of clinical and test data, it is my conclusion that new criteria need to be established by psychology for this newly recognized area of disability. This is largely because of the weight which psychology has in this whole field. In fact, in the schools it is not generally considered necessary to require anything more than a psychological report to make a determination and a decision. Psychologists can and do send to schools and to other referring sources, reports with diagnostic implications which not only are not insightful but may deprive the person tested of the benefit of the treatment required to ameliorate the symptoms, e.g., use of certain indicated drugs. At the same time the reports prescribe counseling, which is often not very effective and one of the most costly of all treatment modalities for school problems resulting from developmental brain damage.

It is my belief that psychological test reports, therefore, ought to contain not only the conclusions of the psychologists, but the data which lead to these conclusions. In order to be maximally helpful, summaries of the raw data in the subtest scores might be regarded as essential material in the reports, just as psychiatric evaluations should include not only diagnoses or conclusions but also the bases for these conclusions. Everyone has a right to his conclusions, but others also have the same right to question or challenge those conclusions. Besides, it removes the report from the realm of the sacrosanct and stimulates the learning process.

Among adults as among children, MBD is expressed throughout the total personality—physically, intellectually and emotionally. In any afflicted person, however, the symptomatology may appear preponderantly, though seldom exclusively, in one sphere. Some are primarily emotional cripples, while others show more marked intellectual handicap or physical malfunctioning.

The Lowest Socio-Economic Level

There is no social, economic or vocational level that is without its problem people, often by reason of MBD. However, the farther down the socio-economic scale one looks, the higher is the percentage of people with this handicap. Let us explore first how it affects the lowest socio-economic level. No systematic study has been carried out to determine the prevalence or incidence of this disability in any non-institutionalized segment of our population, but we do know that the lower the stratum, the greater is its contribution to agency statistics among both children and adults. One survey carried out many years ago indicated that 95 percent of the multiple agency statistics were contributed by five percent of the population. On the basis of routine studies by knowledgeable people, it is increasingly apparent that MBD plays a significant role in our chronic sociologic problems which account for multiple agency statistics.

Frequently there is school failure and dropping out. Poor language arts proficiency may be a factor, especially since the old phonetic system of teaching reading has been bypassed by so many schools. With our emphasis on academic achievement and the factual necessity to be competent in reading, it is not strange that the ghetto or the various poverty pockets of our nation should become "Cities of Refuge." Many students with MBD finish high school, because staying in school is the law of the land, but this does not mean that they can read or do simple arithmetic, or understand money values, or have any practical knowledge of the world in which we live. But having MBD does not necessarily constitute a handicap when it comes to normal appearance, to singing, dancing, partying, boosting (shoplifting), hustling (engaging in prostitution), or even in being a pimp, which is regarded as one of the most lucrative occupations open to males in the ghetto. It is also well known that the illicit drug problem is greater there than elsewhere, which should be a reasonable expectation when one considers that MBD implies a paucity of understanding of cause and effect relationships.

Aside from academic and reading failure, MBD individuals possess many other characteristics which qualify them for a pov-

erty level of existence. Lack of planning and organizational ability not only shuts them out from all but the most menial type of
jobs, but it is reflected in their poor money management, their
family and home mismanagement (to the point of chaos), and
their poor food habits and resulting health implications, which,
in turn, lead to a predisposition to MBD in their children. They
have difficulty in following directions other than those given one
at a time, and their ability to cooperate in such important areas
as pre-natal care is compromised. Impulsivity, or an inability to
stop and weigh and assess the total picture, but responding, instead, to partial or inconsequential details, is the rule. This not
only creates continuing chaos but it frequently leads to encounters
with the law. This is a major contributing factor in crimes of
violence, and ghettos have been primary sources of such crimes.
A good deal of the causality of crimes of violence is attributable to impulsivity, and only a small amount due to premedita-
tion. Over a twenty to thirty year period such felons have been
involved in one or more murders and five to twenty assaults with
deadly weapons. The lack of capacity for imaginative solutions
implies that they are helpless to figure their way out of dilemmas
or even out of unfamiliar situations. This comes up again and
again in their management of children in that they can operate
only as they have been specifically and repetitively taught. An
emergency or an opportunity may stare them in the face, but they
neither recognize it for what it is nor have any ideas as to what
may be required of them in the situation. Some mothers have let
their children die of starvation because they did not recognize
the evidence confronting them, or they respond to illness in the
most inadequate fashion. Their children are frequently poorly fed,
to the point of malnutrition, regardless of income, and one finds
pica almost routinely among them.

When one looks at the ghetto population, it is noteworthy
how many of the commonly recognized symptoms and signs of
MBD can be detected: perseveration or stuckness in a variety of
ruts of action, thought or feeling; inability to assign appropriate
values, not only such as right and wrong, but such as assessing
what is more or less important, and consequently there is a problem with priorities; inability to appraise or determine what is

wrong or how to bring about a correction; inability to exert leadership although they may be extremely verbal and bossy; a lack of capacity for in-depth relationships, but rather in a variety of attachments; and gravitating to situations where they are constantly surrounded by people in the guise of friends who may be essentially strangers. These people are not typically loners, and they do not carry out the schizoid phantasy lives which are the product of psychodynamic rather than of organic factors. There is often a lack of parental control over children, and this in turn predisposes to rebelliousness against authority and even to perseverative preoccupation with "police brutality." It is entirely understandable that when children have grown up with no authority figure and consequently no one to interfere with them, they would likely interpret the hand of the law which interrupted their freedom to do as they pleased as being brutal.

Marriages among MBD people in the ghetto are often unstable, the arrangements are commonly extra-legal, and there is no protection which might be afforded were the unions within the law. One probation officer, who himself had come out of the ghetto, suggested that this type of family instability really made little or no difference, that the important thing was the presence of a male in the home, whether or not he was transient and would be replaced in a few days or a few months by another male. Such a statement staggers the imagination of one who believes that children can prosper and develop some meaningful stability in the form of solid, workable values only when they have the opportunity for continuity in time with significant models.

It is my belief that the most important factor for developing psychological health comes from strong family relationships maintained in continuity. This is the logical ground for development of values which give a sense of identity and of direction. Here one is helped to learn the meaning of caring, of cooperation, of sharing and giving up and giving in, as well as of compromise and postponement. When partners can be endlessly exchanged there is little or no possibility for growth and maturation in the parents, and if the parents don't mature they are certainly poor models for their offspring.

The inability to make out or stick to a budget (admittedly

a difficult problem for those living in poverty), with its implications for disorganized food intake as well as for general household chaos, may be a factor in the production of their innumerable physical complaints and disabilities, although surely only one of many. General irresponsibility, as evidenced by the high costs of doing business in the ghetto, and the failure to abide by the rudiments of honesty and reliability according to the standards of those on the outside, all bespeak value systems that are not attuned to organized societal living. The orientations are narcissistic and egocentric, as is the common manner among people with MBD.

It is generally recognized that slums produce misfits and attract misfits, but one must also be aware that misfits produce slums. In fact, what else could one logically expect them to produce? Slum clearance programs do not change people. If the people have produced slums in their former settings, they will produce them again. They do not know how to behave out of character. Failure to understand this continues to be the occasion for expenditure of endless tax monies without perceptible benefit except for the well-paid administrators of programs.

Crime is also a product of the poverty end of the scale. It begins among the school dropouts. It is one way of gaining status among one's peers, or sometimes even in one's own family, where it is commonly less important where one gets the money, or how, than that one bring home evidences of one's productivity. Drugs enter the picture very early—even children are no strangers to it —and then comes crime, not for status but out of the necessity to support their habit.

Though it is difficult to present accurate figures, it appears that a sizeable proportion of adult offenders are recidivists (repeaters); that their delinquent and criminal careers began long before their admission to adult prisons and jails; that they were formerly wards of the juvenile courts either in or out of juvenile institutions; that their school records evidenced failure in some essential areas; and that there was often inadequate parenting as well as family reliance on welfare. Many of these offenders with MBD were born into welfare of welfare parents who also had MBD, or at least they had the salient characteristics of MBD.

In fact, many have been on welfare for several generations. It is not just that this is a family habit, but with the increasing complexity of society and of job requirements, and the ever rising of the minimum wage level, it has become more and more improbable that people grossly handicapped by MBD would be able to be self-sustaining except in non-socially-acceptable ways. While Congress votes higher and higher minimum wages, they ought not at the same time complain that welfare rolls continue to climb. Welfare rolls likewise are swollen as a result of the nationwide efforts on the part of mental hospitals to empty the hospitals and place patients in the communities, and on the part of courts and prisons to shorten institutional terms through increased use of probation, parole, and keeping offenders in the community.

One of the more obvious places where MBD may be discerned is in the area of the battered child syndrome. Perhaps one of the reasons it is more rare among blacks than whites is that demands on children and consequently need for discipline is sometimes less among blacks. Most of us would agree that in no situation is ingenuity, patience, perceptivity and flexibility more necessary than in child rearing, and these are qualities notably lacking among parents having MBD. Even for normally endowed parents it often seems as though children are made for the express purpose of making parents feel helpless. Add to this the general immaturity which is associated with MBD, the egocentricity, the narcissism, and all of this intensified by our present day emphasis on entitlement to immediate gratification, to fun, to pleasure, and to doing what one likes to do, as inalienable rights, with little or no recognition of or regard for postponement of gratification as necessary ingredients of living and of maturing, and we have gathered together all the necessary elements that would logically lead a young parent with MBD to physically mistreat her baby. It is no wonder that if a parent has been found to batter her child on one occasion, it is more than likely that it will happen again.

There is a higher incidence of abnormal brain wave tracings (EEG's) among delinquent boys than any other known group; however, no routine tracings have ever been made on any sizeable population. In a prison for women, among 700 selected inmates tested in this manner, 349 or 50 percent were found to have definitely abnormal EEG's and an additional 11.5 percent showed possible abnormality. Whereas some inmates with mental retardation had abnormal tracings, this was not an invariable finding. The same was true of inmates who showed marked deterioration from use of alcohol. There seemed to be no reliable correlation between the extent of nervous system deterioration and the interpretation given of their EEG tracings. This clearly indicates that the EEG is not an infallible guide to brain condition or functioning. It certainly is no better than the skill or perceptivity of the expert who interprets the tracing, and even if his skill be outstanding, it is probable that the limits of accuracy or sensitivity inherent in or determined by the mechanism of the EEG machine leave much to be desired.

People tend to come out of prison essentially the same as they went in. Some have learned a few new routines and habits and skills that may be carried away into their lives outside the prison gates, but more are likely to have learned new ways to get rich quick, or how to make desirable impressions on their peers. The very fact of the high incidence of MBD among them precludes the effective use of psychotherapy as a means of bringing about change or correction in them, because their concreteness, their difficulty in moving from the general to the specific, their difficulty in integrating or adding up or putting two and two together, their impulsivity, their perseveration, their lack of empatic capacities (as well as of guilt), and their being highly skillful con artists, make both the intellectual and the emotional aspects of psychotherapy largely futile with them.

It has long been recognized that the psychopathic person does not think or feel or learn as other people do, and in days gone by he was given a label, C.P.I., or Constitutional Psychopathic Inferiority, a label now dropped by psychiatry, but which gave recognition to the belief that the trouble was constitutional, biologic, or inherent, and not the product of interpersonal forces. No doubt the pendulum of opinion will continue to swing and once again there will be a return to a more widespread acceptance of a biologic or organic factor in a sizeable proportion of people exhibiting chronically delinquent behavior.

Mention needs to be made of the problem created by MBD for the courts and for the experts who testify concerning the mental health or illness of persons accused of crimes. Whereas legal and medical concepts differ as to what constitutes mental illness or insanity, it is often difficult to say positively that some particular person is or is not psychotic. Certainly juries have a hard time associating a psychotic label with most people afflicted with MBD who come before the court. Many psychiatrists do, however, see them as suffering from "process schizophrenia," as evidenced by their poor human relations, their disturbed or inappropriate emotional reactions, their unusual perceptions and associations, and the chronicity of their disturbance.

Only when an evaluation of these individuals is superficial and non-perceptive could the assessment be that they are normal mentally. But not being normal mentally does not necessarily imply the presence of either a psychotic state or of mental deficiency or retardation. Whereas the MBD individuals almost certainly would be aware of the attitudes of the larger society and therefore technically would "know right from wrong"—which has long been the legal criterion for sanity vs. insanity—this knowledge might not be incorporated into their own value systems or moral judgments, and they would therefore operate without the moral and emotional deterrents implicit in a true personal incorporation of the moral judgment. Obviously, the experts who testify, as well as the judges and the juries who make the decisions, need to be familiar with this level of aberration in human behavior.

The stress proneness which is characteristic of brain damage, whether acquired early or late, may be seen in temper tantrums in children; general impatience and irritability; impulsive use of a variety of escapes, such as running away or actual physical escape; suicidal gestures or attempts; use of drugs, including alcohol; or development of a variety of physical or psychotic symptoms. It is well known that mentally deficient people frequently develop psychotic behavior characterized by sudden, often explosive onset, non-systematized delusions and hallucinations, and then a gradual return to their norm as the felt stresses are alleviated. There is a similarity in the responses by those with MBD, although at a more orderly and, one might say, more sophisticated level of internal and external functioning. Each person has his or her own private and individual interpretation of what constitutes stress, and those with MBD are no exception.

The descriptive literature on schizophrenia is replete with statements that sound very much like descriptions of individuals with known MBD, and it is my distinct impression that MBD provides excellent soil for the development of schizophrenia, if indeed they are not in many instances one and the same, as I have suggested in my comments regarding expert psychiatric testimony in court.

It should be noted that stress, by and large, may be regarded as whatever causes one to feel helpless, as well as whatever is felt to be threatening to one's pride system. Another way of saying this is that stress is whatever is felt to be threatening to one's physical or one's psychological self-image. When one considers their deficiency in coping mechanisms, their deficit in appraisal capacity, or in their capacity for reasoning and for imaginative solutions, their difficulty in assigning appropriate priorities, and their tendency to be stuck in non functional ruts, it is no wonder that people with MBD are stress-prone, or that when they decompensate or deviate from their usual way of functioning, their symptomatology is an exaggeration of their usual inappropriate patterns interwoven with devices calculated to keep their pride systems intact.

In the physical health area there tends also to be a greater than average amount of disability. Digestive disturbances are almost routine. These begin in infancy and are expressed in colic, difficulty in finding satisfactory formulae, and gas and stool disturbances, often associated with what seems to be reflex upper respiratory tract disturbances, such as ease of developing sniffles or actual colds and fever. Frequently the digestive disturbances persist throughout life. One can hardly help wondering if they do not constitute the army of people always taking some kind of laxative. Allergies tend to be common.

The basic physical equipment may be adequate or sometimes seemingly flawless, but in the low socio-economic level, people with MBD exhibit overall poor management of bodily needs for proper food, for rest, for regular habits of elimination, and for regular activity, often creating problems where none existed initially. Their persisting difficulty in properly appraising bodily states often leads to overanxiety, to over-attention, to over-demand for medical attention or even to excessive demand for surgical intervention. This failure in appraisal capacity also leads to unfortunate disregard and neglect of all kinds of problems in their early stages. It is not easy for most of us to imagine that there are people who do not know when they are chilly, or too warm, or tired, or hungry, or even if they are ill, or how they feel ill, or how bad it hurts, but such people actually exist. It is not strange that they constitute an ongoing problem for medicine. They do not know when to ask for medical help and they cannot give helpful medical histories. If the specific questions are not asked by the doctor it is highly unlikely that making mention of this or that relevant occurrence would enter their minds, for they do not tie things together appropriately or see relationships clearly. Their understanding of bodily functioning is pitifully meager.

Along with these problems there is commonly difficulty in following medical instructions, or their behavior after medical consultation is inappropriate, given the physical disability, because the doctor failed to perceive their global limitations and their inability to use what might be termed common sense. He therefore failed to give the detailed and specific instructions required, either in writing or to some responsible person. It is hard to imagine how handicapped these people can be in the area of use of common sense. If they have not learned how to deal with a problem through habit formation or through structuring it into its elemental steps, it is folly to expect them to come up with logical behavior or answers. Their deficits are often quite surprising because they tend to give the appearance of normalcy. If they only had some recognizable stigmata or blinking lights, our own behavior toward them might be more realistic. These situations also illustrate the fact that whatever symptoms they have, they are usually more troublesome to others than they are to the patient. The patient sees the problem as coming from someone aside from himself.

When one contemplates the morbid effects of people with such vast handicaps on children in their care, or even in their environment, it is easy to see how it would be possible for "the sins of the parents to be visited on the children even unto the third and fourth generations." I suspect it will be a long time before the nationwide drive to keep people out of institutions and to lower the census of these institutions by placing patients in the communities at the earliest possible moment, will have run its course; and, in the meantime, nobody is measuring the lasting cost to families and to communities as a result of their presence.

It is common for pseudo-experts in behavioral science to emphasize the importance of "being wanted," as a criterion for sanction for procreation of children or for keeping them, once born. Such a test is almost wholly without merit, in my estimation, for people who are totally devoid of competence for the job of parenting still "want" their offspring, and commonly delight in the physical softness, the helplessness and the littleness of their children. It is hard to resist the pull of baby kittens, puppies, or, in fact, any baby animal. Becoming pregnant and bringing forth babies may be their one area of competence or achievement. It is not unlike the emphasis males commonly place on their virility—their ability to achieve and maintain an erection, to arouse their partner, and their ability to achieve orgasm. It is quite common to hear men say that they are "no good" merely because they are impotent, and impotence is even used as a reason for contemplating suicide. If we could transfer this emphasis on mere physical evidences of sexual or biologic adequacy to a healthy concern about responsible parenting, some of the major problems of mankind might well begin to be solved.

The Middle Socio-Economic Level

Whereas MBD is more visible at the lower socio-economic levels, it is by no means a stranger as one goes up the ladder. I know of no occupations or professions that are devoid of these problem people. No one has studied the vast reservoir of disabled people constituting the blue collar or even the white collar field. It can be postulated, with a reasonable degree of certainty, that because people with MBD are part of the work force they have less crippling deficits than those in the lower rungs. Probably even more important, one could assume that they have been brought up in homes where they were fortunate enough to have had good and persistent early training in useful habits at the hands of parents who cared for them, had patience with them, and who transmitted their socially acceptable attitudes to them. As a result, they moved easily and naturally into well-structured and routinized work roles; they married and functioned with reasonable adequacy in their narrow circles; and they relied on their union or their religious leaders to guide them morally and politically, so that they became contributing members of their communities. They gave minimal trouble to anyone.

Fortunate outcomes such as this probably depend on such factors as the physical presence of both parents in the home, minimal interpersonal conflict, and therefore general agreement between the parents regarding a host of subjects, including child rearing, goals and values; continuity in care by a single mothering person rather than by a succession of baby sitters without authority; and absence of feelings of frustration by reason of felt deprivation of various conceived rights. Such qualities provide a sense of stability and dependability in the home and the greatest possibility of transfer of these same traits to the next generation. It is my belief that the magnitude of the problem with MBD at all levels today is due less to an increase in the incidence of the disability than to the social upheaval which engulfs us: mass communication; the rapidity of change; the changing role of women; the emphasis on "rights;" the devaluation of the Establishment, as well as of constituted authority, including "God;" the downgrading of traditional values relating to the family, to work, to reliance on self, to sexual continence and other areas of postponement of gratification. Increasing freedom and lack of clear structure constitute a stress for people with MBD.

Where the forces that propel toward adjustment are less strong, the presence of children who are "different" in a variety of ways is a real problem in average middle class homes as well as in the school system and in the community. Occasionally the child with MBD is unusually bright in some particular area, in which case the family may interpret his peculiarities in behavior as deriving from his propensities for genius level functioning. More commonly these different children occasion excessive fatigue in the mother, dissension between the parents and recriminations regarding patterns of child rearing. Relatives, as well as neighbors, complicate matters by blaming the whole uncomfortable situation on the poor disciplinary control in the household.

Not infrequently family doctors have compounded the trouble by attributing the disturbing behavior to such factors as, "It was an unwanted pregnancy," or "The parents just cannot get together on anything," or "The mother is one of those overprotective women," or they quote the expert consultant to whom they have referred the case, saying that there is no evidence of organic factors and the entire picture represents interpersonal stresses which will require some form of psychotherapy. Attitudes such as these, although possibly in part true, nevertheless are not helpful and add their weight to the already heavy burden of the parents, creating more guilt and more helpless rage in them.

When parents can be helped to be realistic, fitting their expectations to the facts of the situation rather than being resentful, either because of the extra time and effort required of them or because of the absence of reciprocal gratification which the child has failed to provide them, there will be fewer problems and less of the crippling psychodynamic overlay developing through childhood and into adulthood. Trusting and comfortable relations with people in childhood predispose to comparable expectations as the child becomes an adult.

The rather typical indiscriminate moving toward people, which has been described among children with MBD as "they never meet a stranger," tends to be a plus factor in their favor. They are not standoffish or reticent and they tend to welcome human contacts even despite their tendency to project all blame and to see themselves as the victims of discrimination or as being picked on. However, despite the initial movement toward people, the relationship matures minimally and fails to grow beyond the initial contact. Sometimes they may talk endlessly about themselves and their doings but fail to be aware of the other person except as a receptacle. They remain strangers because they do not pick up the ordinary cues in human interaction; they never truly perceive the other person, and the observations made or the conclusions drawn about people are commonly so far from the mark that perceptive total strangers might well have done better.

Rarely is sex a comfortable experience for the spouse of the MBD person. Even in marriage, sexual relations may be almost totally absent. Old patterns such as masturbation, peeping, fetishism or homosexuality prevail or are preferred. None of these forms of expression require perceptivity or capacity for enduring relationships. Even relations with prostitutes require no commitment or perceptivity. When sex relations with the spouse do occur they are devoid of mutuality or sensitivity to the partner. The more normal or healthy partner frequently experiences an overall sense of futility, of being used, of isolation, contempt and depression, while the MBD-handicapped spouse may sail merrily on, well liked by many who know him only superficially, and unable to fathom the "peculiarities" of the self-pitying spouse. Indeed, the MBD spouse often succeeds in making the more normal spouse feel like the bad one.

In addition to problems produced by lack of meaningful human relations, there tends to be a work pattern which is below that which many indicators would lead one to expect. They often have many adequacies or competences or even outstanding gifts, but rarely do they achieve the status or the advancement which might seem logical or appropriate. Many factors enter into this. They do not see where they are failing or in error; human relations, which are necessarily more important the higher the level of functioning, are sterile, awkward or inappropriate; and their grasp of the total situation leaves much to be desired. Well-meaning people, including professionals whom they may have consulted for assistance in a variety of areas, sometimes help them move upward on the job-socio-economic ladder, only to find that they have done them a disservice in so doing, because they cannot make the required shifts or they cannot function as independently as required.

It is not unlike the disservice brought to talented black students who have been shifted from their familiar schools into the elite white upper class schools, where the whole setting is so unfamiliar and the stresses are so great that failure becomes inevitable. The need for familiar incoming stimuli is universal; however, when organizing capacity is deficient there is even greater need for maintaining the familiar surroundings.

Advancement in many jobs implies increasingly independent

action and decision making; it implies capacity for perceptivity of human cues; for leadership rather than for merely bossing; the ability to listen with understanding; and it implies minimal rigidity and perseveration or stuckness and a maximum of adaptability. Although, up to a point, essentially automatic promotion does not constitute any serious problem, knowledgeable appraisal of individuals fairly high in civil service does occasionally confront one with almost certain evidence that MBD is in the picture and the person is beyond his depth, for nothing short of this would bring about such dependency, such generous use of cliches, such nonperceptivity, such inappropriate remarks or conclusions, and such chaos in the departmental staff.

Sometimes by dint of luck, excessive effort, phenomenal memory, special abilities in some particular area, or politics, the person completes studies leading to some occupation or profession which is best filled by someone without MBD handicap. If it is possible to lean on or depend on someone else in the situation, things may not be too difficult, but to the extent that the person really is on his own, disorganization, both internal and external, may be the chief products. One psychologist who did a great deal of vocational counseling said to me that the most reliable indicator of how one should expect a person to function is his performance on the Grassi Block Design Test, and this test is, in my belief, one of the most sensitive tests for picking up the level of functional disability in persons with MBD.

Some people are relieved to know something about the nature of their handicap. Others strongly resist the idea that they have any basic defect. Frequently they show a desire for a factual appraisal but are totally unable to comprehend the implications or to use the information as a help subsequently. In a prison for women there often seemed to be an eagerness to have awareness of such a diagnosis in order to have a perpetual alibi. The ones who really need to know the facts of the disability are the parents, if they are intelligent and capable of understanding.

Often it is difficult to catch on to the possibility that MBD is present. There is smoothness of talk, a demeanor which exudes confidence and adequacy, and comments are well laced with nice-sounding cliches or erudite phrases. One may attribute the difficulty in comprehending what the person has said to one's own obtuseness or unfamiliarity with the subject. Only after one has had the opportunity to sit down and read leisurely and carefully what the person has written on some subject does it become clear that the production is merely high-sounding words and phrases, strung along together, and that it is literally incapable of being understood; the logic cannot be followed and the procession of words and ideas leads nowhere. The lack of comprehensibility in direct verbal contacts may be satisfactorily covered over by a perpetual facade or armor of levity, puns, jokes—anything for a laugh. Again, routine devices for bringing a situation under control may be employed. It may be a repetitive rush into sex, listening to records, watching movies, going to museums, driving cars or bikes, relating familiar events or stories, or escaping into golf or television, or whatever repetitious activity provides freedom from stress.

Chronic anxiety tension states and perseverative worry about first one thing and then another are common. Headache, often migraine in type, is a disability that is incapacitating to many people with MBD. Emotional tensions tend to be reflected in the body and are the occasion for the development of an urge on the part of many general practitioners to forsake general medicine and go into training for a psychiatric practice. They recognize the tremendous role of psychological forces, yet they feel handicapped by a lack of expert understanding of the dynamics of the problems or of how to go about being helpful. They are acutely aware that any type of adequate service to these patients who constitute the bulk of their practice is far too time-consuming; a very few patients of this type would seem to constitute an entire practice, and this is economically nonfeasible. As a substitute for time spent with the patient, they have turned to prescribing many of the psychotropic drugs, but they are not satisfied with the results. Then they begin to avoid the patients as far as possible, guilt and frustration take over, and finally they start playing with the idea of transferring to psychiatry where, they are convinced, they will acquire the answers they now lack, and will return to medicine as better doctors.

What is not clearly realized is that psychiatry doesn't have the answers either. Relatively few of the vast numbers of these patients, many of whom are handicapped by MBD, are suitable candidates for analytic psychotherapy, and trying to understand their dynamics or effect their cure with words or with insight would do little good. It is not so much insight these patients need as a type of security derived from an accepting relationship with someone who stands *in loco parentis*. Most often they do best with doctors who appear quite sure of themselves and proceed as if they know exactly what they are doing. They need unhurried, untroubled authority figures. If the doctor cannot afford the time, or the patient cannot afford to pay for private help, there are clinics available in most states, but whether treatment is privately funded or paid for with tax monies it should be clearly understood by the therapist that the goal is rarely insight, with the commonly associated time and cost factors involved, but rather a supportive relationship together with small clarifications and far more directive counseling than is usually regarded as acceptable. To function in this manner, the doctor needs to know a great deal about the current family patterns, as well as values and goals.

Many MBD patients need to be helped to proceed a day at a time, or at least one crisis at a time. Expecting more of the patient than he can deliver is too hard on both the patient and the doctor. Impatience, irritability or avoidance on the part of the doctor, which are the signs of his felt helplessness, derive from unrealistic expectations and serve to intensify the problem. The burden of caring for these patients needs to be borne easily but continuously, for they seldom get over their need for supportive parenting. Their more handicapped peers have, in the past, been comparably helped by the custodial care provided by institutions, when they were geared to be truly asylums rather than our modern mental hospitals, where it is more important to keep the daily census count going down than it is to recognize the basic need of the patients for ongoing supportive care in their vast dependence.

A time ought to come soon, when results achieved as a consequence of investment of endless funds, time, and effort, need to be weighed against the total cost. We ought not to go on indefinitely assuming that because we spend more and more time and money the results are better and better. The real problem may well be the difficulty in getting the younger generation of professional helpers to look factually at the situation, with the long-term rather than the short-term perspective. Having such a perspective would tell us, it seems to me, that efforts should be directed primarily at prevention rather than at treatment, correction or rehabilitation.

The Upper Socio-Economic Level

Whereas the incidence of MBD is much lower as we approach the upper socio-economic level population, there still is no dearth of cases of all degrees of severity among both children and adults. When it occurs in this group, the evidence of their being misfits is more obvious. Not only is there likely to be greater disparity between the handicapped one and the other family members, with consequent intensification of interpersonal stresses, but such deficit as is present is likely to be the cause of greater handicap than a comparable deficit would cause in middle class families. This is probably because there is commonly greater awareness by family members and greater efforts at protection or overprotection. Since financial necessity is not in the picture there is not the pressure on the handicapped one to participate and thus to learn and to be trained, and the handicap is thus intensified or "frozen" rather than circumvented. By reason of the handicap the vocational choices that are within the realm of possible achievement are fewer, and those that are possible tend to be out of step with family tradition and patterns. It thus becomes very difficult to find their comfortable niche in life.

* * * *

Peter was the youngest son in a family of six. Whereas high competence in school and in the world of business and politics was taken for granted in his family, Peter did poorly in school. He had marked dyslexia, to the point where teachers could not understand what he was trying to say, even well into his third year in school, and he was always unhappy because he felt discriminated against, seemingly in every situation, for he assumed he should have all the status, all the privileges and all the benefits he saw coming to other family members.

Not until he moved completely away from home to a far-distant state did there begin to be partial resolution of his problem. There, where he was not visibly in competition with his siblings, he got a simple, repetitive, mechanical job, and with no one to provide implicit or explict disparagement he kept the same job for years. He was completely unable to handle liquor, but with the help of his wife, the church, his job supervisor, and a couple of short stays in a psychiatric hospital, he managed to retain his job until he reached retirement age.

His two children escaped as soon as possible from the stultifying, overprotective prison-like home life he provided them. Although a five-minute conversation with him would leave one baffled, confused and bewildered, he maintained a patronizing attitude of superiority and the right to dominate those in his orbit. It was only when he would return occasionally for visits to the home of his youth that his ability to maintain apparent equilibrium and stability became seriously threatened.

* * * *

Frank was a clergyman who delighted in his ecclesiastical image and he always signed himself "The Reverend Frank Jones." Clearly, there were others who found his sermons difficult to follow, as evidenced by the fact that his second two-year contract was not renewed. He also liked the pastoral counseling role, even if it left him little free time, and at mealtime especially, he could almost always be sure of at least one call for counsel.

Being out of a job did pose certain problems, but his wife turned all her energies into being the breadwinner instead of dividing them between a job and being the traditional model minister's wife to the congregation. He finished writing his book and began sending it to a series of publishers who rejected it, apparently finding it as turgid as did non-professional readers of his opus. He finally gave up finding a job as a clergyman and eventually he established himself as a fairly successful manager of a men's rooming house. He earned more money than he formerly did and he dropped with seeming ease his old custom of saying grace before meals. His wife continued working but complained bitterly about the lack of sleep and rest which were always her lot by reason of his incessant sexual demands on her. He saw no possibility of modifying this pattern.

* * * *

Kendall was the younger of two sons from a well-to-do family. When the father died the older son took over the management of the family department store. Kendall went to college and eventually graduated. He not only graduated but he took graduate courses in forestry. Before long he had to give up working for the Forest Service, partly because of a "weak knee" and partly because he was convinced there was something less than honest going on with government lands and lumber, and by reason of his preoccupation with this conviction he made himself persona non grata wherever he was stationed.

Then he went to another college and took additional postgraduate courses, this time in transportation. In the jobs where his function was routing and managing trucking operations he had continuing difficulties with personnel and with organizing, so that he also found himself without a job in this field. He had one psychotic episode, with delusions and hallucinations, from which he recovered gradually, and it was following this that a diagnosis of MBD was made. He was long past the usual age for marrying because his successes with women were not noteworthy. He seemed to have no difficulty getting first dates, but he rarely got past the initial encounter. He rushed into sex, or he could not seem to get straight in his mind whether the one to court was the girl or her parents; or he failed to understand what was going on. He was quite dependent and often would call his psychiatrist long distance for clarification of quite simple elementary situations. He finally began taking trips to Europe, and returned eventually with a bride. It seemed she attributed the difficulties they had in communication to language barriers. Only time helped her realize language was the smallest part of the difficulty. He finally gave up trying to work in any job situation, for he had been reduced to doing only the most menial kinds of work around the office or the plant. He purchased an acreage in a wooded setting and spent his time studying the stock market and managing his investments, where he did not have to cope with people.

* * * *

A letter which arrived in my mail this week essentially duplicates many I have in my files:

Dear Dr. Anderson: My husband and I have read your article on MBD in *Mental Hygiene* and we were very impressed. Actually, this is putting it mildly. To us it was so fantastic because for the first time in sixteen years (the length of time we've been going to psychiatrists with our daughter) has anyone come so close to describing her. Years of psychiatry have proved fruitless. Waste of time, money, energy.

Jeane was born twenty-nine years ago with the umbilical cord wrapped around her neck, blue from lack of oxygen. It was insignificant to me at the time, unaware as I was of what damage can occur. She was a beautiful, healthy-looking baby but she cried a lot, had temper tantrums, slept little. I thought she was a little spoiled by living with very doting grandparents while my husband, who was a dentist, was overseas during the war. My husband, who was interested in medicine and science, would mention the possibility of brain damage to the various psychiatrists we went to starting when Jeane was age thirteen. This was when her behavior was really becoming odd and she wasn't able to form friendships, or profit by mistakes, etc.—all the symptoms you describe in your article. My husband believes she showed her illness from the time he came home when she was two and a half; probably from birth.

We took so much abuse from psychiatrists whenever he mentioned brain damage, telling us that this is what we would like to hear to salve our own conscience, and we became bitter. We fought with each other, blaming one another, since one doctor said my husband was too strict, another said I was not enough of a mother, a third doctor said that I was too much of a mother. You can understand my bitterness. Today Jeane lives alone in a one-room apartment just on the fringe of society. She rejected us and her other relatives. She blames us for bringing her into a hostile world where she cannot cope. So far we can only see a dismal future for her. I cry inwardly because I want to help her and I can't. I failed to mention her diagnosis. Of course you would know. She was diagnosed as Schizophrenia. Another important question: Has any real progress been made in helping these poor unfortunate victims? You mention prevention before and during birth, but what now?

* * * *

It is quite possible that in the future the limitations of women having MBD will become as obvious as the limitations of men. Up to now it has been the men who were the achievers, the climbers, the competitors and the organizers. Women, in their narrower but probably even more basically important sphere of operation, have not shown up too clearly or often. They have been less in the public eye. We may suspect, however, that the home and family have provided them sanctuary, just as have ghetto living, custodial institutions, and the sparsely populated rural areas of our land. Increasingly, the squeeze will be on, for women as well as for men. The complexities of living multiply fantastically and everyone needs and will increasingly need a good supply of the qualities that permit rather than hamper adaptation to changing conditions. Indeed, the need is for people who can help think of new and yet untried ways of coping and of shaping the events and situations which confront mankind.

REFERENCE MATERIAL

Strauss, Alfred A. and Lehtinen, Laura E., *Psychopathology and Education of the Brain-Injured Child* (New York: Grune and Stratton, 1947).

Goldstein, Kurt, *Aftereffects of Brain Injuries in War* (New York: Grune and Stratton, 1942).

Anderson, C. M., *Jan, My Brain Damaged Daughter* (Portland, Oregon: Durham Press, 1963).

Anderson, C. M., *Society Pays* (New York: Walker and Company, 1972).

Anderson, C. M., and Plywate, H. B., *Management of the Brain Damaged Adolescent;* Amer. J. of Orthopsychiatry, Vol. 32, No. 3, pgs. 492-500.

Anderson, C. M., *Minimal Brain Damage*, Mental Hygiene, Vol. 56, No. 2, 1972.

Wender, Paul H., *Minimal Brain Dysfunction in Children* (New York: Wiley Interscience, 1971).

12

THE NEUROLOGICALLY IMPAIRED
YOUTH GOES TO COLLEGE

Gertrude M. Webb
Associate Professor, Curry College
and
Director, Curry College Learning Center,
Milton, Massachusetts

Through the 1960s, and continuing into the seventies, recognition of the potential of the learning disabled in our schools has become widespread in our country. Emphasis, rightly, has been on early identification and early educational intervention. Thousands of "high risk" children entering our kindergartens and first grades thus are being helped, minimizing the cumulative effect of academic failure. However, a whole generation of current teen-age students has not been so privileged. Neither recognition nor support has been afforded them through their school careers. In today's teen-age population, there are thousands of intellectually able young handicapped people who were not identified or remediated when they entered school as are today's entrants.

Research reports that 8 to 10 percent of our normal school population experience learning disabilities which handicap them in achieving their academic potential. Within that neurologically handicapped group, intellectual abilities range from low normal to average, to superior and very superior. Young people falling within the lower intellectual ability ranges should be counseled toward vocations earlier than those with greater academic potential. Specific skill training in vocational and work-study programs (e.g., carpentry, home economics) affords such learning-disabled students opportunities to develop into productive, useful, and needed members of their communities. Those in the higher and superior ranges of intellectual ability should be offered opportunities equal to those who are not handicapped—opportunities commensurate with their cognitive abilities. Cognitively challenging courses, such as philosophy and logic, provide opportunities to reason and to create at abstract levels which neurologically handicapped young people need if they are to develop to their potenital.

For a number of years, the primary task of Curry College, Milton, Mass., has been training teachers to work with learning-disabled children in elementary schools. In the spring of 1970, Curry College's Learning Center made an assessment of college opportunities for intellectually capable learning-disabled students. This survey showed very clearly that problems in reading, writing, spelling and in organization of ideas on paper have for years prevented intellectually superior neurologically handicapped young people from utilizing opportunities at the college level and becoming truly educated men and women. Very bright, creative young people routinely have been denied college opportunities because of their slowness in reading and their difficulties in presenting their ideas in written form. Few attempts have been made to assess their thinking capabilities, their potential contributions to the college community, to themselves and to society in general.

"I was constantly told to be a janitor, to work with my hands," says one current participant in the Curry College Program of Assistance in Learning (CCPAL).

"I've had my skills and abilities evaluated and a local counseling agency told me, 'Forget college—you have a good head—but you can't prove it on paper—you'll never make it in college.' " Even when such people have been admitted to college, no provision has been made to assist them in their learning.

Five years ago David was a very discouraged young man. He had entered a western university with high expectations. In his freshman year, he was given the option of dropping out or flunking. "I just couldn't keep up with the books," David said of those days. "People thought I was stupid. I was on the verge of accepting the label myself."

He left the university and returned to his home near Boston. A friend encouraged him to visit the state department of special education. There he was told that he was "perceptually handicapped." "That was news to me," David said. "In fact, I really didn't know what that meant." How little others understood the problem was soon evident. While the youth spent an hour each day in a state language clinic, he was given a job in the institution's library. Later, when that didn't work out, he was hired by a bank. "Neither job was suitable," David explained. "Both required reading, and I would get mixed up and mess things up."

After applying to a number of colleges, the young man was accepted by a local junior college. He thought he would have an opportunity there because the school took "special students." But David soon discovered that "special" did not mean a program geared to his needs but that "special" meant a semester's probation. "I was in regular classes and had no special help," David recalled somewhat bitterly. "The Profs didn't understand my problem. When I tried to tell them, they said, 'I've heard everything now; don't con me.' " Curry's assessment of college opportunities for learning-disabled students revealed discouragement of neurologically handicapped, intellectually able candidates, and lack of support in the few colleges that did admit such students.

Is there justification, in a technological society such as ours, that routinely uses tapes, recorders, computers, and typewriters to help us record our ideas, to deny able young people educational opportunities for enrichment? We at Curry College think not. Our Program of Assistance in Learning (PAL) is our response to these young people. At Curry we chose to pick up the challenge of able young handicapped people eager for learning and to assist them in helping themselves toward a successful college career and more rewarding self-actualization.

What are the characteristics of the young people involved in our program? How do they differ from the regular student body? Appearancewise they run the gamut from very small to very tall, and most of the boys enrolled lean to being slight in stature. Our population includes a football hero and a hockey star, but also several boys who need help in body coordination. The boys outnumber the girls in a five to one ratio. The students' faces on arrival express optimism and hope associated with their anticipated success through the PAL program. They are alert, animated, and intense—almost as if within each burned a flame searching for a path toward effective learning.

Orally, most communicate well, making their points effectively, although a few have expressive language problems and appear on first meeting to be very quiet. Overall they are curious, interested, intelligent and eager to participate in oral discussions. Many exhibit fine motor problems and difficulties in their visual and auditory integration systems.

As a result of these handicapping conditions, and although their oral performance is adequate, their written performance lacks any order. Sentences are fragmented; ideas are not sequenced; handwriting is illegible; spelling is bizarre. Punctuation and capitalization virtually are nonexistent or incorrect at best. As with the written word, most are several grade levels behind in their reading ability. Both speed and comprehension are generally depressed. These characteristics differentiate the PAL student from the general Curry student, but they make him no less a potentially able student—rather an able student with special needs.

Even as we generalize about the characteristics of the PAL population, we hasten to explain that no PAL student has all the handicapping conditions described. One may have physical prowess and need help in building auditory skills so that he can better take in his professors' remarks. His neighbor, however, may have fine motor coordination and visual memory difficulties, which cause him not to be able to write or to easily remember much of what he has read. Still a third may be in trouble getting her ideas in order so that the teacher can follow, while yet a fourth needs help getting his ideas expressed on paper.

Applicants to the PAL program are screened so as to insure the appropriateness of their candidacy and the probability of the program's meeting the students' needs. Examination of any previous neurological and medical evaluations and of high school records is also made. Many neurologically handicapped young people have academic histories of failure attributable to the inflexibility of the institutions they attended—to the lack of willingness or lack of ability of these schools to "harmonize" their messages with the powers of the child at the moment. At a personal inter view with the director of the program, explanations for low grades may be evaluated as the student views historically his academic strengths and difficulties.

Some of the perspectives of "their learning at school," as students told it at the Winter Meeting of the Massachusetts Association of Children with Learning Disabilities in 1972, are worthy of our attention.

"Our schools are set up only for the success stories. Anybody else can forget it!"

Maybe that's one reason why sixteen out of twenty men on "death row" are people who have learning disabilities.

Some boys who have learning problems told what it felt like to move from "stupid" to delinquent and back again.

Bill was the town bad boy. When a school was broken into it was Bill behind it. The homemade bomb was Bill's handiwork. "I couldn't read or write, but I learned how to talk and get around the teachers or I wouldn't have survived. The football field was the only place where I wasn't a flop for nine years, but I wasn't great, even there. The only way that I could look good to the other kids was to make a reputation for being the biggest nuisance."

To John, making the hockey team was the only thing that kept him in school in an affluent suburban town. His mother tried to tell the principal that he had dyslexia in the fifth grade. The principal said that teachers know best, that John was lazy.

When his guidance counselor called John in for the first time and asked what was wrong with his home life, John walked out on him. If he hadn't found a language tutor who was able to establish a trusting relationship, John would have run away from both home and school.

Mike refused to tell what school he went to because it had given him such a bad time. "I am 25 now. I was 21 before I found out that I had learning disabilities. School was just a mill grinding us up if we weren't at the head of the class. Every so-called expert told me a different thing. One said that I had a disease that was catching. Another told me that all I needed was to be kept back a few years. The people who do the most harm are the biggest experts: the guidance counselors."

Ask the kids who are the learning losers what they want to be most and they say: "I want to be a graduate!"

Bill went from tutor to American College in Switzerland before getting along well enough to get into Bowdoin.

John is still a sophomore at high school. Mike couldn't make it at a junior college but now he is getting the help he needs at Curry College's Learning Center, which preps students with learning problems for the college's four year liberal arts program. Mike is sensitive about admitting to 25 years of heartbreak, but if it will save other kids from similar fate, he is willing to shout it from the housetops: "It was neccessary for me to make something out of my life. If you don't make it in school, you don't make it."

Our most recent experiences with guidance people, unlike those reported earlier by the above students, have been very supportive of their candidates. Guidance people from local school systems, as well as from ones many hundred miles away, visit or call to endorse the candidacy of one of their students. They commend him as being able to think and to be a contributing member of their respective peer groups, even though they are learning disabled. Some counselors report that their high schools are beginning to make accomodations in their classrooms for students with recognized learning disabilities (e.g., oral exams). Others openly admit their failure to create special programs for cognitively able handicapped students.

Parents, like guidance counselors, have also come to speak in behalf of their able children. In truth, some have come with not so academically able children, hoping that the PAL program might in some miraculous way transform their children. It is a difficult task to counsel parents to accept their child of low intelligence as he is, to appreciate his non-academic abilities—to help him find the many wonderful places and settings in society that do not require college competencies. PAL is not an appropriate program for such students, and thus part of our screening process must be an initial individual assessment of college-level ability.

Academic success or failure seems to be rooted as deeply in concepts of the self as it is in measured mental ability, because feeling good about one's self allows one to act, to adjust, to do more than merely respond to a stimulus. It gives one the freedom to take the next step. Conversely, a poor self-image absorbs one's psychic energy and prevents one from moving into new areas of learning. We are reminded of the lines of Alexander Dumas:

> A person who doubts himself
> Is like a man
> Who would enlist in the ranks of his enemies
> And bear arms against himself.
> He makes his failure certain by himself
> Being the first person to be convinced of it.

Since we at Curry are trying to help the academically able who really want to learn, an assessment is made of the student's desire to go to college—to Curry in particular—to *work* toward success. We subscribe to the Psychology of Use that says in essence, "It's not what one has but rather how one uses it that counts."

Having satisfied ourselves that ability and readiness for college are present in the prospective candidate, we ask for writing samples from a visual stimulus and from an auditory stimulus. In the first case, a picture of a panoramic scene is given the student. He is asked to describe in two or three paragraphs what he sees in the picture or what he imagines might be going on there. In the second instance he is asked to write about some relevant issue, e.g., the lowering of the drinking age to eighteen. The writing samples are also windows to the applicant's syntactical and grammatical difficulties.

PAL's screening program aims to select students who can profit from the program's offerings and, accordingly, to exclude those whose strengths would better be used in a setting other than college.

After screening and upon acceptance into the program, a more detailed assessment of the strengths and weaknesses within the students' informational processing system and learning style is effected. A battery of diagnostic tests is given to isolate areas of special strengths and needs along the pathway of the development of the individual's integrative systems as depicted in the following two models of learning.

INFORMATIONAL PROCESSING SYSTEM—Model A

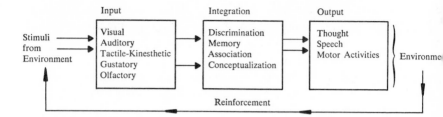

LONGITUDINAL INTELLECTUAL DEVELOPMENT—Model B

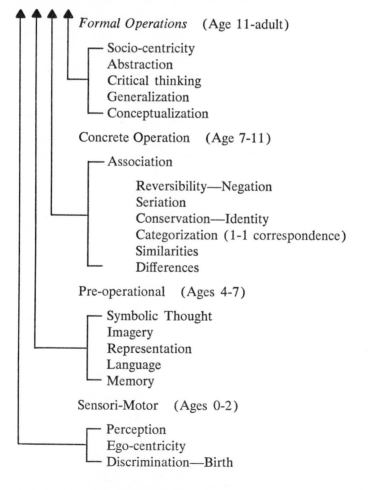

Formal Operations   (Age 11-adult)

— Socio-centricity
  Abstraction
  Critical thinking
  Generalization
— Conceptualization

Concrete Operation   (Age 7-11)

— Association

  Reversibility—Negation
  Seriation
  Conservation—Identity
  Categorization (1-1 correspondence)
  Similarities
— Differences

Pre-operational   (Ages 4-7)

— Symbolic Thought
  Imagery
  Representation
  Language
— Memory

Sensori-Motor   (Ages 0-2)

— Perception
  Ego-centricity
— Discrimination—Birth

Individual profiles include measures of intellectual development and of the deficit and strong areas within the auditory, visual, motor and "self" systems. A typical profile follows:

Tom's profile of strengths and weaknesses include: Verbal measure of intelligence—120, Performance measure—98, Full Scale—111. Tom's scores indicate verbally superior intellectual functioning and a 22 point discrepancy with the performance aspects of intelligence. Such a pattern no doubt has caused Tom academic problems in getting on paper and on examinations the ideas he can express verbally. Such a discrepancy between the verbal and performance areas is characteristic of some learning-disabled students.

Tom's high verbal score indicates good practical judgment, ability to associate and reason, and an understanding of expected behavior. His weak performance in the block design, digit symbols and digit span indicates problems in visual-motor areas and both visual and auditory memory areas. *Visual Survey Tests* revealed problems (with glasses) in near vision, particularly with the right eye. A recommendation for a medical-visual examination was made and pursued by Tom. Adjustments were made in his lens structure to afford Tom better control of his nearsightedness in relation to distance vision. Additional testing revealed other problems in visual-motor and visual-memory areas. *Auditory Discrimination Tests* revealed some difficulty in distinguishing differences in similar though unlike sounds. Language screening revealed problems in sentence structure, punctuation, capitalization, sequencing of ideas, and relating minor to major ideas.

Projective testing showed Tom to be very much in this world—realistically aware of himself and his problem in his world. Tom's problem areas are ones which no doubt have hampered his use of his full intellectual potential.

The completed individual diagnosis is interpreted to the PAL student—causes for his difficulties in reading, writing, and organization of thought are explored with the student. Often this is the first recognition of the "why" and "where" of his disabilities and, more important, his abilities. An honest presentation of his learning profile is critical to his understanding of his special needs and the program to be designed to meet them. We cannot overemphasize the need for forthrightness at this point. Many of these students react with comments such as: "No wonder I'm reading slowly if I'm misreading some small words in each sentence. I lose the meaning and have to reread. Can I be helped? What do I need to do? Why didn't someone tell me the truth before?"

An individual prescriptive program is written for each student in the PAL program. Tutorial support is given in his special areas of need twice a week for 1½ hour periods. Accordingly, some spend much time developing critical listening skills, while others pull main ideas out of taped material and organize in outline form. Still others, working from an outline, expand ideas into paragraphs. Full compositions and term papers, attending first to the sequencing of ideas and then to effectiveness of the presentation, are drafted and improved upon in these sessions.

All students work to improve sentence structure and grammatical and syntactical constructions. Emphasis is placed on language—speaking, listening, reading, writing—on getting the ideas translated to or from another person. The fine art of communication is the heart of the program.

The development of reading skills gets particular attention for all students in the PAL program. Students know whether they are visual or auditory learners and are helped to use their strengths accordingly. Machines, such as the shadowscope, are also used to help students speed their reading. Probably one of the most effective parts of their reading program is that all the students' textbooks are on tape at the PAL Resource Room. The student comes to the Center to "listen" to his books. He is requested in addition to read visually as he listens. Students report that listening to the correct information prevents them from reading the text incorrectly and having to go back to reread to get the meaning. Accordingly, they save much reading time as they more satisfactorily comprehend what they are reading. Former frustrations with the written page become a memory as the pleasures and the fruits of understanding the texts become theirs. Taping of the books is done by readers of the National Braille Press as well as by the Milton's Women's Club.

Particular students are invited to participate in a motor program where body control is developed through training on a trampoline. Problems in spatial orientation (e.g., north, south, east and west—necessary for success in a geology course) and difficulties in mathematical computation are dealt with in individually programmed instruction. Auxiliary counseling services are available to PAL students on the campus and are integrated with the Program.

The individually designed PAL program is above and in addition to the regular college curriculum. All PAL students are integrated into the college for their regular courses. They select core and elective courses just as any other of the 900+ students enrolled at the college. They carry a full academic load. They are in no way segregated from the regular population and they participate in all kinds of social, athletic and extracurricular activities.

Professors of all PAL students are alerted to their enrollment in the program and to their individual special needs. The cooperation between the general faculty and the PAL students cannot be too highly lauded. Typical accommodations made by the professors have been the acceptance of examinations on tape and/or the reading of examinations to the students. Curry faculty members take time to encourage PAL students to say what they think. Typical feedback from the professors describing the students is, "I'd rather have PAL students. They really mean business." Without the support of the faculty, the students, even though they are individually strengthening their skills, would encounter frustration in the general classroom. Happily, this is not the case at Curry, which is a small liberal arts school where professors care about their students and respect their individuality.

The faculty has long recognized the fact that language skills constitute the core problems for the learning disabled student. Accordingly, each time a PAL student has requested exemption from the foreign language requirement, the recommendation of the curriculum committee, supported by a Faculty vote, has been affirmative. PAL students have thus been exempted from the study of the language itself but have been required to study the life and culture of a foreign people. Such intelligent handling of the neurologically handicapped student gives him the needed opportunities for enrichment without putting him in a position of failure. Sponsors of the PAL program students feel very fortunate to be interacting at the college level with such a responsive and supportive faculty.*

As we complete the second year of the PAL program and plan for the year to come, we look at our population and its place in the college society for an evaluation of the worth of the program. Of the four students enrolled in the pilot program in the first year, two are currently on the dean's list, one in the highest honors range. The other two students are doing better than they have ever done academically, though one asked to have his texts continued on tape. All four are actively participating in college activities and one is co-captain of the hockey team. Another student has organized and directed a successful college Career Opportunities Exposition for the benefit of prospective Curry graduates. The success of this venture has strengthened the ego and the productivity of a young man who for many years was told to forget college.

This year the program is four times its original size and all the students are holding their own academically. Two students felt, at the completion of the first semester, ready to continue without support. One withdrew because of illness. All others are working very hard in cooperation with the PAL instructors and Curry faculty, and we anticipate continued academic success at the completion of one year. PAL is designed as a one-year supportive program, a year in which the goal is to develop within the enrollees the language-oriented, thinking-based skills which will allow them to function successfully on their own in the college setting. Our experience at this point is that if the students are adequately screened, one year's support should achieve the described goal. We strongly feel the record of academic achievement of the PAL enrollees proves without doubt the worthiness of their college candidacy.

Currently parents and teachers are asked, "How should we prepare our able learning disability children for a potential college career?" In response we can only suggest, that silly as it may

---

* It is our feeling that K-12 schools could adopt this or similar programs within a special education budget.

sound, the answer probably is at the beginning, at birth or prior to it. The research on fetal life currently being done holds the potential for answering many of the questions on the genetic, chemical and neurological issues that cause learning problems. A search of the literature (including the reading of this book) may well give prospective parents enlightened insights into these problems.

In the very first few weeks of life, the child's acceptance within his family helps to begin in him the development of a sense of being a "good me in a good world" or, negatively, a "bad me in a bad world."[1] This begins the development of the child's self, which from that point develops in direct proportion to the satisfaction of his basic needs: his sense of security, his sense of belonging, his feeling worthwhile, his developing independence. Assuming his basic needs are well met, the young child develops a strong self concept which in turn allows him to bring sufficient psychic energy to learning.[2] Should the opposite be true (his basic needs not being met and his self concept a negative image), his chances of ever getting to college are diminished even at this early stage of development.

In the pre-school years, the familial educational aspirations affect the developing child's desire for continuing enrichment and growth. Accordingly, the stimulation of the child—the opportunities to explore and to learn—and the balance of such freedom with some limits in this world, ready him for academic learning.

These precursors of academic success developed in the home demonstrate themselves in the child's: (1) perceptual motor development, (2) social-emotional development, and (3) cognitive development. School readiness implies having moved from thinking about oneself alone; it implies thinking; it implies thinking about others; it implies having adequate language to express one's thoughts; it implies having gross and fine motor skills to do school tasks.

As the child enters school, an assessment of his development

---

[1] Harry S. Sullivan, *Interpersonal Role of Psychiatry* (New York: W. W. Norton, 1953).

[2] Ernest Wilson, *The Emerging Self* (Unity Village, Mo.: Unity Books, 1970).

along these lines is in order. The parent, at the outset, should be involved in a realistic appraisal of the child's potential and needs. Teachers and parents, the two most significant groups in the child's development, must work together if the child is to succeed. If they were building a house they would test the soil to see if it were made of clay, rock or sandy soil—to insure its holding the structure. Similarly, they should cooperatively assess the child's physical, intellectual, social and emotional accomplishments to determine how they can help prepare him for academic success. The school is then in a better position to establish a baseline for individual functioning and, accordingly, design an appropriate program as the child embarks on the long school road (thirteen years) of academic development. The school (like the home in the first few weeks of life) has an opportunity at the outset to develop a sense of trust with the child—a relationship which tells him he is either a "good academic me in a good academic world" or the reverse side of the coin. Once the assessment has been made and a learning environment created, where should the school take the child if he is eventually to make it to college? We suggest the model on the following page.

For each child who is not moving along the anticipated road, a detailed analysis of his learning style and possible causes for his not learning are mandatory. The data should be analyzed and a diagnostic hypothesis and teaching plan formulated. Needless to say, ongoing evaluation through the thirteen years of school are crucial to the child's success.

If the child is to succeed at college, the schools should put special emphasis on thinking skills—not on reading alone and not on mathematical relationships alone. The child should be helped to go up and down his "learning ladder" from discriminations to generalizations, from the concrete to the abstract. Such a thinking-learning program should help those learning-disabled young people with native college-level ability to develop educational aspirations and ability to succeed in college—hopefully with the support of a program such as PAL. We recommend the model to other colleges as one for replication.

Perceptual	Socio-Emotional	Cognitive
Discrimination	Check the satisfaction of the child's five basic needs:	Concrete operations
Letters		Association
Numbers	1. Security—to be safe and relatively free of threat.	Names to numbers.
Body parts recognition use	2. Loved and accepted unconditionally.	Names to sounds.
	3. Belonging—to be part of a group.	Names to letters.
Memory	4. Recognition, to gain approval, to feel significant and accepted for the way in which one functions.	Relationships
Sequencing	5. Independency—to take responsibility and to make choices.	Time
		Space—near, far, north, south
	numerical	
	logical	Classification
		Categorization
Language Development—receptive	Language Development—integrative	Language Development—Expressive oral written

Mathematical skills
Conceptualization
Planning ability
Organizational skills
Anticipation of consequences of one's actions.

Mathematical skills
Conceptualization
Planning ability
Organizational skills
Anticipation of consequences of one's actions.